BY WHAT STANDARD?

BY WHAT
STANDARD?

God's World...God's Rules

Edited by

JARED LONGSHORE

FOUNDERS PRESS

Published by
Founders Press

P.O. Box 150931 • Cape Coral, FL • 33915
Phone: (888) 525-1689
Electronic Mail: officeadmin@founders.org
Website: http://www.founders.org

©2020 Founders Press
Second Printing August 2020
Printed in the United States of America

13 ISBN: 978-1-943539-21-5

Interior Design by Samuel Dickison
Cover Design by Jordan Singer

CONTENTS

CONTRIBUTORS

TOM ASCOL

Tom serves as the President of Founders Ministries. He has served as a Pastor of Grace Baptist Church since 1986. He has earned the MDiv and PhD degrees from Southwestern Baptist Theological Seminary in Ft. Worth, Texas. He has served as an adjunct professor of theology for several seminaries in North America. He and Donna have six children, as well as 3 sons-in-law and a daughter-in-law. They also have 12 grandchildren. Tom has edited and contributed to several books, including *Dear Timothy* and *Redeeming the Gospel and Reforming Churches*. He has authored *From the Protestant Reformation to the Southern Baptist Convention* and *"Traditional Theology" and the SBC*.

VODDIE BAUCHAM

Dr. Voddie Baucham serves as Dean of Theology at African Christian University in Lusaka, Zambia. Previously he served as pastor of Grace Family Baptist Church in Spring, Texas. Dr. Baucham is the author of numerous books, including *Expository Apologetics: Answering Objections with the Power of the Word*, *The Supremacy of Christ in a Postmodern World*, and *Family Shepherds: Calling and Equipping Men to Lead Their Homes*.

TIMON CLINE

Timon Cline is a native of Memphis, TN and grew up in Dakar, Senegal where his parents were missionaries. After graduating from Wright State University he concurrently earned a J.D. from Rutgers Law School and a M.A.R. from Westminster Theological Seminary. His writing has appeared in various publications including the *Founders Journal*, *National Review*, and *Areo Magazine*. He writes regularly on law, religion, and politics at *Conciliar Post* and *Modern Reformation*. He lives in Philadelphia with his wife, Rachel.

MARK COPPENGER

Mark Coppenger is retired Professor of Christian Philosophy and Ethics at Southern Baptist Theological Seminary. He's also been a professor, whether full-time or adjunct, at Wheaton College, Midwestern Baptist Theological Seminary, Trinity International University, and Elmhurst College; a pastor in Arkansas and Illinois; a denominational worker with Indiana Southern Baptists and the SBC Executive Committee, where he was founding editor of *SBC LIFE*; and an infantry officer. He received a B.A. from Ouachita, Ph.D. from Vanderbilt, and M.Div. from Southwestern Seminary. In the last decade, his articles have appeared through the online postings of *The American Spectator*, *Providence*, *The Philadelphia Inquirer*, *The Washington Post*, The Gospel Coalition, and Founders Ministries. His most recent books include *Moral Apologetics* (B&H) and *Cases and Maps: A Christian Introduction to Philosophy* (Wipf and Stock).

JARED LONGSHORE

Jared is Associate Pastor of Grace Baptist Church in Cape Coral, Florida. He serves as a board member and Vice President of Founders Ministries. Having served in pastoral ministry since 2007, he has earned MDiv and PhD degrees from the Southern Baptist Theological Seminary in Louisville, Kentucky. He and his wife Heather have seven children. Jared has edited and contributed to several works, including *A Noble Company* and the *Founders Journal.*

Tom Nettles

Tom J. Nettles retired from his position as Professor of Church History and Historical Theology at the Southern Baptist Theological Seminary in 2014 having begun his career in teaching at The Southwestern Baptist Theological Seminary in 1976. In his writing, he has sought to tap into the historical foundations of present theological issues. He and his wife Margaret live in Louisville, KY, where they are active at LaGrange Baptist Church and he serves when needed as Senior Professor of Historical Theology at the seminary.

Chad Vegas

Chad Vegas is the founding pastor of Sovereign Grace Church, where he has served since 2006. He is also the Founding Board Chairman for Radius International; a missionary training organization. Chad received his M.A. from Talbot School of Theology. He also served 3 terms as an elected Board member of the largest high school district in California. He has been married to Teresa since 1994, and they have 2 children.

INTRODUCTION

Either God created the world, or He didn't. Elijah asked what is still a pertinent question, "How long will you go limping between two different opinions" (1 Kings 18:21)? If Yahweh is God, follow Him. If man is God, follow him. In any case, "Choose this day whom you will serve."

Many have failed to see that a false religion is afoot. But it is getting harder to ignore. The philosophy and empty deceit which says man is the measure of all things has been with us since Protagoras. Yet it materialized in 1960's America in life-altering ways. Having thoroughly worked its way through our educational institutions, this vain ideology now advances in nearly every aspect of our civil and cultural experience.

This false religion is the same one God gave people up to in Romans 1. We have turned from worshiping the Creator to worshiping the creature. This religious system teaches that man is God and the human will is the holy standard. Salvation masquerades as that future state of universal equality attained by strict adherence to the Hegelian dialectic. But, in reality, it consists of satiating the unrestricted human appetite by any means necessary. So we do not leap upon altars crying out to Baal to send fire while cutting ourselves (1 Kings 18:26ff). But we do leap up on cars as we riot in fiery streets, cutting down people's livelihoods while crying out to finite, governmental gods. We do not sacrifice our children to Molech (Leviticus 18:21). But we do sacrifice them to Planned Parenthood.

The book you hold in your hand contrasts this false religion with the true Christian faith. It is an attempt to flesh out some of the message found in the film By What Standard (available at www.founders.org). Contributors address a variety of topics, including vain philosophies, cultural Marxism, race, manhood, womanhood, sexuality, and justice. These topics are set forth in the light of Scripture, providing insight into the times and how to live Christianly in them.

Jared Longshore

ONE

HOLLOW AND DECEPTIVE PHILOSOPHIES

By Tom Ascol

S ometimes I wonder how anybody makes it to heaven. Think about all the warnings the Bible gives to those who are walking with God through this world. We are constantly being opposed by that unholy trinity of the world, the flesh, and the devil, which means we have enemies around us, within us and above us.

In both Old and New Testaments, the Lord has seen fit to issue repeated warnings to His people to be on their guard against dangers that surround them at every step of their journey to the Celestial City. We are repeatedly warned about the deceitfulness of our own hearts, the strategies of the devil, and the enticements of the world.

In the Old Testament false prophets were regularly a threat to God's people. Moses gives specific instructions to resist false prophets and "worthless fellows" who will try to lead the people astray in the land of promise (Deuteronomy 13:12-13).

Jeremiah 9:6 says such false teachers heap "oppression upon oppression, and deceit upon deceit," and they refuse to know the Lord. In Jeremiah 23:16 the Lord says, "Do not listen to the words of the prophets who prophesy to you, filling you with vain hopes. They speak visions of their own minds, not from the mouth of the Lord." Jesus plainly warned about such people in Matthew 7:15, "Beware of false prophets, who come to you in sheep's clothing but inwardly are ravenous wolves."

Psalms and Proverbs are filled with calls to be on our guard against those who would lead us away from God, especially when they come to us with smooth talk and flattering words (Proverbs 26:23-26; Psalm 55:21ff).

Paul warns about such smooth talkers in Romans 16:17-18, where he writes, "I appeal to you, brothers, to watch out for those who cause divisions and create obstacles contrary to the doctrine that you have been taught; avoid them. For such persons do not serve our Lord Christ, but their own appetites, and by smooth talk and flattery they deceive the hearts of the naive."

Peter says that the devil prowls around like a roaring lion seeking someone to devour, so we must be sober-minded and watchful (1 Peter 5:8). He admonishes us in 2 Peter 3:17, to "take care that you are not carried away with the error of lawless people and lose your own stability."

In one of the most touching scenes in all of the Bible Luke records Paul's final words to the elders of Ephesus in Acts 20:28–30. He told them: "Pay careful attention to yourselves and to all the flock, in which the Holy Spirit has made you overseers, to care for the church of God, which he obtained with his own blood. I know that after my departure fierce wolves will come in among you, not sparing the flock; and from among your own selves will arise men speaking twisted things, to draw away the disciples after them."

Later, in the last letter we have from him, just a few months before he died, he tells Timothy in 2 Timothy 4 to preach the Word. Then he tells him why that is so important in vv. 3-4, "For the time is coming when people will not endure sound teaching, but having itching ears they will accumulate for themselves teachers to suit their own passions, and will turn away from listening to the truth and wander off into myths."

I could multiply such passages as these and you are probably as familiar with them as I am. But as we reflect just on these that I have noted—the very words of God to us—doesn't it highlight just how serious the danger is that confronts us? It is true—the world is filled with devils and they *do* threaten to undo us.

One of the reasons that I love Bunyan's *Pilgrim's Progress* is because he so graphically and helpfully depicts the life of a Christian as a dangerous journey. Yet, I fear, that we tend not to think of the Christian life that way today. We much prefer to think that we are safe; we are OK; that we really don't have much to fear about our spiritual lives and therefore don't really need to beware—to be careful.

Such complacency has set up modern evangelicals to be played. What I mean is that we are in the midst of a very subtle, intentional, and deadly maneuver by the devil that is designed to lead pastors, evangelical leaders and churches away from allegiance to the gospel of Jesus Christ, and the authority and sufficiency of His Word.

Theologian Kevin Vanhoozer has wisely noted that pastors and churches today must particularly brace ourselves for a particular kind of spiritual warfare, "For," he says, "we wrestle not against flesh and blood, matters in motion, but against isms, against the powers that seek to name, and control, reality."[1]

That is precisely what I see going on today. There are godless ideologies that have spread throughout Western civilization in recent decades with a vengeance and with their agenda to "name and control" reality. In other words, they are telling us what we are supposed to see; naming it and defining it for us, and then demanding that we reorder our lives on the basis of this new, supposed reality.

---

1. Melvin Tinker. *That Hideous Strength: How the West Was Lost* (Welwyn Garden City, UK: Evangelical Press), 2018, 33.

In recent years many of these ideologies have been smuggled into many evangelical churches and organizations through the Trojan Horse of what is commonly called, "social justice." In the name of racial reconciliation, honoring women and showing love and respect for the sexually confused, evangelicals have welcomed in ways of thinking that undermine the very teachings of God's Word that actually do promote true love and true justice through the life, death and resurrection of Jesus Christ.

The devil has been very effective in confusing people about what constitutes real justice and what actually working for justice entails. We are being played precisely at this point. God is the only true source of justice. He is the righteous One who has created this world and He has defined justice for us in His Word. Yet, in the name of seeking justice many evangelicals are being told that we must see the world and work for certain outcomes on the basis of ideas and ideologies that are contrary to Scripture.

We are being played, manipulated, maneuvered, and deceived. Proponents of hollow and deceptive philosophies are telling us what we must see, think and do if we are to be faithful in pursuing justice in the church and the world.

PAUL'S WARNING TO THE COLOSSIANS

In Colossians 2:8 Paul specifically warns us not to allow anyone to deceive us in this way. I want to look at that verse in this chapter in order to understand what is going on and what we must do about it.

In the letter of Colossians Paul begins with an introductory expression of thanksgiving and prayer for the church. He then launches into a profound explanation of the supremacy of Christ in 1:15. Beginning in 1:24 he describes how that awareness of Christ informs his own ministry as an apostle and minister of the gospel. Our text is found in the middle of that description. Paul gives an admonition in vv. 6-7; then a warning in v. 8; followed by reasons to heed the warning in vv. 9-10.

Colossians 2:6–10 (ESV) — Therefore, as you received Christ Jesus the Lord, so walk in him, rooted and built up in him and established in the faith, just as you were taught, abounding in thanksgiving. See to it that no one takes you captive by philosophy and empty deceit, according to human tradition, according to the elemental spirits of the world, and not according to Christ. For in him the whole fullness of deity dwells bodily, and you have been filled in him, who is the head of all rule and authority.

I like the way that JB Lightfoot renders v. 8. He puts it like this:

Be on your guard; do not suffer yourselves to fall prey to certain people who would lead you captive by a hollow and deceitful system, which they call philosophy. They substitute the traditions of men for the truth of God. They enforce an elementary discipline of mundane ordinances fit only for children. Theirs is not the gospel of Christ.[2]

In this text Paul calls on us to be so grounded in Jesus Christ that no one can take you captive with hollow and deceptive philosophies. Paul sticks with his theme of the greatness and sufficiency of Christ as he admonishes us in vv. 6-7 "walk in Christ." Just as we received Christ by faith—taking Him at His Word—so we are to live in Him, being rooted, built up, and established in the faith just as we have been taught the faith from the beginning of our relationship with Christ.

In v. 8, he warns us not to be taken captive by hollow and deceptive philosophies which are not according to Christ. Then in vv. 9-10 he buttresses his argument by reminding us that in Christ the whole fullness of deity dwells and we have been filled in Him. In other words, why in the world would you let anyone lead you astray from the simplicity and fullness that is in Jesus!

Let's look at v. 8 more closely: "See to it that no one takes you captive by philosophy and empty deceit, according to human tradition, according

---

2. Joseph Barber Lightfoot. *Colossians and Philemon*, Crossway Classic Commentaries (Wheaton, IL: Crossway Books, 1997), 89-90.

to the elemental spirits of the world, and not according to Christ."

This is the goal of our spiritual enemies. They want to take us captive. Paul uses a very rare word, used only here in the Bible and rarely anywhere else. It means to plunder; to take the spoils that come from being victorious in battle. This term indicates that Paul sees the threat as spiritual warfare. He says we must not allow this to happen: "See to it!" "Watch!" "Be on guard!"

This is what a Lieutenant says to his platoon as they move through enemy territory. Paul says that we must take care that *no one* takes us captive. He may have had specific people in mind who were propagating dangerous ideas in Colossae. But we must remember that such teachers spread deceptive philosophies as instruments of the devil, whether wittingly or unwittingly. And the devil's desire is always to take people captive to do his will (2 Timothy 2:24-26). Paul says: Do not let this happen! Be on your guard.

So the goal of our spiritual enemies is to take us captive. But what methods do they employ? The methods of our spiritual enemies are philosophy and empty deceit. Now this is not a prohibition of all philosophy. While this is the only time Paul uses the word, we should not understand Paul to be rejecting philosophy in general. What he has in mind is a system of teaching used by the enemy to capture God's people. He is saying there are ideas at play, intellectual arguments, which will lead people astray from the living God. Moreover, he is pointing out the problem with a specific kind of philosophy. One that is empty deceit.

The description is tightly woven. All three words are qualified by one definite article. There is one idea here. That is why I take Paul to refer to any hollow and deceptive philosophy. It is a way of thinking that is spiritually bankrupt. It is a way of thinking that is deceptive—that is, it sounds impressive and helpful. But in reality, it is deadly. Three sources of this hollow, deceptive philosophy are identified. Each one is introduced by the same preposition: "according to."

First, this hollow, deceptive philosophy is according to human tradition. Now again Paul is not putting down all tradition. He speaks of tradition favorably in 2 Thessalonians 2:15. The problem is that it is merely human, a tradition that is separated from God. It is not in keeping with that which God has revealed. This is precisely the problem with the Pharisees as Jesus pointed out when He applied Isaiah 29:13 to them in Mark 7:6-7, "Well did Isaiah prophesy of you hypocrites, as it is written, "'This people honors me with their lips, but their heart is far from me; in vain do they worship me, teaching as doctrines the commandments of men.'"

As the Huguenot Pastor, John Daille put it, teachings coming from mere human tradition are "all of them nothing but folly and vanity in the sight of God,… And though men boast of their utility, they are extremely hurtful, as they pester consciences, and busy them about things which God has not ordained, and turn them aside from his pure service to things which do not profit."[3]

Second, this empty philosophy is according to the elemental spirits of the world. Now this is a notoriously difficult phrase to interpret. Some say it refers to basic elements of the world: earth, wind, fire, and water. Others, that it signifies basic elements of an idea or system—the "A,B,C's" of it. Some claim the phrase implies connection to supernatural beings.

It seems that the third of these ideas fits more closely with the way Paul thinks of spiritual warfare, but whatever his precise meaning is by this phrase, the real danger is found in the third description of this hollow philosophy's source. And that is that it is not according to Christ. It doesn't come from Christ. It is not revealed by God. It isn't compatible with a right understanding of the person and work of Christ. In other words, it is incompatible with the gospel. Curtis Vaughan puts it like this: "Christ is the pole-star of theology, the standard by which all doctrine is to be measured. Any system, whatever its claims or pretensions, is to be rejected if it does not conform to the revelation which God has given us in Him."[4]

---

3. John Daille. *Exposition of Colossians* (National Foundation for Christian Education, 1968), 290.

4. Curtis Vaughan. *Colossians and Philemon, Founders Study Guide Commentary* (Cape Coral, FL: Founders Press, 2016), 71.

This is always the great danger that we face—that we will be led away from Christ by ideas or practices that do not conform to the revelation that God has given us in Christ. This is the very concern that Paul expresses for the Corinthians as he warns them about the false teachers in their midst. He writes in 2 Corinthians 11:3 (NASB95), "But I am afraid that, as the serpent deceived Eve by his craftiness, your minds will be led astray from the simplicity and purity of devotion to Christ."

We must work hard to be so grounded in Jesus Christ that no one can take us captive with hollow and deceptive philosophies. How can we guard ourselves against being taken captive in this way? By having an unwavering, unqualified, unembarrassed, submission to the Holy Scriptures as the authoritative, sufficient Word of God. Let our cry be that of Isaiah 8:20, "To the law and to the testimony: if they speak not according to this word, it is because there is no light in them" (KJV).

I believe that what Paul has written in Colossians 2:8 directly applies to what we are facing today in the so-called "social justice" movement. This is a movement that has its origins in the unbelieving world and has made rapid, and at some points, very deep inroads into Christian churches and institutions.

In fact, Colossians 2:8 is in a significant sense a main impetus behind the Statement on Social Justice and the Gospel which was recently published. I was involved in helping to write that statement that consists of 14 articles of affirmations & denials. The first line of the Introduction to the statement explains the concerns of the original framers of it—and presumably of the more than 11,000 people who have signed their names to it in support.

The statement begins like this: "In view of questionable sociological, psychological, and political theories presently permeating our culture and making inroads into Christ's church, we wish to clarify certain key Christian doctrines and ethical principles prescribed in God's Word."[5]

---

5. Statement on Social Justice: February 26, 2020, https://statementonsocialjustice.com.

Those "questionable sociological, psychological and political theories" need to be identified, understood and kept in their proper places. In the time that I have left, I want to try to do just that by looking at the worldview by which the modern social justice movement is being driven. It is, at its heart, antithetical to biblical Christianity. As a result, when Christians uncritically embrace and promote today's social justice movement they are in danger of being taken captive by unbiblical ideologies and led away from Christ.

Professor Thaddeus Williams of Biola explains it this way:

> The problem is not with the quest for justice. The problem is what happens when that quest is undertaken from a framework that is not compatible with the Bible. And this is a very real problem, because the extent to which we unwittingly allow unbiblical worldview assumptions to shape our approach to justice is the extent to which we are inadvertently hurting the very people we seek to help.[6]

It is precisely because I believe that this is happening that I oppose the social justice movement. Let me say it this way. I oppose the social justice movement because I am for *biblical justice*. I oppose the modern social justice movement not because I deny the existence of injustices that we face, but because many of the proposals that come from that movement are based on dangerous ideologies that lead away from Jesus Christ and His gospel.

SOCIAL JUSTICE

What is meant by "social justice?" It is a difficult term to define precisely because it is used in so many different ways by its proponents. Antonio Martino, an Italian economist and politician has astutely noted that

---

6. Thaddeus Williams, "Interview: How Should Christians Think About Social Justice." Josh McDowell Ministry, July 22, 2018, https://www.josh.org/christian-social-justice/.

social justice . . . owes its immense popularity precisely to its ambiguity and meaninglessness. It can be used by different people, holding quite different views, to designate a wide variety of different things. Its obvious appeal stems from its persuasive strength, from its positive connotations, which allows the user to praise his own ideas and simultaneously express contempt for the ideas of those who don't agree with him.[7]

Luigi Taperelli, an Italian Jesuit priest, is the first to use the term in the late 18th century to describe principles for a just society. Many, I dare say, most people who use the term today are not thinking in terms of 18th and 19th century Roman Catholic social theory. Most people today have a less sophisticated approach to social justice and usually mean by it that laws, cultural practices, economic policies, and such should be "just" and fair. Of course, that leaves us asking, "just and fair by what standard?"

One of the standard college textbooks on the subject (Readings for Diversity and Social Justice) defines social justice as "the elimination of all forms of social oppression."[8] Where oppression exists, justice seeks to eliminate it. That is a good thing, right? After all, God commands us to do this in Isaiah 1:17, doesn't He, when He says, "learn to do good; seek justice, correct oppression; bring justice to the fatherless, plead the widow's cause." And Psalm 82:3, "Give justice to the weak and the fatherless; maintain the right of the afflicted and the destitute."

It is precisely at this point that I fear the sleight-of-hand comes in that results in many Christians being duped. Because the question that must be answered is this: Who determines who the oppressed are? And what does it mean to seek justice for them? Or, as we should again ask, *by what standard?*[9]

---

7. Ronald Nash. *Social Justice and the Christian Church* (CSS Publishing, 2002), 5-6.

8. Maurianne Adams. *Readings for Diversity and Social Justice* (New York, NY: Routledge, 2013), 483.

9. Founders Ministries, *By What Standard?* A Founders Ministries Cinedoc, https://founders.org/cinedoc/.

Cultural Marxism & Critical Theory

For more than 150 years, Marxism has been offering answers to that question, first in terms of economics and more recently in terms of culture or sociology. This latter neo or cultural Marxism has been a dominant influence in the academy and politics in helping to shape our understanding of oppression in society.

Joe Carter, of the ERLC, published an article at The Gospel Coalition entitled, "Kinism, Marxism and the Synagogue Shooter." In that article and some later exchanges I had with him, Carter says that the term, "cultural Marxism," is racist jargon that "originated from a racist worldview perpetuated by anti-Semites."[10] In a brief twitter exchange, Joe said that the use of "cultural Marxism" is "a racist and antisemitic [sic] dog whistle that...should be abandoned by Christians." He then urged me to quit using the term.

Obviously, I have not acquiesced to his request because I believe that it remains helpful in understanding the play that is being made against our culture in the West and increasingly against many evangelical and reformed churches and organizations.

Al Mohler helps us understand why Carter and those like him object to the use of the term, as he explains how widespread this ideology is in the academy. Commenting on an article by David Brooks in the NY Times, Mohler explains that

> many on the left are saying that cultural Marxism is the boogie man of the right, that it's an invented position amongst conservatives, but that is not so....What is driving the left is indeed nothing less than a form of cultural Marxism, which has been taught on college and university campuses for a long time, and is now...the lingua franca. It is the symbolic universe in which the younger progressives live.[11]

10. Joe Carter, "Kinism, Cultural Marxism, and the Synagogue Shooter." The Aquila Report, May 2, 2019, https://www.theaquilareport.com/kinism-cultural-marxism-and-the-synagogue-shooter/.

11. Albert Mohler, "The Briefing." Albert Mohler, November 29, 2018, https://albertmohler.com/2018/11/29/briefing-11-29-18.

Cultural Marxism is an adaptation of classical Marxism moving it from an economic theory to a cultural and social one. Classical Marxism saw class conflict between the bourgeoisie and the proletariat—or the "haves" and "have-nots." Cultural Marxism views such conflict as between the oppressed and the oppressors; between those with privilege and those without it. The working class has been replaced by minorities. Majority groups are defined as "privileged" and "oppressive." Minority groups are regarded as "underprivileged" and "oppressed."

Whites, men, heterosexuals, and cisgenders are all majority groups and therefore inherently oppressive. They comprise the "dominant culture" and wield "hegemonic power" against sub-dominant cultures. Hegemony comes from a Greek term that means "to have dominance over." Those who do not fit into such groups are "sub-dominant" minorities and by definition, in the cultural Marxist scheme, oppressed. Those in the dominant culture exert their hegemonic power over minorities by manipulating them—oftentimes inadvertently—to accept their cultural assumptions, mores, and values.

This way of viewing the world (cultural Marxism) has given rise to a philosophical movement or ideology known as Critical Theory (CT).

It is critical to grasp the true nature of Critical Theory. Michael Thompson explains,

> Critical theory is not, however, simply a subfield within social theory, philosophy, or the social sciences. It is a distinctive form of theory in that it posits a more comprehensive means to grasp social reality and diagnose social pathologies. It is marked not by a priori ethical or political values that it seeks to assert in the world, but by its capacity to grasp the totality of individual and social life as well as the social processes that constitute them. It is a form of social criticism that contains within it the seeds of judgment, evaluation, and practical, transformative activity.[12]

---

12. Michael Thompson. *The Palgrave Handbook of Critical Theory* (New York, NY: Palgrave Macmillan, 2017), 1.

Critical Theory's agenda, therefore, is to see the overthrow what it deems oppressive groups and the deconstruction of those structures that enable them to wield their hegemonic power, all in the name of love and compassion for the oppressed.

This ideology is already on full display across our nation in our political system (see Alexandria Ocasio-Cortez) as well as on our college and university campuses (google Professor Brett Weinstein of Evergreen State University). It is seen in everything from the innocent sounding "diversity departments" to the violent silencing of those heretics who dare to question its orthodoxy.

You can see how problematic this ideology becomes if it is allowed to define who the oppressed are and what constitutes seeking justice for them. Yet, that is precisely what is happening across our nation and it has begun to make inroads into the evangelical world. Consider three especially problematic principles of Critical Theory.[13]

First, your fundamental identity is not who you are as an individual but arises from the groups to which you belong. What matters most is whether you are a part of privileged, dominant "oppressor" groups or sub-dominant "oppressed" groups. This is how you can be racist, misogynistic and homophobic even though you personally harbor none of those sinful attitudes. If you are part of the white, heterosexual, cis-gender, male hegemony, you are guilty of systemic oppression.

Second, your fundamental moral duty is to work for the liberation of oppressed groups. This is what it means to do justice. If you are not undertaking this work in behalf of the oppressed then you are complicit in their ongoing oppression.

Third, when it comes to knowing oppression, your lived experience far outweighs objective evidence and reason. In fact, this standpoint epistemology argues that using objective evidence and reason is exerting he-

13. Neil Shenvi and Pat Sawyer, "Critical Theory & Christianity," Free Thinking Ministries, August 17, 2018, https://freethinkingministries.com/critical-theory-christianity/.

gemonic power over those in sub-dominant cultures (minorities) and is itself an act of oppression. This is why those in the hegemony need to sit down and listen rather than speak.

Note a few examples of evangelicals writing about justice issues in ways that betray the influence of critical theory on their thinking.

Timothy Isaiah Cho (MDiv, Westminster Theological Seminary), a contributor to White Horse Inn and writer for Core Christianity has said:

> The Bible is written from the lens of the marginalized. If you come from a group or community that is historically not marginalized, you need these voices and perspectives or else your understanding of the Word, the gospel, and the Christian life will be thin and weak.[14]

> If the references in your pastor's sermons, the books used in small groups, the resources passed between the laity, the music sung in worship, & even the reflection quotes in your worship bulletins are predominantly by White men, your church is promoting a truncated Christianity.[15]

Andy Draycott, Associate Professor of Theology and Christian Ethics at Talbot School of Theology, Biola University, presented a paper at the 2018 ETS entitled, "Walking Across Gender in the Spirit? The Vocation of the Church and the Transgender Christian."[16] He asked the question, "Should we consider 'transgender Christians' as having a good self-understanding?" He gave an unqualified, "yes." Further, he used the ordinance of baptism as an analogy as a way to help us think about "transgendered Christians." They have died to their old, biological identity (the one they were born with), and have risen to a new life as transgendered.

---

14.   Timothy Cho, Twitter, September 16, 2018, https://twitter.com/tisaiahcho/status/1041357588770648064.

15.   Timothy Cho, Twitter, January 31, 2019, https://twitter.com/tisaiahcho/status/1091108240660656129.

16.   Andy Draycott, "Walking Across Gender in the Spirit? The Vocation of the Church and the Transgender Christian." Word MP3, 2018, https://www.wordmp3.com/details.aspx?id=33607.

The pushback against his paper was so strong after the ETS meeting that Draycott issued a statement of apology for his "lack of clarity" in his presentation and basically contradicted what his paper actually says.

In the weeks leading up to Mother's Day 2019, some evangelical women announced that they would be preaching in their churches that Sunday. The most prominent among them was Beth Moore. In the inevitable controversy that erupted the language defending Mrs. Moore and other women preachers included accusations of misogynistic oppression and the need for women to be liberated from such oppression.

I am not accusing any of the people I have named of being Cultural Marxists or of consciously promoting Critical Theory. What I am saying is that the influence of that worldview is apparent in what they are advocating and how they are contending for what they believe to be justice.

Such examples could be multiplied many times over, but my main concern is not to highlight all of the ways and places that the worldly philosophy of CT has infiltrated evangelical thinking, but to sound the alarm that it is doing so and to call us to recognize that this way of viewing the world is not according to Christ. You cannot buy into the world view of cultural Marxism or Critical Theory and maintain a commitment to the Bible as the Word of God written.

God's World, God's Rules

Christ has given us His Word and that Word is authoritative, sufficient, and final. It teaches us that God is the Creator of this world. He has ordered it and has done so in various ways including ways that include some hierarchies in relationships and distinctions between people. He made men stronger than women and adults to have more maturity than children. He created human sexuality to be binary. In other words He created two and only two sexes: Male and female He created them. He providentially orders the times and places of our existence. He is the One who says plainly in His Word that the office and function of elders are restricted to qualified men.

He alone is righteous and He has revealed His righteousness to us in the moral law. Sin is any transgression of or lack of conformity to that law. To live justly is to live lawfully. Injustice is failure to live lawfully.

In a phrase, *this is God's world and He gets to set the rules.* If we want to live in it well, then we must live in it in keeping with His design. Our fundamental problem is that we have shattered His design by our own rebellion against Him. We do not have the righteousness that He requires and we cannot pay the penalty that our sin has incurred. Our only hope is His sovereign grace and that grace is exclusively revealed in Jesus Christ. If we are going to be reconciled to God we must come to know Him on His terms, through faith in His Son to whom we bow as Lord. In submission to Jesus Christ, we accept what the Bible says is right and wrong, good and bad, just and unjust. And we commit ourselves in faith, to keep His commandments.

Our world is a spiritually dangerous place. It has always been so since the fall of our first parents. The dangers confronting us are particularly insidious because of the subtlety with which they have entered into our ways of thinking and viewing the world. So let us face these days with the boldness and confidence of Martin Luther and sing his hymn after him:

And though this world, with devils filled, Should threaten to undo us,
We will not fear, for God hath willed, His truth to triumph through us:

The Prince of Darkness grim, We tremble not for him;
His rage we can endure, For lo! his doom is sure,
One little word shall fell him.

That word above all earthly powers, No thanks to them, abideth
The Spirit and the gifts are ours, Through Him who with us sideth:
Let goods and kindred go, This mortal life also;
The body they may kill: God's truth abideth still,
His Kingdom is forever.

TWO

Cultural Marxism

By Voddie Baucham

I have been talking about Cultural Marxism for a long time. It is a topic that most people didn't want to hear me talk about in the past. But now for some strange reason, people are finding it more relevant. 1 Chronicles 12 has a reference to the sons of Issachar. It says they were "men who had understanding of the times, to know what Israel ought to do" (1 Chronicles 12:32).

In context, David is about to inherit the kingdom. There are swords, shields, mighty men of valor. You need all that. But you also need some men *who understand the times* so that you know what you ought to do. That's what I hope this chapter will be about. I hope that it will be about us trying to understand the times. Now I don't want to just offer a dry introduction to the topic of Cultural Marxism. Rather, what I want to do is put this in a context to help you understand why it is important, why it matters.

One of our current challenges is that we often opt for name-calling rather than honest debate. For example, some topic comes up and one person says it is a social justice issue. Another person calls him a Cultural Marxist. Then the former turns around and calls the latter a racist. That's about all the debate that you get. This is just name-calling and things get short-circuited because of it. Often neither side is being completely honest, and we know it.

Too often the person who is looking at his brother saying, "You're just a Cultural Marxist," doesn't necessarily mean what he is saying (even though he may believe his brother is espousing some of the ideas that come from Cultural Marxism). Likewise, the person that turns back and says, "You're just a racist," knows better. But both sides recognize the way to shut the other down. Because right now these are not issues that are being debated. These are not issues that are being discussed. In fact, in many instances, the mere act of debating and discussing these issues can get you labeled a Cultural Marxist or a racist.

Similarly, today if one person says that a particular event was an injustice and is challenged on whether or not that is indeed the case, a standard response is *"How dare you?* I just told you this was an injustice. How insensitive of you not to acknowledge it!"

One person genuinely points out what he sees as injustice and is called a Cultural Marxist. Another disagrees and is called a racist or bigot. The result is that we end up not addressing the issues in any kind of helpful way.

That is a great irony here. Some issues need to be dealt with. There are issues we need to discuss. But this has been declared ground where we are not allowed to fight. Merely deciding to debate and argue these issues can disqualify you. For some people it even disqualifies you from being a Christian. You're no longer a brother or a sister if you're not right on these issues.

In light of these realities let me tell you what I'm not saying. I'm not saying that all who disagree with me are Gramscian Cultural neo-Marxists. I don't believe that. I believe that there are some people within certain movements, who hold to this ideology that I'm talking about. Others don't hold to the ideology but unfortunately have decided to use the terminology. And that's a problem.

I'm also not here to state that all of the ideas with which I disagree in the current debate are Marxist. While I'm not a social justice warrior, an advocate of intersectionality, or a proponent of systemic racism theory, I don't believe that everyone who is an advocate of those things is necessarily a Marxist. We have to be careful with that label. We are dealing with brothers and sisters here. I would love to be treated with that level of brotherly love and respect. Even so, I can't demand it. I won't demand it. But I have to give it.

My goal then is to lay out a sketch of Cultural Marxism. We won't be able to go into every aspect of this ideology. But I want to show where the idea comes from and what we are talking about when we use the term. I hope to make it clear why and how I and others use the term and what we mean by it. I do use the term and have done so for a while. It is appropriate to use the term. Although it is unfortunate because when people hear it a sense of offense comes. So we have to be careful.

In addressing Cultural Marxism it is critical to see that *ideas matter*. Words matter. We need to understand the words that we use. Whichever side of this thing you find yourself on it is important for you to understand the words you use. You cannot assume that people know what you mean when you throw out those words.

It truly is important to address these issues. We are at a critical juncture with a critical issue. Things are at stake here that are of the utmost priority. Certain ideas are being embraced today. Some of those ideas are antithetical to the gospel that we love and preach. We need to find a way forward. Sticking our head in the sand is not an option. We find ourselves at this crossroads within evangelicalism. We must battle these things out, understand each other, get clarity, and find ourselves on the same page.

Let me say upfront without hesitancy or equivocation: Racism is real. It is sin. I find it sad that people argue that those of us who have been a part of the Statement on Social Justice and the Gospel have somehow made a statement that we don't believe that racism is a sin. Racism is real. It is a sin. Oppression is real. It is sinful.

I'm not avoiding real issues. Enough already with the people saying, "You just use terminology like Cultural Marxism so that you don't have to address these real issues." Nothing could be further from the truth. Too many people have been killed by police officers. There are too many police officers who have been killed by citizens. We have serious problems with immigration. There are far too many educational resources in this country for so many people to have so poor an education. These are problems for Christians to address.

So simply because I'm going to argue and will not stop arguing against Cultural Marxism, it does not follow that I am unwilling to acknowledge or to engage on these real issues. It is insulting, unfair, and unbrotherly to suggest otherwise. Just as much as it is to say that anybody who emphasizes these issues more than I would somehow doesn't love the gospel.

My Background

I want to help you understand why this is something I've been addressing. I was raised in South Central Los Angeles. I was raised by a single teenage Buddhist mother. So yes I was a fatherless young black man growing up in the ghetto in South LA, drug infested, gang-infested South LA. The police who policed my neighborhood were from the famous or infamous (depending on who you were asking) Rampart Division. You don't even have to be from LA to have heard about the Rampart Division. The Rampart Division was the baddest gang in LA. They made sure we knew that. Several family members of mine have spent most of their adult life in prison. There are two first cousins of mine who have been gunned down in the streets.

It is rather ironic that some who hear me teach on these issues think that I'm not in touch with blackness or the black experience. It is especially ironic when some of those people who have the audacity to say such things have seen virtually nothing in the way of real oppression.

I come from a family of activists. I come from a family that was associated with black power, black nationalism, the nation of Islam, protests, and the whole civil rights movement. I didn't grow up with my father, but I knew my father. He was always an advocate. He worked in the criminal justice system as a counselor in juvenile detention centers and a boy's home. My mother was a victim's advocate until she retired in San Antonio, Texas where she worked in the legal system. My first three jobs were in group homes because of the influence of the people who raised me.

All of this is true, yet I *despise* Cultural Marxism. I'm not a social justice warrior. I reject ideas like white privilege, intersectionality, and systemic racism theory absolutely and unequivocally—and not just since yesterday.

I started writing about Cultural Marxism in the mid-2000s. I wrote about it intensely in 2007 during the election because of what I saw as the incredible threat of Barack Obama, who was a massive Cultural Marxist. In my opinion, he was a dangerous man then and still is now. He is so on many fronts and for several reasons. I interviewed on CNN before the election talking about some of these issues. I only got to do that one time. And that was pretty much it. The lady said after the interview was over, "We will have to have you back." And I knew at that moment that I would never be back on that person's show again.

Barack Obama was acquainted with Cultural Marxism not only from his university days but even in his church. He sat under an overtly Marxist pastor, Jeremiah Wright, for decades. Wright was not just a Cultural Marxist he was a Classical Marxist.

In addition to his teachers, Obama's position on certain issues betrayed Cultural Marxist proclivities. His homosexual agenda was a clear example. He was the most radical pro-homosexual politician that I had ever seen or experienced in the mainstream. His position on abortion and infanticide was radical. His position on judicial activism and hate crimes legislation was highly problematic. I said openly on many occasions that I believe this man's presidency would make race relations in America worse not better.

So don't think that I write this because now Cultural Marxism is a trump card that can be used in this particular debate. For nearly a decade and a half now I've been addressing this issue. So with that in mind let's look at it.

Classical Marxism

First, Cultural Marxism and Classical Marxism are two different things. Karl Marx was an economist. Classical Marxism is an economic system. You have the bourgeoisie and the proletariat along with the familiar phrase, "From each according to his ability to each according to his need." The goal was to produce the uprising of the masses to overthrow capitalism. Marx saw capitalism as oppressing the masses. He also saw religion as the opiate of the masses that allowed them to be oppressed by capitalism. He was rabidly atheistic. Most Christians would not identify with Marxism. That in part is why it is difficult to talk about Cultural Marxism. So we must mark the difference between the two.

Marx believed that history had three stages or epochs (the ancient stage, the feudal stage, the capitalist stage). He thought he was witnessing the rise, and would see eventually of the fall, of the capitalist stage. He also advanced the idea of class consciousness. Each one of these societal epochs contained internal contradictions. These internal contradictions are what would lead to struggle and would eventually lead to the next phase. Then came his idea of historical determinism. Ultimately capitalism would fall. Capitalism had to fall. Why? Because his view of history was one of struggle. History was a series of struggles or conflicts. He was a disciple of Hegel. So this was his dialectic (thesis, antithesis, synthesis).

He envisioned the workers of the world would be uniting and revolting. His vision came to pass, but not everywhere. Toward the end of his life and during the life of his followers, they tried to understand and explain why capitalism didn't fall. If capitalism is the exploitation of the masses, and if history is all about these conflicts, and if this conflict is going to come, and if the next thing that is going to come is a post-capitalist society, then why have we not seen it all come to pass?

Antonio Gramsci and The Frankfurt School

Enter the cultural Marxists. Marx died in 1888. But his ideas did not. If you are going to understand Cultural Marxism then you must know Antonio Gramsci, an Italian Marxist, and a group of individuals known as the Frankfurt School. One of their goals was to explain why the revolution didn't occur as Marx thought it would.

To understand Cultural Marxism you must understand Gramsci's idea of cultural hegemony. Listen to the way one sociologist puts it, "cultural hegemony refers to domination or rule maintained through ideological or cultural means. It is usually achieved through social institutions that allow those in power to strongly influence the values, norms, ideas, expectations, worldview, and behavior of the rest of society."[1]

Cultural hegemony? That's the power. By the way, this idea of cultural hegemony explains something. Have you ever wondered why women, who make up more than 50% of the population, are considered a *minority*? Because women are not seen as part of the cultural hegemony. The cultural hegemony is patriarchal. The cultural hegemony in our society is white, male, heterosexual, cis-gendered, able-bodied, native-born, Americans. Everybody who is not *that* is a minority. Everybody who is not *that*, is a victim of the cultural hegemony established by *those* individuals. This is a recipe for war.

---

1. Nicki Cole, "What is Cultural Hegemony?" ThoughCo, January 6, 2020, https://www.thoughtco.com/cultural-hegemony-3026121

Cole explains, "Gramsci developed the concept of cultural hegemony to explain why the worker-led revolution that Marx predicted in the previous century had not come to pass. Central to Marx's theory of capitalism was the belief that the destruction of the economic system was built into the system itself since capitalism is premised on the exploitation of the working class by the ruling class."[2]

Why didn't Classical Marxism take root everywhere? Because the situation is deeper than economics. Culture must be addressed. Gramsci would argue that Marx missed this part. The revolution that comes doesn't need to be an armed revolution or a revolution of force. It needs to be a hegemonic revolution. In other words, we need to change the cultural hegemony.

Gramsci argued that to change the cultural hegemony you must control the robes of society—judges, professors, pastors, and politicians. Leverage those positions to educate and mobilize the masses against the hegemonic power. Use the educational system, the political system, and the judicial system to overturn the cultural hegemony. Does that sound at all familiar?

This is how you gain power. By the way, you gain political power by promising various groups of people that you will advocate for them. That's why you can have so many white, male, heterosexual, cis-gendered, able-bodied, native-born, American politicians who present themselves as representatives of the people who are not any of those things! That's how Cultural Marxism works.

The Frankfurt School refers to a collection of scholars in Frankfurt, Germany. They were known for developing Critical Theory and popularizing the dialectic method of learning by interrogating society's contradictions. It is most closely associated with the work of some German philosophers during the early 20th century. They saw a couple of things that for them explained why the revolution didn't happen. Part of it was the

---

2. Ibid.

fact that people were receiving so much information through mass media.

So one of the main goals of the Frankfurt School was to leverage those tools to bring about the change in the hegemonic powers. They saw people becoming passive recipients of political and ideological information instead of being activists. They believed that this explained why the revolution didn't take place. They theorized that this experience made people intellectually inactive and politically passive as they allowed mass-produced ideologies and values to wash over them and to infiltrate their consciousness. Because of what happened in WWI they left Germany. In 1933 they went to Switzerland. But they only stayed there for a couple of years. In 1935 they came to New York where they became affiliated with Columbia University.

There's a man by the name of Balint Vazsonyi who came to the United States fleeing the Nazis in Hungary. He wrote a book called *America's 30 Years War*. Essentially his thesis was that he ran away from what was happening in Europe by force only to come to the United States and watch it happen gradually throughout a generation. So what do these guys give us?

Identity Politics, Intersectionality, and Cultural Hegemony

One thing they give us is Critical Theory. Many in evangelical circles have spoken recently of Critical Race Theory. It is a grandchild of the Frankfurt School along with political correctness and multiculturalism. As a result of these ideologies we have all been taught over time through media and educational systems to view ourselves not as part of a whole but as part of sub-groups. We have learned to identify with sub-groups which in some way are being oppressed by the hegemonic power that rules our culture.

When we talk about elections now we don't talk about candidate A being ahead in the polls. We say candidate A is ahead with red-headed, left-handed, white people from the south. While candidate B is getting the vote of second-generation migrant workers, with eczema. Why do we talk like that? Why do we think about politics that way? Why do we think about each other that way?

Why do ideas like intersectionality from Kimberle Crenshaw gain such popularity that people use it like we know what it is? To understand intersectionality start with the hegemonic power: white, male, heterosexual, cis-gendered, able-bodied, native-born, American people. That's *the man*. The man is keeping us down.

Intersectionality, in a nutshell, is the idea that to the degree that you don't have those "identities," you are oppressed. So if you are male, heterosexual, cis-gendered, native-born, able-bodied, American—by the way also attractive, there's pretty privilege too—if you are all of those things but you're not white, then your oppression is limited to that area. But what if you're not white but you're also not male? Now that place where your not whiteness and your not maleness intersects, that is where you feel the weight of your oppression. But what if you're not white, not male, and not heterosexual? Well now the oppression is even worse because you have these three intersections of oppression. Intersectionality says that the level of oppression and the kind of oppression that you experience combines itself in these areas and layers itself in these intersections. But what is that if not a grown-up expression of Cultural Marxism?

This framework sheds light on the confusion of racism charges today. When people call you a racist they could be charging you with racist, prejudicial ideas or actions. Or, they could just be saying that you are a part of the cultural hegemony which is inherently prejudiced against people who are not white, male, heterosexual, etc. All of this means that you now have racism without a racist. How in the world do you handle *that*? If racism is in the heart of an individual, let's go to the book. Let's call that what it is. But the racism that exists because of cultural hegemony? How do you fix that? Now instead of a preacher, you've become a politician.

Intersectionality breeds confusion on many societal issues. A prime example is the Michael Brown case. On the one hand a guy 6 foot 4 inches, 300 and some odd pounds, reaches into a police car and grabs the gun of a police officer. Everybody knows if I have a gun and you reach to grab my gun then one of us is in trouble. If you get it, it's me, if you don't, it's you." Hands up, don't shoot? Never happened. It was a complete fabrication.

So a guy who had just strong-arm robbed somebody in the store was stopped by a policeman. He acted aggressively against the policeman and got shot and killed. Tell me the story of the police officer who acted inappropriately and we can go together to seek justice. But there was no racism or injustice in this story. Unless, the problem is not one police officer and his actions, but a cultural hegemony that has established structural racism that disproportionately targets black males. Therefore, every time something like that happens it is another piece of evidence. This is why you have people who say things like, "The facts of that case don't matter."

It is even worse when people say, "Oh now you're blaming the victim." The result of that is people don't engage, discuss, or interact. Whatever your answer is, if it doesn't line up with what the Cultural Marxist says it ought to be then you're wrong and racist—or in my case, a sell-out who is trying to curry favor with white people.

An Agenda That Must Be Stopped and Problems That Must Be Solved

Cultural Marxism is not just an idea. It is a *disruptive, transformative, agenda*. It is an agenda that needs to be recognized and confronted. The result of this agenda is a real pain, real sin, and real brokenness that doesn't get addressed. As someone who grew up in a drug-infested, gang-infested South LA, the son of a single teenage mother, I look at the Mike Brown situation and I want to say to all of the young black boys like him who were young black boys like me, *we can't live like that*. To all of the fathers who were not there, to the tune of nearly 75% among black children, we have a problem that needs to be addressed. We can't live like this. We have to deal with this. There is brokenness here that has to be addressed. But the way things stand now to say that is to blame the victim.

That means that whatever pathologies there are that need to be addressed *don't get addressed!* It is the system's fault. Again, I am not arguing that there is no racism, brokeness, or injustice. We have way too many people in prison in this country. There's something broken about that. Especially when a large number of those people are in there because of addiction to drugs. But what we have done is created an environment where everyone is divided up into constituencies, which is incredibly ironic because that leads to stereotypes. We look at everyone's issues in relation to the system, what the system is doing, has done, and needs to do. Doing so has the potential to move us away from addressing individuals and their sin, their pain, and their brokenness.

We don't have to be either-or. Why do I have to choose between advocating for laws to change in the area of abortion, which disproportionately affects people who look like me, or proclaiming the gospel to change the hearts of young women so that they won't kill their babies? We don't have to choose between those two. Why do I have to choose between acknowledging the fact that there are huge problems and pathologies both among individuals *and* cultures or systems?

Love the Gospel and One Another

Galatians 3:28 says, "There is neither Jew nor Greek, there is neither slave nor free, there is no male and female, for you are all one in Christ Jesus" But sadly, one of the things that this Cultural Marxism has exposed recently is a false unity. We have people who for years have been talking about how unified we are in Christ. But now are suddenly dismissing one another because of where they fall on a particular social issue.

There's an ideology at work. That ideology has an endgame here. We see it in the world of politics. If you visit a university campus you will see this. It has to be addressed. It has to be addressed because there are issues, real brokenness, real sin, real problems. And if we're not careful, we will render ourselves unable or unwilling to address them because of these ideologies that we've imbibed.

We have to love the gospel enough and love one another enough to address these things. Here's a great irony. The great irony is that in a way, I'm borrowing language from the other side now. Because the other side is always saying, "check your privilege." And I'm kind of saying that. But here's the difference. I'm saying it to everybody. I'm not saying that if you're white, male, heterosexual, cis-gendered, able-bodied, native-born, American then you should check your privilege. I'm saying if you are a member of the body of Christ, and in this discussion and debate, you have learned how to shut down the other side, regardless of who that other side is, check that... *check that*. And that's going to require boldness, both in terms of trusting our brothers and sisters in Christ and in terms of willingness to speak to issues that in this day and age will get you outright castigated. But the truth is worth it.

THREE

THE RELIGIOUS ROOT OF OUR SEXUAL PERVERSION

By Jared Longshore

It is no secret that the state of sexuality in America is perverted. We live in days of sexual anarchy. We twist God's design in every conceivable way, resolved to fashion a sexuality that is right in our own eyes. The sexual chaos around us runs all the way down to the foundations. We've got big problems down there.

The cracks down there produce all kinds of difficulties up here in our daily experience. It's like we are in a house with the walls falling in. We're a bit distracted by the walls. Who could blame us when not too long ago there was an 11-year-old boy dressed like a girl taking off his clothes at a gay bar in New York while men threw dollar bills at him.[1] That's the kind of thing that leaves us asking, "What *is driving* this sexual perversion?"

---

1. Doug Mainwaring, "11-year-old 'drag kid' dances in popular NYC gay club as patrons toss money at him." Life Site, December 17, 2018, https://www.lifesitenews.com/news/11-year-old-drag-kid-dances-in-popular-nyc-gay-club-as-patrons-toss-money-a.

The answer goes deeper than you might think. *Our current sexual perversion is the fruit of a false religion.* This false religion worships the creature rather than the Creator. Our sexually immoral culture, then, is not merely a prodigal son slipping up in a moment of lust, soon to come back to his senses. In that setup, the prodigal son has his senses to come back to. He engages in activity contrary to his foundational beliefs. Our sexually immoral culture is doing just the opposite. It is acting in accordance with first principles. A deep, systematic ideology spawned the sexual pollution all around us. And that ideology didn't just start growing yesterday.

Ross Douthat, a contributor to the New York Times, has written an article called "The Return of Paganism." He identifies paganism as the belief "that divinity is fundamentally inside the world rather than outside it, that God or the gods or Being are ultimately part of nature rather than an external creator, and that meaning and morality and metaphysical experience are to be sought in a fuller communion with the immanent world rather than a leap toward the transcendent."[2]

Peter Jones, a Presbyterian minister, has spoken of this paganism as well. He calls it Oneism, which is a worldview that claims all is one. There is no distinction between the Creator and the created. At a recent Ligonier Conference, Jones said, "The rising generation, the millennial generation, is the first generation of our modern era to receive a fully developed neo-pagan cosmology masquerading as the correct view of history and demanding to be inscribed in public policy. It is indeed a well-worked out cosmology, that is a worldview, about the nature of existence. And it is thoroughly pagan."[3]

This paganism, as defined by Douthat and Jones, is the religious root of our sexual perversion. This Oneist worldview is upon us. It is subtle,

---

2. Ross Douthat, "The Return of Paganism." New York Times, December 12, 2018, https://www.nytimes.com/2018/12/12/opinion/christianity-paganism-america.html.

3. Peter Jones, "Paganism in Today's Culture." Ligonier Ministries, February 25, 2015, https://www.youtube.com/watch?v=0C5caA2Q13Q.

having flown under the radar of many Christians. Yet the Christian faith is incompatible with such a worldview. Paganism is at odds with reality as God has structured it in this world. Therefore it can only lead to despair.

Especially when it comes to our sexually polluted moment, if we miss this undergirding belief structure, then we will fail to do justice, love kindness, and walk humbly with our God. We will very likely fail to do it while thinking we are doing it. We are in danger of doing *injustice* while being told by many we are doing justice, *hating kindness* while being told we love it, and *walking proudly* while being cheered as those who walk humbly with God.

Now for a few qualifications upfront. When I point out the religious root of our sexual perversion, I do not mean that everyone who identifies along the LGBT spectrum is self-consciously pagan. We could surely find many who would claim to believe in a distinct creator. And I *certainly do not* mean that any person who experiences sexual lust, be it homosexual or otherwise, is outside of the Christian faith. Many Christians sin sexually and then proceed to repent. My point is instead that, generally speaking, grievous sexual sin is itself God's handing over of those who have already turned away from Him to worship the creature. Consider Romans 1:18-32

> For the wrath of God is revealed from heaven against all ungodliness and unrighteousness of men, who by their unrighteousness suppress the truth. For what can be known about God is plain to them, because God has shown it to them. For his invisible attributes, namely, his eternal power and divine nature, have been clearly perceived, ever since the creation of the world, in the things that have been made. So they are without excuse. For although they knew God, they did not honor him as God or give thanks to him, but they became futile in their thinking, and their foolish hearts were darkened. Claiming to be wise, they became fools, and exchanged the glory of the immortal God for images resembling mortal man and birds and animals and creeping things.

Therefore God gave them up in the lusts of their hearts to impurity, to the dishonoring of their bodies among themselves, because they exchanged the truth about God for a lie and worshiped and served the creature rather than the Creator, who is blessed forever! Amen.

For this reason God gave them up to dishonorable passions. For their women exchanged natural relations for those that are contrary to nature; and the men likewise gave up natural relations with women and were consumed with passion for one another, men committing shameless acts with men and receiving in themselves the due penalty for their error.

And since they did not see fit to acknowledge God, God gave them up to a debased mind to do what ought not to be done. They were filled with all manner of unrighteousness, evil, covetousness, malice. They are full of envy, murder, strife, deceit, maliciousness. They are gossips, slanderers, haters of God, insolent, haughty, boastful, inventors of evil, disobedient to parents, foolish, faithless, heartless, ruthless. Though they know God's righteous decree that those who practice such things deserve to die, they not only do them but give approval to those who practice them.

Sexual immorality is the fruit of creature worship. There are not many more texts that illustrate our times more clearly than this one. Taking these verses as a guide, consider the progress of our sexual perversion, the principles which have given rise to this sexual perversion, and what Christians should do about it.

The Progress of our Sexual Perversion

The progress of our sexual perversion has come about because of the work of sexual revolutionaries. These sexual revolutionaries had (and have) a goal. Their goal is not merely to attain some sense of equality. I recently heard a Christian leader apologizing to the LGBT community on behalf of Christians because Christians have not sought justice for them. Quite honestly, I think that pastor is getting played. That's precisely how some really bad people driving all of this want him to feel. They want Christians to believe this is about justice and equality. But it's not.

Take, for example, the Gay Liberation Manifesto of 1971. It said, "Equality is never going to be enough. What is needed is *a total social revolution*, a *complete reordering of civilization*. Including society's most basic institution, *the patriarchal society*."[4] Along the same lines, there is the key leader in the second wave of feminism in America, Kate Millett. She was a homosexual woman and author who held meetings in one of which the following call and response were heralded:

> "Why are we here today?" "*To make revolution*," the group answered. "What kind of revolution?" "*The Cultural Revolution*," "And how do we make Cultural Revolution?" "By destroying the American family!" "How do we destroy the family?" "By destroying the American Patriarch," they cried exuberantly. "And how do we destroy the American Patriarch?" the leader replied. "By taking away his power!" "How do we do that?" "By destroying monogamy!" they shouted. "How can we destroy monogamy?" "By promoting promiscuity, eroticism, prostitution, and homosexuality!"[5]

The goal of the sexual revolution was a complete leveling of authority. The adherents of the sexual revolution didn't really hate men. They hated *hierarchy*. They hated order and objectivity. They did not hate fathers; they hated the Father. The agenda of the sexual revolutionaries is often lost on Christians. For example, a very prominent Southern Baptist pastor recently said in a message on homosexuality that to be like Jesus, "churches *must be known* as the friends of the LGBT community." It is just here that our present challenge comes into high relief. Christians should certainly be friendly to LGBT people. Jesus was a friend of sinners. My family and I have had homosexual neighbors with whom we enjoyed a friendly

---

4. Manifesto Group. *Gay Liberation Front Manifesto.* (London, UK: Gay Liberation Front), 1971.

5. Gene Veith, "Mallory Millett's Critique of Her Sister's Feminism." Patheos, February 12, 2018, https://www.patheos.com/blogs/geneveith/2018/02/the-other-ms-milletts-withering-critique-of-feminism/.

relationship. But my concern is the claim that "churches must be known as friends to the LGBT community." In our times, there is a world of difference between being a friend and *being recognized as a friend by those who don't know Christ*. If your goal is to be known as a friend, you may end up being no real friend at all.

Here's where the concern hits home. This same pastor, shortly after saying these things, called for "the tearing down of all hierarchy." Many well-meaning Christians are being played at precisely this point. They are in danger of adopting the operating principles of the world while thinking those principles accord with biblical kindness and justice.

To grasp the progress of the sexual revolution you must see its goal, but you also need to mark its extent. You don't usually have this big of an impact upon society if you lack a worked-out system of ideas driving your agenda. Note the different spheres it has impacted.

Our sexual perversion is *cultural*. A man has competed in the Miss Universe Beauty pageant.[6] Homosexual unions and modern families are common themes in today's television programs. It touches on *athletics*. A male has won gold in women's cycling.[7] It impacts *education*. Drag Queen Story Hour at the library is becoming more common.[8] Our sexual confusion is *political*: Obergefell has created more problems than we can count. It is *financial*. A biological male received 20 thousand dollars for being dismissed from a woman's football team.[9] It is *extreme*: Sexual transition-

---

6. Lindsay Lowe, "Miss Universe contestant is making history as the first openly transgender contender." Today, December 14, 2018, https://www.today.com/style/angela-ponce-first-openly-transgender-miss-universe-contestant-t144729.

7. Peter Hasson, "Biological Male Wins Women's Cycling World Championship." The Daily Signal, October 21, 2019, https://www.dailysignal.com/2019/10/21/biological-male-wins-womens-cycling-world-championship/.

8. Drag Queen Story Hour, https://www.dragqueenstoryhour.org.

9. Evan Frost, "Transgender football play prevails in lawsuit against Minnesota team, league." MRP News, December 22, 2018, https://www.mprnews.org/story/2018/12/22/transgender-football-player-prevails-in-lawsuit.

ing advances in our society. A judge in Ohio recently took an adolescent female out of her home because her parents would not let her begin hormone therapy to try to become a man.[10] This sexual perversity invades the *religious* realm seen in the drift of Mainline Protestantism and the Revoice Conference. Finally, it is *deadly*, which is evidenced by abortion and suicide statistics. Many reports have shown that youth identifying as LGBT are much more likely to commit suicide than are their heterosexual peers.

I don't mention this extent to be a fearmonger. I am not recommending that you hide your kids and pull the shades down. But I am pointing out that we are dealing with a well-conceived, well-developed ideology that has given rise to the outlandish levels of sexual immorality we have now attained. That ideology is so pervasive in our society that many Christians are in danger of imbibing its principles unawares. So what are some of those principles?

THE UNDERLYING PRINCIPLES OF OUR PRESENT SEXUAL PERVERSION

Many underlying principles drive our sexual perversion. I want to point out three. The sexual perversion of our times is driven by the worship of a pagan god, the approval of a pagan law, and the cultivation of pagan desire.

A Pagan God

First, our sexual confusion is fueled by the worship of a pagan god. We worship the creature rather than the Creator. In Romans 1:21, Paul says, "For although they knew God, they did not honor him as God or give thanks to him." Thus far, we are good. The unbelievers don't believe; they don't worship God. Christians do not have any trouble understanding this one. But that is not all the apostle says. He goes on in verse 24 to

---

10. Jen Christensen, "Judge gives grandparents custody of Ohio transgender teen." CNN, February 16, 2018, https://www.cnn.com/2018/02/16/health/ohio-transgender-teen-hearing-judge-decision/index.html.

say, "Therefore God gave them up in the lusts of their hearts to impurity, to the dishonoring of their bodies among themselves, because they exchanged the truth about God for a lie *and worshiped and served the creature rather than the Creator.*"

The unrighteous did not stop at atheism. They did not hunker down happily in their agnosticism. We should know better than to assume that they would. We know that our hearts are idol factories. Man will worship something. If he does not worship the Creator, then he will worship the creation. We are in a "not whether but which" situation. It is not whether we will worship God, but rather which god we will worship. There is no middle ground. There is no neutrality.

Why should we read the progress of sexual immorality in our times as the fruit of creature worship? Because Paul goes on in the very next verse explaining the connection. After mentioning creature worship in verse 25, he says in verse 26, "For this reason God gave them up to dishonorable passions. For their women exchanged natural relations for those that are contrary to nature; and the men likewise gave up natural relations with women and were consumed with passion for one another."

You cannot raise an entire generation on sayings like, "Believe in yourself. You can be whatever you want to be when you grow up," and then when the boys grow up and want to be women say, "Oh no, we didn't mean it." If you train people to think that they are god, come to find out, they end up thinking they are.

The challenge is that a lot of this thinking flies under the radar. The church would reject the teaching that directly claimed man was God. But bad ideas usually don't come knocking on the front door. For example, the *Greatest Showman* was a recent, popular movie in which a lady with a beard sang center stage at a circus. After being excluded from a party for her androgynous appearance, she sings her power ballad, *This Is Me:*

Look out 'cause here I come
And I'm marching on to the beat I drum

I'm not scared to be seen I make no apologies,
this is me...
and I know I deserve your love
'cause there's nothing I'm not worthy of.

Many people think the bearded lady is justified—"She was excluded wasn't she?" But is the Christian confession, "I know I deserve your love 'cause there's nothing I'm not worthy of?" Furthermore, her claim is based on making no apologies and being true to her own drum beat. Interestingly, last year at the *Revoice Conference*—a gathering to empower gay Christians—this very song was quoted as a way for homosexual Christians to find strength in their suffering for being gay.

A Pagan Law

Our sexual perversion is not only driven by the worship of a pagan god, but also the approval of a pagan law. Here again, it is not whether but which. It is not whether you will approve a law, but which law you will approve. Romans 1:32 says, "Though they know God's righteous decree that those who practice such things deserve to die, they not only do them but *give approval* to those who practice them." Notice they did not merely neglect God's decree and go about their business quietly. No. They disapproved of God's standard and approved of another one in its place.

The pagan law driving our sexual perversion is the human will. How could it be any different? If man is God, it follows that man's standard is the divine standard. So it is common for people to look at Christians and object, "Who are you to tell me how to live, what to believe, and how to think?" Such an objection from unbelievers is not really the new development. The new development is that many Christians don't know how to respond. "Well, I don't know. I thought I was supposed to evangelize, but I'm not quite sure how to answer your question." There is a perfectly good answer to that question: "I am a representative of Christ Jesus, and before He commissioned me to tell you these things, he said, 'All authority in heaven and on earth has been given to me.' You're breathing His air with

His lungs, oxygenating His blood. And He has told us plainly what the real standard is."

It takes courage and submission to Christ as Lord to speak that way. And we're losing these things. You cannot raise a generation on Elsa's *Frozen* anthem "Let it go, let it go... no right, no wrong, no rules for me, I'm free," and then expect them to grow up and obey Jesus, much less tell other people to obey Jesus. I know people just love that movie. Watch away, just counsel that poor girl when it gets to that part.

The replacement of God's standard with man's standard has left us terribly confused about honor and shame. People call what is honorable shameful and what is shameful honorable. The church is caught in the middle, trying not to call shameful things too shameful and trying not to call honorable things too honorable. We kind of want to smooth things out and make sure everybody gets a trophy or at least a ribbon. The question ever before us is, "By what standard?" By what standard is something honorable or shameful? The answer to that question is God's standard, not man's. We do people no good by failing to call shameful acts shameful. That is not the way to relieve people of their shame. It actually leaves people in their shame. We fail again when we do not give honor where honor is due. By failing to do so, we fail to cultivate God's good standard in the world.

Here are the two directions of our honor and shame confusion on sexual matters. On the honor end, Hebrews 13:4 says, "Let marriage be held in honor among all, and let the marriage bed be undefiled." Let marriage be highly esteemed. Marriage is a marvelous, miraculous work of God. The two shall become one flesh. This is a holy union. In our present moment, people attempt to make a mockery of marriage. On the shame end, Romans 1:27 speaks of homosexual acts as "men committing shameless acts with men," and we have forgotten how to blush. Jeremiah 6:15 says, "Were they ashamed when they committed abomination? No, they were not at all ashamed; they did not know how to blush." Listen to the outcome, "Therefore they shall fall among those who fall; at the time that

I punish them, they shall be overthrown."

You do not serve people when you empower their homosexual life-style. You do not love them. You serve their destruction by helping them not to blush. We should be like the apostle who upheld both God's law and His gospel. Although he took no pleasure in the grief of the Corin-thians, he rejoiced they were grieved into repenting.

A Pagan Desire

Along with a pagan god and pagan law, our sexual perversion is fueled by the cultivation of pagan desire. That is desire unhinged from any ob-jective reality. God's goodness, truth, and beauty have nothing to do with the way this desire ought to take shape. A pagan understanding of desire is pervasive among us.

The Revoice Conference went wrong at just this point. Ron Belgau, one of the speakers, has written the following, "I believe gay sex is sinful, and that the desire for gay sex, though not itself sinful, is a temptation."[11] But the problem with this, of course, is that the desire is itself sinful. The tenth commandment makes plain that it is not only a sin to take your neighbor's wife; it is a sin to covet your neighbor's wife. Likewise, it is not merely a sin to engage in homosexual acts. It is a sin to desire to commit those acts.

There is more and more talk in the Christian world about same-sex attraction. But even this language of attraction illustrates the battle that is raging for the dictionary. The apostle Paul does not speak of a sinless attraction. He says in Romans 1:24, "God gave them up in the *the lust of their hearts.*" Again, in verse 26, he speaks of "dishonorable passions."

Christians then must reassert the cultivation of Christian desire. They must develop their desire in accordance with God's revealed truth. Doing so is hard work. But it must be done for it is not whether we will cultivate desire, but which desire we will cultivate.

---

11. Denny Burk and Rosaria Butterfield, "Learning to Hate our Sin without Hat-ing Ourselves." Public Discourse, July 4, 2018, https://www.thepublicdiscourse.com/2018/07/22066/.

The vast majority of people in our day, given our highly pragmatic understanding of education, have not been taught to think well on this front. C. S. Lewis identified the problem some time ago in his work, *The Abolition of Man*. He recounted the story of two children who went to a waterfall. Upon looking at the waterfall, one child said, "This is sublime." The response came that the boy should not have said, "This is sublime," but only, "I have feelings of sublimity." Lewis explains that the foolish respondent claimed there is no objective sublimity in the waterfall. Thus it calls for no sublime feelings in the child. Feelings don't work that way, they say. Feelings just fly around willy-nilly disconnected from objective truth. Lewis laments that the result of such thinking; we raise men without chests. We train the next generation without the capacity to cultivate affections that rightly respond to reality.

This pagan notion of desire yields some ugly fruit. Pornography and sexual abuse are two examples. We have such high levels of these sins in part because we have only trained the hands and minds of children. We have left them unable to admire what is beautiful, love what is lovely, and disdain what is ugly.

Along with the cultivation of Christian desire, we must reteach the destruction of ungodly desire. Colossians 1:5 says, "Put to death therefore what is earthly in you: sexual immorality, impurity, passion, evil desire, and covetousness, which is idolatry." For many, the very idea that we must kill something in us seems barbaric, self-defeating, and consistent with landing a man in an insane asylum. We have so highly exalted human desire that it cannot be questioned, much less executed. Christians, however, display the true beauty of holy desire as they put to death what is earthly in them by the Spirit.

What Should Christians Do?

I want to conclude by answering the question, "What should Christians do about all this?" Our current sexual perversion is the fruit of a false religion. Sex reassignment surgery? 11-year-old boys dancing in drag at gay bars? Men competing in a Miss Universe beauty pageant? These things are sexual anarchy. They are windows into our society's growing religious commitments. Those religious commitments lead to Nihilism, to utter despair. What should Christians do? Here are three exhortations.

First, don't be fooled. Stay sharp. Watch for the softening of Christian foundations. Worship the Creator. Uphold God's law. Ask continually, "By what standard?" Crucify your sinful desires and call others to do the same. Remember that ideas have consequences. Recall that bad ideas strike at your blind spots, advance when you are asleep, and lurk at the back door.

Richard Weaver, in his book *Ideas, Have Consequences*, highlights the process in which corrupt notions infiltrate our thinking. He warns of the Great Stereopticon. The work of this great machine is to "project selected pictures of life in the hope that what is seen will be imitated. All of us of the West who are within the long reach of technology are sitting in the audience."[12] The Great Stereopticon consists of the press, the motion-picture, and the radio (or television). The press does not want an exchange of ideas. It thrives on friction, so it exaggerates and colors beyond necessity. The motion-picture plays stories that are wrong at the root. The modern public misunderstands the danger of the motion-picture. They want censorship of long kisses and vile jokes, but it is the entire plot that is deadly. The radio or television (which in our day must include the internet) has the most significant reach of them all. It is always discipling. You can stay away from the movies or skip sections of the newspaper, but the message unceasingly comes through this third arm of the great machine. The point is not to avoid technology, news, and stories. The point is to know you are always being discipled. So stay awake.

Second, don't fear. Stay courageous. Don't pack up your toys and go home when you find out other people think you are a transgressor. Re-

---

12. Steve Weaver. *Ideas Have Consequences*. (Chicago, IL: University of Chicago Press), 2013, 85.

member what they said about our Lord. When people claim you are homophobic, racist, sexist, or misogynist, and then even other Christians begin to think you're a bit too stiff and maybe even a little judgmental, don't fear. Jesus tells us to do the opposite, "Blessed are those who are persecuted for righteousness' sake, for theirs is the kingdom of heaven. Blessed are you when others revile you and persecute you and utter all kinds of evil against you falsely on my account. Rejoice and be glad, for your reward is great in heaven, for so they persecuted the prophets who were before you" (Matthew 5:10-12).

Third, advance with the good news. We have to advance, knowing that we need a miracle from Jesus. We need to storm ahead, believing that if the Holy Spirit doesn't make this arrow hit the target, then we are doomed. We need the kind of deep love for people that's even a little crazy. Love that goes to a rebellious people willing to be rejected and ridiculed that they might have salvation. Our Christ did just that. He came to seek and save the lost. It was a risky, messy, painful work. But for the joy set before Him, He endured the cross. So should we.

We desperately need the good news to blow up all the silliness going on. So I have to close with this good news to any and all who are sexually polluted and confused. I don't care if you are gay, lesbian, bi-sexual, transgender, hear this, *Jesus Christ came to save sinners.* Jesus the Righteous One was sexually pure as snow. He was flayed on a cross so wretched sinners like you and me would never know condemnation. I don't care what kind of sexual depravity you've been involved in. I don't care if you've had sex reassignment surgery or hormone therapy. I don't care if you've been a polygamist or incestuous. I don't care if you've slept with animals. I don't care if you've sexually assaulted people in your past. If you repent of your sin and believe in Jesus Christ *you will be saved.* You will be washed. Your shame will be taken away. And you won't go on in your sexual immorality. You won't go on identifying with the sin or sinful desire you once lived in. The gratitude you will have for the free grace you've received will abound in a life of increasing purity.

I'd like to leave off with a final word for Christians. If we want to lessen the shame of certain kinds of sinners *who don't come to Christ*, and feel uncomfortable with the shame being removed from other types of sinners *who do come to Christ*, then we should see just how badly we've been compromised. If we would do justice, love kindness, and walk humbly with God in the days ahead, then we must preach Christ without compromise.

FOUR

White Privilege: The New Original Sin

By Tom Ascol

I n his classic book on Holiness JC Ryle wrote this: "The man who is content to sit ignorantly by his own fireside, wrapped up in his own private affairs, and has no public eye for what is going on in the Church and the world, is a miserable patriot, and a poor style of Christian."[1] (Holiness, 292). It is because I agree with Ryle that I write this chapter.

I believe in the devil. He is a wicked, powerful being who, together with his demons, operate as principalities, cosmic powers and spiritual forces of evil in heavenly places (Ephesians 6:12). I believe that he has specific goals and designs to wreak havoc among the people of God by mimicking and corrupting the work of the gospel (2 Corinthians 2:11; Matthew 13:24-29). I further believe that we are living in a time in the

---

1. J. C. Ryle, *Holiness* (Carlisle, PA: Banner of Truth, 2014), 292.

West when the devil and his minions have been particularly effective in carrying out their designs by seeding the culture with deadly, damnable ideas that have been wrapped in deceptive packaging to look like love and compassion.

With Paul, I am afraid that just as the devil deceived Eve by his cunning, the thoughts of many Christians in our day are in danger of being led astray from a sincere and pure devotion to Christ (2 Corinthians 11:3). And we shouldn't wonder because we have been warned that Satan disguises himself as an angel of light. Neither should it surprise us "if his servants, also, disguise themselves as servants of righteousness" (2 Corinthians 11: 14-15).

Brothers and sisters, this is what the church is always up against. There are forces of darkness that are arrayed against us and against which we have been called to contend. If we forget this or fail to take seriously what the Bible says about such spiritual warfare, then we will be easily led astray and be derelict in our duty to stand firm in both the defense and confirmation of the gospel (Philippians 1:7).

That is precisely why this book has been published. Many of these chapters seek to address godless ideologies that have spread throughout Western civilization in recent years with a vengeance and with their agenda to manipulate reality. In other words, they are telling us what we are supposed to see; naming it and defining it for us, and then demanding that we reorder our lives on the basis of this new supposed reality.

The foremost ideology that Christians in the West are facing today is Cultural Marxism. This is an adaptation of classical Marxism from an economic theory to a cultural and social one.

Classical Marxism saw class conflict between the bourgeoisie and the proletariat—or the haves and have-nots. Cultural Marxism views such conflict as between the oppressed and the oppressors; between those with privilege and those without it. The working class has been replaced by minorities. Majority groups are defined as privileged and oppressive. Minority groups are regarded as underprivileged and oppressed.

Whites, men, heterosexuals, and cisgenders are all majority groups and therefore inherently oppressive. Those who do not fit into such groups are minorities and by definition, in the Cultural Marxist scheme, oppressed. The agenda then is to see the overthrow of these oppressive groups and the structures that keep them in power—all in the name of love and compassion for the oppressed.

This ideology is on full display in our political system as well as on college and university campuses across our nation. It is seen in everything from the innocent sounding "diversity departments" to the violent silencing of those heretics who dare to question its orthodoxy.

The worldview to which this ideology has given rise has rapidly swept across our culture such that it is on its way to becoming the predominant worldview among the younger generations. In other words, the Judeo-Christian worldview in which the older generation of American Christians grew up is long gone. While pollsters have tried to tell us this for some time, they have miscalculated what has arisen in its place. Researchers have told us a great deal about the rise of the "Nones"—those who mark "none" when asked for their religious preference.

For example, a December 10, 2018 article in Religion News claims that "Nones" now comprise 35% of the American population.[2] But among those under 45 years old, that percentage increases to nearly 45%. Most have interpreted this as an increase in the secularization of America, but I believe that is a mistaken analysis.

What we are witnessing is the rapid rise of new religion. As David French has written in the National Review,

> It was foolish for anyone to believe that a less Christian America would be a less religious America. As Solomon said in Ecclesiastes, God "put

---

2. Jana Riess, "Religion Declining in Importance for Many Americans, Especially for Millennials," Religion News Service, December 10, 2018, https://religionnews.com/2018/12/10/religion-declining-in-importance-for-many-americans-especially-for-millennials/.

eternity in man's heart." Traditional Christianity and Judaism aren't just being removed from American life; they're being replaced.[3]

If true Christians do not wake up and realize what is happening, we will be ill-prepared to contend for and defend the gospel in this pivotal, cultural moment. We must resist the temptations of both liberalism and pietism. That is, we must neither uncritically buy into the agenda of Cultural Marxism by embracing its presuppositions, critical theories and assessments, nor simply ignore it or dismiss it as insignificant as long we are being left alone to preach the gospel.[4]

Rather, we must identify this new religion, expose it as an all-out assault on biblical Christianity, and refute it. We must do so by simply and accurately teaching God's Word, and proclaiming the simplicity and fulness that is in Christ. In this new religion spawned by Cultural Marxism:

- Orthodoxy is political correctness—so you must toe-the-line or be branded a heretic.
- Holiness is accrued by the number of victim statuses that you can claim (or, if you are so sinful that you don't have any or many such statuses, then your pursuit of holiness is limited to recognizing the intersecting levels of oppressions and honoring those to whom they apply).
- Conversion or being born again in this new religion is becoming awakened to Cultural Marxist categories of oppression or, as it is sometimes called, "woke."
- Original sin is "privilege," the most notable of which is "white privilege."

---

3. David French, "Intersectionality: Religion for Deep-Blue America | National Review," National Review, March 6, 2018, https://www.nationalreview.com/2018/03/intersectionality-the-dangerous-faith/.

4. Melvin Tinker, *That Hideous Strength: How the West Was Lost* (Welwyn Garden City, UK: Evangelical Press, 2018), 20.

Definition

Privilege is treated as the original sin of those who are born into a society that is imbalanced in their favor so that they cannot help but internalize prejudices and assumptions that make them part of the oppressor class. Thus, if you are a heterosexual, cisgender, white Christian male who was born in a society that is majority white, male, heterosexual and Christian, then you have multiple levels of privilege which means that you came into this world as a racist, sexist, homophobic, religious bigot.

Dr. Robin Diangelo, Professor of Education at University of Washington, and author of *White Fragility: Why it's So Hard for White People to Talk About Racism*, explains white privilege by contending that to be born white in America is to be complicit in maintaining and promoting the ideology of White Supremacy. She explains her meaning by using herself as an example.

> Think about it like this: from the time I opened my eyes, I have been told that as a white person, I am superior to people of color. There's never been a space in which I have not been receiving that message. From what hospital I was allowed to be born in, to how my mother was treated by the staff, to who owned the hospital, to who cleaned the rooms and took out the garbage. We are born into a racial hierarchy, and every interaction with media and culture confirms it—our sense that, at a fundamental level, we are superior.[5]

It is this innate condition that has been dubbed, "white privilege," by the promoters of Cultural Marxism. And this terminology is being employed in the name of racial reconciliation. It is a system of unearned privileges and advantages that have been unjustly provided to white people simply because of their race.

---

5. Sam Adler-Bell, "America's White Fragility Complex: Why White People Get so Defensive about Their Privilege," Salon, March 18, 2015, https://www.salon.com/2015/03/17/the_white_fragility_complex_why_white_people_gets_so_defensive_about_their_privilege_partner/.

Traces of this idea can be found in W. E. B. Du Bois in the 1930s. He spoke of a psychological wage that every white man earned each day simply by being white. The idea was refined and given new expression in a 1988 essay written by Peggy McIntosh, who is a radical feminist and Senior Research Associate of the Wellesley Centers for Women. She wrote an essay on Male Privilege and White Privilege that was quickly released in its shorter form entitled, "White Privilege: Unpacking the Invisible Knapsack."

The essay is a personal account of McIntosh's perceptions of her own life of privilege. She attributes many of the benefits and advantages she has to the fact that she is white and then extrapolates that to all white people. Her analogy is that all white people have a knapsack full of privileges that they enjoy but which they "have been carefully taught not to recognize."[6] Thus, their knapsacks and privileges are invisible to them. McIntosh lists 26 privileges that whites possess unthinkingly, and includes everything from being able to be in the company of people of their own race most of the time to being able to purchase "flesh-colored" band-aids and have them match their skin tone.

The Problem

There are many problems with this way of thinking. I will point out three of them.

First, this racialized way of thinking about privilege completely ignores the inevitable realities of culture, namely, that the majorities who create and lead cultures do so in ways that benefit them. This should not be surprising nor is it inherently evil. Old Testament Israel developed a culture that provided a better life for devout Jews than for pagan Gentiles. For a Gentile—even a proselyte—to complain about Jewish privilege

---

6. Peggy McIntosh, "White Privilege: Unpacking the Invisible Knapsack," *Peace and Freedom Magazine*, August 1989.

would be ridiculous. The same could be said about modern China, Japan, or any other nation. Their cultures will naturally tend to benefit those who constitute the majorities in them. So you wouldn't visit Beijing and complain that everyone there speaks Chinese because of Chinese privilege.

Second, the concept of white privilege is too hasty to lay the blame for disparities upon systemic racism. There indeed are systems of oppression in the world. In our own land unjust laws and policies have been employed by arrogant and malicious people. But it does not follow that systemic racism is a universal principle causing the different outcomes in life. God simply has not arranged His world to fit the egalitarian spirit of this age.

Men and women are inherently different. Some people are inherently stronger than others; some inherently smarter. Some are born into Christian homes. Some into pagan homes. Not every disparity between people of different races can be attributed to racial privilege or oppression. Furthermore, very often greater disparities can be found within a race than between races. Tom Brady and I are both white, but that is about all that we have in common.

A third major problem with the concept of white privilege is that once you accept it on the terms of the Cultural Marxism that spawned it, you place major obstacles between the gospel and people, whether they be white or black.

The concept of white privilege places a stain on white people that can never completely be removed and can only be partially lessened if they commit themselves to a lifelong "cultural identity journey." That's what Daniel Hill calls it in his book, *White Awake: An Honest Look at What it Means to be White*. According to Hill, the process of this journey is designed to transform white people "from blindness to sight." He describes seven stages of this journey: "encounter, denial, disorientation, shame, self-righteousness, awakening, and active participation."[7]

---

7. Daniel Hill, *White Awake* (Westmont, IL: InterVarsity Press, 2017), 49.

Those who cannot or will not stay on this journey are diagnosed with "white fragility" and will remain asleep and enslaved to their privilege until they consciously "check their privilege" (that is, repent) and get back on the pathway to awakening. Do you see what this does? It prevents the white person who accepts the Marxist notion that he is cursed with white privilege from ever being justified. He must live in a state of perpetual guilt because of something over which he has no control. He cannot check his privilege enough; He cannot repent enough to make amends for his privilege. But the gospel of Jesus Christ says that there is therefore now no condemnation for those who are in Christ Jesus! (Romans 8:1) And if the Son sets you free, you are free indeed (John 8:36).

The concept of white privilege also sets up barriers between black people and the gospel. It encourages black people to see themselves primarily as victims whose identity is determined by those more privileged than they are. This sends the false message that no matter what they do, they cannot overcome the unearned privilege of those who are white.

Such an attitude is bigoted, disrespectful and rooted in unbelief. "Therefore, if anyone is in Christ, he is a new creation. The old has passed away; behold, the new has come" (2 Corinthians 5:17). No person should be made to feel that he or she is inevitably underprivileged in the kingdom of God because of skin color. In Christ "there is neither Jew nor Greek, there is neither slave nor free, there is no male and female, for you are all one in Christ Jesus" (Galatians 3:28).

Where this reality is ignored or violated due to prejudice, bigotry or any other reason, Christians must fight against it. But we must do so on the basis of what God's Word teaches not on the basis of Marxist philosophy.

Any teaching that encourages people to think of themselves primarily as being victimized, whether on the basis of race or something else, is contrary to the ways of Christ. Our Lord suffered the greatest injustice in history. Yet never once did He speak of Himself as being a victim. In fact, in the greatest injustice that the world has ever seen—an injustice that resulted in the execution of the only righteous man who has ever lived—Jesus was doing His greatest work of conquering sin, death and hell for all who trust in Him. Anything that encourages His followers to see their own victimization as a key ingredient in their identity cannot be from Christ.

GOD'S WORD

Scripture calls us to accept responsibility for our own lives, no matter how privileged or underprivileged we may be. In the parable of the talents, Jesus makes the point that three servants were given unequal amounts of money—or we might say, privilege—but each one of them was expected to exercise wise stewardship over what they were given (Matthew 25:14-30). The servant who received five talents made five more. He was commended and rewarded. In the exact same way the servant who received only two talents was commended and rewarded. Only the servant who buried his talent and did nothing with it was rebuked and condemned by the master.

The Bible teaches us to see all of life as grace and to recognize that we stand before Him as His image-bearers who are accountable to Him. Whether He puts one, two, or five talents in my hand, I must recognize that it is more than I deserve and I must make the most with what has been entrusted to me. That is, I must use whatever gifts and opportunities—whatever privileges—God gives me to honor Him by doing good.

I am not to covet those who have more nor disdain or neglect those who have less. Rather, I am to rejoice with those who rejoice and weep with those who weep. Any ideology that discourages me from doing that is contrary to the ways of Jesus Christ and must be rejected.

The rhetorical question Paul asks in 1 Corinthians 4:7 (NKJV) should shape the way that we see ourselves and others: "For who makes you differ from another? And what do you have that you did not receive? Now if you did indeed receive it, why do you boast as if you had not received it?"

I am not saying that everyone who uses the language of "white privilege" is consciously grooving on cultural Marxism. But what I am saying is that it is dangerous—indeed often disastrous—for followers of Christ to employ concepts that have been spawned by vain philosophies of the world. Paul warns of this very thing in Colossians 2:8, "See to it that no one takes you captive by philosophy and empty deceit, according to human tradition, according to the elemental spirits of the world, and not according to Christ."

It is sadly and undeniably true that the sin of racism remains in this country and too often in our churches. But, as we must do with all sin, where we find it, let's attack it with the gospel of Jesus Christ as given to us in the Word of God.

I appeal to my fellow Christians who are tempted to buy into this ideology in an attempt to promote racial reconciliation: Please back up and reexamine the foundation of the tools you are employing. David would never have killed Goliath had he employed Saul's armor—as attractive and impressive as it was. Neither will we be able to fight effectively the racial sin that remains among us by relying on carnal weapons instead of the Sword of the Spirit. God has placed that Sword in our hands to make us thoroughly equipped for every good work.

FIVE

BIBLICAL JUSTICE AND SOCIAL JUSTICE

By Tom Nettles

Now we know that whatever the law says it speaks to those who are under the law, so that every mouth may be stopped, and the whole world may be held accountable to God. For by works of the law no human being will be justified in his sight, since through the law comes knowledge of sin. But now the righteousness of God has been manifested apart from the law, although the Law and the Prophets bear witness to it— the righteousness of God through faith in Jesus Christ for all who believe. For there is no distinction: for all have sinned and fall short of the glory of God, and are justified by his grace as a gift, through the redemption that is in Christ Jesus, whom God put forward as a propitiation by his blood, to be received by faith. This was to show God's righteousness, because in his divine forbearance he had passed over former sins. It was to show his righteousness at the present time, so that he might be just and the justifier of the one who has faith in Jesus (Romans 3:19-26 - ESV).

GOODNESS, JUSTICE, AND GRACE

Discussions of the subject of justice peer into the very essence of God and the relation of His creatures to Him. The grand scheme of the world is the revelation of God's goodness. Creation, providence, special revelation, and most profoundly, redemption all cooperate in this inexhaustible display. God's own eternal being overflows, as it were, into the creation of other beings brought into existence for the very purpose of expressing, on God's part, and, on ours, viewing, loving, and enjoying the goodness of the triune God.

When Moses requested a view of God's glory, God responded, "I will make all my goodness pass before you" (Exodus 33:18, 19). God's goodness was originally expressed in the freedom of the creature to enjoy everything in creation under the governance of sovereign prerogative expressed in law. The single positive prohibition revealed that the greatest enjoyment of God's goodness would be experienced in a proper understanding of the creature/Creator relationship. Justice in this case was the creature's glad submission to the Creator's goodness in defining the terms of fellowship. This daily fellowship prospered in the context of creaturely recognition of the transcendent excellency and consequent inviolability of divine prerogative.

Adam, however, fell. The creature claimed the divine prerogative as his own and in so doing, subjected himself and his entire covenantal posterity to the just curse of death in all its forms. A most sobering demonstration of man's disregard to righteousness confronts us when the elect nation redeemed from slavery in Egypt rebelled in the same moment God was revealing His just laws to Moses (Exodus 20, 32). Just before God gave the law a second time and renewed the covenant with Israel, in answer to the request of Moses for a sight of God's glory, God expressed His goodness beginning with the words, "I will be gracious to whom I will be gracious, and I will have compassion on whom I will have compassion" (33:19). God's goodness would be displayed in the sovereign disposal of grace and compassion. Then, as Moses took two newly cut stone tablets up Sinai, God hid Moses in the cleft of a rock, passed by him so that the glory he saw, though true and pure, was not the killing vision that a full display would have brought. In this muted vision, Moses heard God's words, "The Lord, the Lord God, merciful and gracious, longsuffering, and abounding in *goodness and truth*, keeping mercy for thousands, forgiving iniquity and transgression and sin, by no means clearing the guilty, visiting the iniquity of the fathers upon the children and the children's children to the third and fourth generation" (Exodus 34:6, 7).

This revelation of glory that abounds in goodness and truth presents the problem that only could be solved by the incarnation of the Son of God. How does God forgive when He will by no means clear the guilty? In the gospel we find it stated this way: "Christ also suffered once for sins, the just for the unjust, that He might bring us to God" (1 Peter 3:18). Paul said, God set forth Christ "as a propitiation by his blood, through faith, to demonstrate his righteousness (because in his forbearance God had passed over the sins that were previously committed) to demonstrate at the present time his righteousness, that he might be just and the justifier of the one who has faith in Jesus" (Romans 3:25, 26). The reason that God honored Moses's prayer, "Go among us, even though we are a stiff necked people; and pardon our iniquity and our sin, and take us as your inheritance" (Exodus 34:9) was the provision of a reconciler made in the eternal covenant of redemption. He would make a just recompense for the sin of the remnant of Israel and the elect of all nations. The necessity of the atoning work of Christ, yet future, kept Israel intact. The revelation of God's goodness, therefore, as exhibited in mercy and forgiveness as well as fully executing a due recompense on the guilty, consummates in the full execution of justice on the covenant representative of the people to receive forgiveness. God is just and merciful and neither of these elements of goodness suffers in the manifestation of the other. The overarching reality of the divine/human relationship both prior to and subsequent to the fall is justice.

JESUS AN EXAMPLE OF PROVIDENTIAL, UNJUST, PURPOSED SUFFERING

During His vicious treatment before and during His crucifixion, Jesus did not retaliate nor make threats for behind the unjust actions of men were the just actions of God. "When they hurled their insults at him, he did not retaliate; when he suffered, he made no threats. Instead, he entrusted himself to him who judges justly. He himself bore our sins in his body on the cross" (1 Peter 2:23,24). In Christ's sufferings, God judged justly the sins of His people. Also, He will judge justly the sins of those who remain unforgiven, for He will by no means clear the guilty.

God's law indicates the perfect holiness and righteousness of God which necessarily is expressed in justice. The relationship of the Christian to justice is one of infinite debt personally, fully paid by Christ so that if we have the grace of confessing our sins, He is "faithful" to His covenant promise "and just" in receiving the perfect ransom and redemption to "forgive us our sins and to cleanse us from all unrighteousness" (1 John 1:9).

God's revelation of Himself in terms of justice and His salvation to sinners in perfect harmony with that justice calls on us to consider two applications of justice. One, how do we respond personally to perceptions of injustice toward ourselves and our fellow believers? Jesus, above all, knew that His unjust treatment in the hands of men arose from a purpose of justice in the decree of God. Peter gives Christ's suffering as an example of how we should endure wrongful suffering (1 Peter 1:6; 2:19). Two, how do we respond to perceptions of injustice in culture in general and the world at large?

We may not have perfect answers to either of these questions, for we are dealing, to some extent, with the hidden purposes of God in both areas. But, through what is revealed, we can seek to establish principles within which we can talk and act as Christian brothers and sisters.

It Will be Worth it All When We see Jesus

We can be certain that there are only two points within the entire span of time when perfect justice will be reified among men. The first, as already indicated, is in the atoning work of Christ. Christ died the "just for the unjust" in a redemption designed to give perfect execution of God's wrath for all the sins of all His elect. The last farthing was paid and those who are thus ransomed certainly find ultimate deliverance. It is this certainty that explains the present patience of God with the moral tailspin of the world, not willing that any of His elect should perish, but that all should come to repentance (2 Peter 3:9). He will rescue the righteous man and "hold the unrighteous for the day of judgment" (2 Peter 2:7-9). Believers are received as just, though we are unjust, for perfect justice has been done by God Himself in bruising His Son for our iniquities.

The second point of perfect justice will occur when the final judgment comes and many will hear, "Enter into the joy of your Lord," and others will hear "Depart from me ye workers of iniquity." Paul was confident, in light of the perfectly just operations of the covenant of redemption, he would be given a "crown of righteousness" by "the Lord, the righteous judge," along with all "who are unflinching lovers of His appearing" [my translation]—both His humble appearing for redemption and His glorious appearing for the perfect consummation of all things (2 Timothy 4:8). Peter gives more detail to this manifestation of perfect righteousness both in judgment and redemption in depicting it as "the day of judgment and destruction of ungodly men," the meltdown of this present heavens and earth, and the presentation of a promised "new heaven and new earth in which righteousness makes its abode" (2 Peter 3:7, 12-13).

Another striking revelation of the perfect justice to be enacted when Christ returns appears in Paul's words to the Thessalonians in the middle of a time of persecution. Note the emphasis on righteousness and justice in which we may confidently hope though no apparent relief looms before us in this life:

> This is evidence [that is, their present persecutions and afflictions] of the righteous judgment of God, that you may be considered worthy of the kingdom of God, for which you are suffering—since indeed God considers it just to repay with affliction those who afflict you, and to grant relief to you who are afflicted as well as to us, when the Lord Jesus is revealed from heaven with his mighty angels in flaming fire, inflicting vengeance on those who do not know God and on those who do not obey the gospel of our Lord Jesus. They will suffer the punishment of eternal destruction, away from the presence of the Lord and from the glory of his might. (2 Thessalonians 1:5-9 ESV).

Paul goes on to pray that God would make them "worthy of his calling," having introduced the section with the assumption that their suffering for the kingdom was indeed evidence that they would be considered "worthy." We know that this worthiness is not the merit of eternal life gained only through perfect obedience to the moral law. It does reflect, however, that the moral character of the kingdom is reflected in the developing character and confidence in divine goodness that is shown in a patient endurance of present suffering for the sake of future glory in the presence of God.

I agree with the vision perceived by Eric Mason in his *Woke Church* when he wrote, "We can't let these issues of race make us forget that Jesus is coming back. We may think anger, and picketing, and legislation, and hashtags change things. But there's a real revolution coming. He will set all things in order. . . . Yet here we're seeing the equality of all people who have been washed by the blood of the Lamb and made worthy through Christ to be able to stand before God. They're not standing in themselves; they're standing in the Lamb. They're not proclaiming how great they are or what they did for Christ. They're standing and they're showing how worthy Christ is!"[1]

In between these two perfect displays of justice, the cross and final judgment, how should Christians look at the principle of justice and

---

1. Eric Mason, *Woke Church* (Chicago, IL: Moody Publishers, 2018), 168, 171.

righteousness revealed in Scripture?

THE PERFECT STANDARD

The standard of righteousness, and therefore of justice, is divine law. Because righteousness is impossible without the love of righteousness (the crown of righteousness is given to those whose affections are constantly set on his appearing), the highest form of purely just living is to love God with all of our being. As the greatest of beings who is infinitely worthy of praise and whose goodness is immutable, God stands as the object of supreme love, both of benevolent love and of complacent love. To love him constitutes, therefore, the first and greatest commandment. Righteousness and justice find full exhibition in love for God. Precisely this constituted Jesus as the exalted Savior-King in the Hebrews application of Psalm 45: "But facing the Son he says, 'Your throne, O God, extends into eternity, and you rule your kingdom with perfect uprightness. You loved righteousness and hated lawlessness; on account of this, God your God, anointed you with the oil of exuberant joy above your companions.'" (Hebrews 1:8, 9 [personal translation]).

The second commandment also calls for love of the righteousness that it expresses: "Love your neighbor as yourself." John gives a perfect correlation to love and righteousness in saying, "Whoever does not practice righteousness is not of God, nor is he who does not love his brother" (1 John 3:10). We are not allowed to bless God but curse men, for humankind is made in the image and likeness of God (James 3: 9, 10).

Even within the commandment of love for neighbor, we find a hierarchical application of the duty related to divine righteousness as Paul relates the work of the Spirit to the moral love intrinsic to the law. He expounds love for neighbor as doing "good to all people as we have opportunity, particularly those of the household of faith" (Galatians 6:10). This point is precisely what Jarvis Williams, an African-American New Testament scholar, affirms in saying, "Practicing racial reconciliation means that I regard a white Christian as my brother, but not an African-American who is a non-Christian. Hence, my love and service to my Christian brothers and sisters should transcend any love, affection, favoritism, devotion and service that I offer someone from my race, because Christians are part of the family of God. Membership in the Christian family is much more important than association with any ethnic group or club."[2]

The second great commandment, therefore, is to be kept purely and conscientiously, with both benevolent and complacent love. Because the beings loved, however, are finite both in nature and being, loving them is dependent on the Being and excellence of God Himself. Their excellence, even if sinless, is less glorious than that of God. Both benevolence and complacence toward them, therefore, arises from their own relation to God. Jesus introduces us to the intensified covenantal love when He said, "Here are my mother and my brothers! Whoever does God's will is my brother and sister and mother" (Mark 3:34). Omitting any discussion as to how "perfect hatred" (Psalm 139:22) is a proper response to God's enemies and a reflection of God's own moral perfection (Psalm 5:5; 11:5; Malachi 1:2, 3), we must recognize that sometimes love for God will result in separation from and resistance to fellow creatures (cf. Luke 14:26; Mark 10:29). The regard we have for their ways compared to the moral imperative of knowing, following, and loving Christ will seem like hatred.

These relationships—justice, righteousness, and love [with its perfect corollary, hatred of evil]—inform us as we seek to investigate how the Christian responds to injustice in the world, both toward himself and toward others.

The Imperfect World

We are faced immediately, however, with the sad reality of a fallen world, that we all presently live below the original and immutable stand-

---

2. Jarvis Williams, *One New Man* (Nashville TN: B & H, 2010), 136.

ard of righteousness. Subsequent to the fall of Adam we will note perfect justice only in the cross and in the judgment. We still are governed by a law of perfect justice but never experience its beauty and power until heaven. We have been given, therefore, certain accommodations to help with stability and to point beyond the accommodation to a better way.

Government:

One accommodation is that civil government is given the sword. In an unfallen world, the sword would be unnecessary; its present functions fall beyond the perfect standard of justice implied in the Law in which all would love their neighbors as themselves and there would be no murder, or other destructive evils. Nevertheless, taking a life becomes an obligation in a fallen world: "Whoever sheds man's blood, by man his blood shall be shed; for in the image of God he made man" (Genesis 9:6 NKJV). And then in Romans 13, "Therefore, whoever resists the authority resists the ordinance of God, and those who resist will bring judgment on themselves . . . for he does not bear the sword in vain, for he is God's minister, an avenger to execute wrath on him who practices evil" (Romans 13: 2, 4 NKJV). In an unfallen world the execution of wrath would be unknown either from the hand of man or the hand of God. Presently, however, in order that we might enjoy a "peaceful and quiet life, godly and dignified in every way," we make "supplications, intercession, prayers, and thanksgivings" for all kinds of governing authorities (1 Timothy 2:1,2). This necessary accommodation can be abused and often is. We submit to it as better than anarchy but with determination to establish as nearly as possible a more perfect integration of freedom, law, and justice.

Marriage:

A second accommodation is in the provisions related to divorce.: "When a man takes a wife and marries her, and it happens that she find no favor in his eyes because he has found some uncleanness in her, and he writes her a certificate of divorce, puts it in her hand, and sends her out of his house" (Deuteronomy 24:1 NKJV). In such a case she is not to be received back by him if she goes and marries another. This provision of divorce God used as an image of His attitude toward a disobedient Israel, "Then I saw that for all the causes for which backsliding Israel had committed adultery, I had put her away and given her a certificate of divorce" (Jeremiah 3:8 NKJV). When this question arose in the ongoing attempt of the Pharisees to catch Jesus in some heresy, He said, "Because of the hardness of your heart he wrote you this precept" and then contrasted it with the original intent of God in creation. Further accommodation is seen in the phenomenon of a person who has become a believer while the spouse remained an unbeliever. "If the unbeliever departs, let him depart; a brother or a sister is not under bondage in such cases. But God has called us to peace" (1 Corinthians 7:15 NKJV). Peter instructs believing wives with unbelieving husbands to be submissive so that they, "without a word, may be won by the conduct of their wives, when they observe your chaste conduct accompanied by fear" (1 Peter 3:1 NKJV).

Again, we often see gross abuse even of this accommodation. The Samaritan woman in John 4 provides a potent illustration of rampant disregard not only of original intent but of the measured accommodation.

Masters and Slaves:

A third major accommodation in the relations within society is the relation of master and slave. In an unfallen world, this relation would not exist and so would not have to be regulated. Slavery for the Gibeonites (Joshua 9) was an accommodation to their coexistence with the Israelites for they had shrewdly gained a covenantal commitment from them to let them live. When they found out that they actually were close neighbors in the land that was to be cleansed of all of its idolatrous peoples, they spared them but used them as slaves. Joshua said, "Now therefore, you are cursed, and none of you shall be freed from being slaves—woodcutters and water carriers for the house of my God" (Joshua 9:23). Though this accommodation was not the ideal of godly freedom, for the Gibeonites it was preferable to annihilation and for the Israelites it represented a compromise between their covenantal promise and their failure to execute the command of God utterly to destroy them.

Since the presence of slavery in America is foundational to most social justice ideas, we should look more carefully at that phenomenon. While we do not find the Bible condemning the relationship of slavery as, in every case, an immoral institution, several biblical factors work as leaven in a fallen world to eliminate slavery in human relations. One, in Israel, "If a man is found kidnapping any of his brethren of the children of Israel, and mistreats him or sells him, then the kidnaper shall die; and you shall put the evil from among you" (Deuteronomy 24:7 NKJV). Two, this specific law combined with the word in the ten commandments, "Thou shalt not steal," serves as the foundation for Paul's listing of "kidnappers," or "Man-stealers" in 1 Timothy 1:10 as a violation of the law and as a trait of the "lawless and insubordinate." Three, the preface to the Ten Commandments in which God identified Himself as the one who brought Israel "out of the land of Egypt, out of the house of bondage," says that the goal of God for His people is freedom. He wants them to have an internal manifestation of the law and of personal discipline and love so that it is not necessary that any kind of forceful restrictions be placed on them. The extension of this image into the New Testament as a purpose of the gospel gives a powerful incentive to "walk by the Spirit" so we will not "gratify the desires of the flesh." The spiritual analogy of freedom from slavery to sin, freedom to be bound to Christ, shows that freedom is preferable to slavery. "So, brothers, we are not children of the slave but of the free woman. For freedom Christ has set us free; stand firm therefore, and do not submit again to a yoke of slavery" (Galatians 4:31, 5:1, 16 ESV).

Four, Paul's word to the Corinthians in 1 Corinthians 7 also serves as leaven to seek to serve God in freedom instead of in slavery:

> Only let each person lead the life that the Lord assigned to him, and to which God has called him. This is my rule in all the churches. . . .

Each one should remain in the condition in which he was called. Were you a slave when called? Do not be concerned about it. (But if you can gain your freedom, avail yourself of the opportunity.) For he who was called in the Lord as a slave is a freedman of the Lord. Likewise, he who was free when called is a slave of Christ. You were bought with a price; do not become slaves of men. So, brothers, in whatever condition each was called, there let him remain with God" (1 Corinthians 7:17, 20-24 ESV).

The condition of slavery can be seen as an "assignment" from God, and as an assignment it is to be viewed as that "to which God has called him." A slave who is a Christian sees his bondage to Christ as so transcendently real, that he need not regard himself as a slave to men. If, however, legitimate opportunity for freedom comes, take it, for freedom is a better condition than slavery. In a condition of freedom, one may more readily fulfill Paul's admonition "Let him labor, doing honest work with his own hands, so that he may have something to share with anyone in need." (Ephesians 4:28).

Fifth, the admonition that slaves and masters both serve the same master in heaven (Ephesians 6:9; Colossians 4:1) and are to consider one another as "beloved brothers" tends toward the freedom of the slave (Philemon 16).

It is because slavery is the most restricting, limiting, and personally galling relationship that exists in the fallen world that Paul and Peter give very careful and clear instructions to both slaves and masters. Perhaps the most succinct summary of the manner in which slaves were to conduct themselves is found in 1 Timothy 6:1. "Let all who are under the yoke as slaves regard their own master as worthy of all honor, so that the name of God and the teaching may not be reviled. Those who have believing masters must not be disrespectful on the ground that they are brothers; rather they must serve all the better since those who benefit by their good service are believers and beloved."

Does Scripture guide us to fitting responses when we are treated unjustly? In writing to slaves about unjust treatment from brutal masters,

Peter said, "For it is commendable if a man bears up under the pain of unjust suffering because he is conscious of God" (1 Peter 2:19). Are we to we to complain against Peter and think that he should have advocated rebellion as a justifiable action? Paul adds, "Exhort bondservants to be obedient to their own masters, to be well pleasing in all things, not answering back, not pilfering, but showing all good fidelity, that they may adorn the doctrine of God our Savior in all things" (Titus 2:9, 10) And after Paul admonished slaves to serve their masters "with fear and trembling, in sincerity of heart, as to Christ," he told masters, "And you, masters, do the same things to them, giving up threatening, knowing that your own master also is in heaven, and there is no partiality with him" (Ephesians 6:9).

Even as we cannot hold the spouse sinful who is separated from the unbelieving spouse on the basis of the unbeliever's unwillingness to live in harmony, or the government as sinful that uses the sword in a responsible way to enforce the good and lawful and suppress the evil and unlawful, nor can we find the slave/master relationship *per se* as intrinsically sinful. There are better options in all of these relationships, but these accommodations are not condemned.

Most social justice application in the United States, arises from an assumption of the absolute evil of slavery even as an accommodation in a fallen world. In his 1963 presidential address at the Southern Baptist Convention Herschel Hobbs preached, "In like fashion take the institution of slavery. It would be blasphemy to say that Jesus approved of it. However, not one word of condemnation of it fell from His lips." He goes on to affirm that the principles Jesus instilled in human society "sounded the death knell for human slavery" and everything which "degrades men made in the image of God."[3] If, however, one receives the principle of accommodation, it would not be blasphemous at all to observe that, in this fallen world, Jesus did not consider slavery an absolute moral evil or that masters were, *ipso facto,* to be condemned for their position. Perhaps he

---

3. *Annual of the Southern Baptists Convention,* 1963, 93.

did not utter a word of condemnation of it because the relation of master and slave was not condemnable.

Real Injustice:

We also are instructed personally, however, as to how we should respond in truly unjust situations. When Paul was imprisoned, it certainly was unjust, but he prayed that "utterance may be given to me, that I may open my mouth boldly to make known the mystery of the gospel" (Ephesians 6:19). He told the Philippians that his imprisonment "had turned out for the furtherance of the gospel" (Philippians 1:12). He requested of the Colossians to pray "that God would open to us a door for the word, to speak the mystery of Christ for which I am also in chains" (Colossians 4:3). He invited Timothy not to be ashamed of the "testimony of our Lord nor of me his prisoner, but share with me in the sufferings for the gospel according to the power of God" (2 Timothy 1:8). Paul expressed nothing but confidence in divine providence in these situations. He invoked his legal standing as a citizen of Rome on four occasions in order to escape unjust treatment and gain a broader hearing for the gospel (Acts 16:37; 21:39; 22:25-29; 25:11, 12)

When James preached strongly against wealthy farmers who fraudulently withheld wages from their workers, he warned them that the cries of the oppressed would certainly come to the Lord of Hosts. This fearlessness in oppression was the spirit of personal indulgence and love of position that consummated itself in the killing of the Lord Jesus Christ. The only righteous one was subjected to their perversion of justice. In light of that, James told those who were mistreated so to "be patient, brethren, until the coming of the Lord. . . .Do not grumble against one another. . . .Take the prophets who spoke in the name of the Lord, as an example of suffering and patience" (James 5:1-10). Is such biblical admonition a fearful capitulation to the arenas of power in the world? Can we not really believe that when a thing reaches the ear of the Lord of Hosts, it certainly will be set right, either here or in eternity. It will be most complete and satisfying in eternity.

How do we respond to the theory of social justice and the remedies it sets forth for seeking just resolution of its perceptions of injustice? In what way does gospel justice form the response that a Christian has to unjust situations in the world? How should admonitions of patience and submission to providence inform the Christian response to the principles of social justice? How do we evaluate terms of repentance when we believe we have been wronged? How should we act when certain aspects of injustice are within our reach? How should we respond when others are beyond our reach? Does the gospel reality that we already have received perfect justice in the framework of infinite mercy in God's gracious provision of His Son as Redeemer and that He Himself will execute perfect justice on wrongdoers influence our perceptions of how justice is defined and sought in secular culture?

Moral Law Among Non-virtuous People

In this life, the perfect standard of justice is the moral law. The whole of it is a schoolmaster designed to lead us to Christ in His redemptive work. Then it defines for us the constant standard for sanctification in our conformity to Christ in loving God and also loving man. The ceremonial law is done away with for Christ has filled it full in His own person and in His sending of the Spirit. The spiritual truths within the civil law were to be applied to the new people of God in the church. A good example of that is found in 2 Corinthians 6:14-7:1, where physical punishment in Israel is replaced by spiritual discipline in the church and the covenantal status of Israel is given over to a Gentile congregation.

Under the new covenant, we do not argue for the institution of the first table of the commandments in civil society, but we do work to be leaven in the society by preaching the gospel. Any society that ignores the provisions of the second table will be a very unstable, dangerous, immoral, and, by definition, an unjust society. Even the most stable outwardly just society, however, only masks the true virtue that is indicated by a real engagement with the requirements of the Law. In addition, we find it pragmatically appropriate that certain disciplined accommodations are made in a fallen world in order to obtain the highest level possible of safety, stability, and justice for the highest percentage of the population.

How do we negotiate these treacherous waters of seeking justice in a fallen world, for fallen people, from fallen people. Before suggesting several areas in which the Social Justice movement imposes an alien agendum on the principles of gospel justice, I want to suggest several points of which we must be aware if we are to come out of this discussion with more light than fight, more love than hate, more truth than caricature.

Rules of Engagement

First, we must acknowledge that many of those with whom we take issue on this difficulty are professing and cordial evangelicals. They believe the Bible, accept the Trinity, believe that Christ died to redeem sinners, and that He is coming again. We want a meeting of the minds in a fraternal discussion.

Second, with all candor we must acknowledge that some of the difficulty has been created by the number of times Southern Baptists, among other evangelical denominations, have passed resolutions concerning public justice, particularly concerning race, that only slowly have had any substantial effect in conduct or real resolution of cultural tension. Since 1845 a variety of resolutions was passed concerning the "colored population," and then after the civil war regular statements concerning evangelism, education, church planting among the same population. As early as 1923, Southern Baptist were prompting cases of conscience on these social issues and their relation to the evangelistic task of the church. Complicated by the Social Gospel movement and its development of an aberrant non-evangelical theology, the report said, "some people . . . think . . . there is some sort of conflict between social service and the gospel" but, while denying an essential conflict, insisted that "Southern Baptists will never preach social service as a substitute for the work of grace in the individual heart." The implication is that though we have a distinct priority for preaching the gospel, the other should not be left undone.

In May 1954, a Supreme Court decision abolishing segregation of public schools evoked from the much-admired senator from Mississippi James O. Eastland the comment, "The South will not abide by or obey this legislative decision by a political court . . . Education cannot thrive in a climate such as would result from the mixture of the races in the public schools." One representative said flatly, "The white and Negro children of my state are not going to school together."[4]

In 1961, in the midst of nationwide aggressive action seeking to implement the seven-year old Supreme Court decision, a resolution of the Southern Baptist Convention was adopted just prior to some of the most sorrowful, disgusting, and eventually murderous manifestations of division, injustice, and hatred that characterized the mid-twentieth century.

> This Convention in years past has expressed itself clearly and positively on issues related to race relations. Today the solution of the race problem is a major challenge to Christian faith and action at home and abroad. Because Southern Baptists are the largest Christian group in the area where racial tensions between whites and Negroes are most acute, we feel an especially keen sense of Christian responsibility in this hour. We recognize that members of our churches have sincere differences of opinion as to the best course of action in this matter. On solid scriptural grounds, however, we reject mob violence as an attempted means of solving this problem. We believe that both lawless violence on one hand and unwarranted provocation on the other are outside the demands of Christ upon us all. We believe that the race problem is a moral and spiritual as well as social problem. Southern Baptists accept the teachings of the Bible and the Commission of Christ as our sole guide of faith and practice in this area as in every other area. We cannot afford

---

4. Carson Clayborne, *Reporting Civil Rights: Part One - American Journalism 1941-1963* (New York, NY: The Library of America, 2003), 208. This book contains nearly 1000 pages of immediate reporting of civil rights violations, often brutal and murderous, as well as more long-term reflective articles.

to let pride or prejudice undermine . . . either our Christian witness at home or the years of consecrated, sacrificial missionary service among all the peoples of the world. We therefore urge all Southern Baptists to speak the truth of Christ in love as it relates to all those for whom he died. We further urge that this Convention reaffirm its conviction that every man has dignity and worth before the Lord. Let us commit ourselves as Christians to do all that we can to improve the relations among all races as a positive demonstration of the power of Christian love.[5]

The tortured history of race relations and the lamentable tardiness of Baptists in the South to come to terms with the moral implications of racial prejudice left the principles of gospel justice and Christian discipleship threatened by clinging to sinful prejudices. Refusal to be willing to suffer for and with others in real issues of justice—legal, gospel, and moral—can blunt the arguments that we might maintain against the driving philosophy of social justice theory. If we would evaluate social justice ideas as honestly and accurately as possible, none of us can turn a blind eye to the real, and often radical, purely racist meanness that has often been a dominant force in society.

A Personal Pilgrimage

Born and reared in Mississippi 1946-1968, I came of age during the thick of some of the most blatantly racist activities in both society and church. I was 9 years old when Emmett Till, a fourteen-year old was lynched, beaten, shot, and thrown into the Tallahatchie river for supposedly whistling at a 21-year old white woman. The accusation was apparently false. His murderers were acquitted by an all-white jury though identified by three eye-witnesses, all of whom were black. In 1962, I remember feeling strangely disconnected from, and morally resistant, to the rage that surrounded the enrolment of James Meredith in the University of Mississippi, and amused at Ross Barnett's charade of moral courage in

---

5. *Annual of the Southern Baptist Convention,* 1961

opposing Robert Kennedy's enforcement of the process. A bit later, I was sixteen going on seventeen and beyond when sit-ins in Jackson, Mississippi, at the Woolworth's lunch counter were part of civil rights actions. Jackson is twelve miles from my home town of Brandon. These resulted in the rampant verbal insult, physical assaults and eventual jailtime for students from Tougaloo, some from Jackson State, some from local black high schools and others from out-of-state.

The assassination of Medgar Evers in the summer of 1963, shot in the back by Byron De la Beckwith, gradually brought an end to the demonstrations. On the weekend after the funeral for Evers, attempts to enter churches, including some Baptist churches and First Baptist church of Jackson resulted in their being turned away by deacons. Finally, they were welcomed to an Episcopal church and sat quietly through the service, were welcomed by several of the parishioners, and were invited to return by the minister. One year later, the murders of Chaney, Goodman, and Schwerner, civil rights workers took place in Neshoba County Mississippi, at the hands of the KKK. That was the summer before I entered college. This is the reality behind the Statement on Social Justice that says, "believers can and should utilize all lawful means that God has providentially established to have some effect on the laws of a society."[6] And, we can add, the enforcement of those laws and the necessity of being a conscientious goad to those responsible for such enforcement.

A refusal to recognize that behind the movement for social justice are real and often grotesque instances of injustice can lead to a failure to deal with the remnants of any kind of indwelling sin including racism. Eric Mason graphically described how the history of racism affected his early perceptions as a black man reared by older parents who experienced the worst of the Jim Crow South.[7] Jarvis Williams also described the humili-

---

6. The Statement on Social Justice, https://statementonsocialjustice.com.

7. Mason, *Woke*, 75-77.

ation of racial snideness and meanness that accompanied his childhood in a "small and racist town in eastern Kentucky."[8] In all of our personal histories, only the gospel has the power to operate as leaven to heal the fears, insecurities, pride, and sinful responses of tension-filled relationships. Persons on both sides of this historic cultural dynamic need the humbling and curative powers of gospel truth; nothing else will cure deeply enough.

My gradual coming to terms with the cruel reality of this environment was initiated by the 1954 world series win of the New York Giants and a consequent life-long intense admiration of the ability of Willie Mays. Second, the female woman of color from Laurel, Mississippi, Leontyne Price, whose voice both in raw talent and in perfection gained by training has never, in my opinion, been equaled by any other. These palpable examples of clear superiority in highly competitive professional disciplines escalated my sense of the stupidity as well as the moral indefensibility of the atmospheric prejudice of my environment. This pilgrimage culminated when combined with the most profound and lasting of change agents, the doctrines of the gospel. All humans have descended from Adam and, in him, are corrupt and condemned. All who come by faith into Christ are justified and are not under condemnation. All who are indwelt by the Holy Spirit will be sanctified, fitted for heaven, and eventually glorified. The greatest standard of justice to which we must conform is God's righteousness communicated to us by Jesus Christ in His perfect obedience. The greatest healing we need is not from any kind of environmental and cultural denigration but from the ravages of indwelling sin. All this occurs without respect of persons. Each of us should trace our journeys in these matters to uncover any remnants of sinful dispositions in this matter. Most of you will not have as far to go as I did. As all of us objectify our stories, we must recognize that law does not conform to our history, but remans impartial when applied in its purest form.

---

8. Jarvis Williams, *Removing the Stain of Racism from the Southern Baptist Convention,* (Nashville, TN: B & H, 2017), 17-19.

SOCIAL JUSTICE COMMANDEERS THE GOSPEL

While we must be earnest in these matters of opposing real evil in society, we should also recognize that some principles in the Social Justice movement, if applied uncritically, will lead away from the Bible's concept of gospel justice and Christian discipleship and tend to substitute cultural engagement for gospel proclamation. Observation of certain inequalities, both real and supposed, legitimately makes persons look for solutions. The appearance of racism, economic disparity, supposed prejudicial distribution of job opportunities opens the door to solutions that borrow from anti-Christian world views.

Plausible Philosophical Leaven

The ideas of the Hegelian and Marxist dialectic that views the world in terms of a developing perfect synthesis drives social justice theory. Immanuel Kant (1724-1804) argued that ideals of good are isolated in an unseen—a noumenal—world, and all we experience and can verify is the phenomenal expression of tangible realities, for no moral values can be proved empirically. Practical reason, however, needs virtue and freedom for culmination of the moral imperative, the sense of duty that must govern all human interaction. God must exist in order to give perfect unity to freedom and responsibility in a state of immortality. G. W. F. Hegel (1770-1831), sought a method by which Kant's noumenal world would actually be given empirical reality in this life. The movement of thesis, antithesis, synthesis in an ongoing pattern is supposed to yield a reality in which a perfect equilibrium in social relations, political justice, development of arts and science, educational theory, and economic standing is achieved in the Absolute Idea. Kant's noumenal can become the phenomenal by the logic of history. Karl Marx (1818-1883) dropped the idealism of Hegel and opted for material reality as the only viable reality since that was the only palpable phenomenon of human experience. The Kantian concept of the necessity of God's existence in order to give substance to the categorical imperative, amounts to an invention of religion. The positing of God and religion, therefore, causes tolerance of present inequality and is on that account a mere opiate, a mirage good only for the oppression of the masses. Belief in God is simply manufactured to relieve the existential stress between classes. Material equilibrium and equality will be the final synthesis and can only be achieved when the opiate of the people is eliminated. Pure Marxism encouraged revolution through class struggle, often violent. This was designed to speed along the process so that the ultimate synthesis of material equality (government control of all means of production) soon would come to be a present phenomenon.

Others who accepted the dialectic did not want to destroy religion in the process, but to use it and its already-embraced ideas as the tools for promoting the social changes envisioned. Antonio Gramsci (1891-1937) was an Italian Neo-Marxist who dropped the absolute materialistic determinism of Marx and sought to incorporate elements of other intellectual traditions such as critical theory, psychology, existential philosophy, and religion. To achieve hegemony, one does not reject the language of God and theology but inject new concepts into their received meaning and put the energy of religion into the desired social revolution. Liberation theology was the master stroke of this theory. In the same way, when this philosophy is combined with a mental concept enforced by the biblical language of justice, reconciliation, original sin, oppression we have fertile ground for the plausible ideology of social justice. What we actually have, however, is not the biblical idea of justice and its outworking in Law and Gospel, the development of Christian character through patient endurance, but an interpretation of the Christian faith that is infused with Hegelian and Marxist goals. The theory must identify the final antithesis, an evil composed of all forces that oppose the final goal. The oppressive agent in society in a general way is "whiteness." Depending on how many moral categories one is willing to jettison, it is more critically *straight, white, maleness*. The final synthesis is a remediation of all these social and cultural inequalities by means of a perfect intersectionality of offended groups. We are called on to help develop this final synthesis, combining both the ideal and the material, as a matter of Christian discipleship.

Civil Law and Biblical Standards

When we embrace certain principles of social justice, we must be careful to distinguish what we accept as just and right in society and civil equality from our commission as proclaimers of divine revelation. If we defend the right of women to equal treatment in the marketplace to job opportunity, salary, education, and positions of administration we do not forsake or relativize the biblical standard that the gift of elder, bishop, or pastor-teacher is limited in Scripture to men, not based on passing cultural ideas but rooted in fundamental doctrinal precepts. We do not argue that the rights of women extend to sovereignty over "her own body" in a way that legitimizes abortion. If we defend the rights of gay people to a wide latitude of rights in job markets, social interaction, we do not reject the biblical teaching or the necessity of our preaching it and governing our churches in accordance with the biblical condemnation of homosexuality as unnatural affection that is evidence of a judgment on society and on individuals. We will not cease to call for repentance from the sin and warnings that that, along with all sexual immorality, embraced without repentance, will come under the eternal judgment of God.

The social justice principle of intersectionality presses toward unifying all those who identify themselves as oppressed as a single complainant and can easily press Christian teachers and churches into owning causes that are anti-scriptural. One need only read *A Theology for the Social Gospel* by Walter Rauschenbusch to realize how these issues can press theology toward pure immanence and social remediation and forsake the reality of transcendence, cross-centered redemption from the consequences of sin, and the centrality of our hope in the transformation that comes at the appearing of Jesus Christ in glory.

Impact of Social Justice Theory

I think acceptance of social justice categories presents several challenges to orthodox, evangelical theology and alters the biblical worldview in several observable ways.

Exegesis:

Social Justice encourages exegetical accommodation that has unwarranted doctrinal implications. For example, reconciliation of Ephesians 2:15 is interpreted as a subjective-attitudinal operation of the Spirit. In turn, this is seen as an essential and definitional element of the gospel apart from which one has not fully understood or embraced the gospel, and includes racial reconciliation with all its historical assumptions as endemic to gospel understanding. In the midst of some excellent and helpful exegetical work, the interpreter inserts the idea that the "Gentiles were racially separated from God's promises" when the textual emphasis is that they were covenantally separated, separated by requirements of the ceremonial law. This shift leads then to the liberty of stating that "Jesus himself provided the model for this racial reconciliation in that he preached this gospel of peace to Jews near the promises and the Gentiles far away from these promises."[9]   Paul's argument, however, is that in reconciliation an objective cross work of Christ abolishes all distinctions necessarily consequent upon the ceremonial law and brings elect human sinners, both Jew and Gentile, as one redeemed body into Christ's substitutionary, propitiatory death giving all of them peace with God. God's enmity toward them, prompted justly by personal transgression and original corruption, has been removed in Christ.

The writer states, "The gospel includes both entry language (repentance and faith, justification by faith and reconciliation with God) . . . and maintenance language (walking in the Spirit . . . reconciliation between

---

9. Williams, *Stain,* 40, 42.

Jews and Gentiles . . . , and loving one another in the power of the Spirit. Walking in the Spirit is a gospel reality because Jesus died for our sins to deliver us from this present evil age (Gal 1:4) so that Jews and Gentiles would receive the blessing of Abraham which is the Spirit (Gal 3:14b)." The writer goes on to say, "Because of much confusion among evangelicals about the meaning of the gospel, I further develop below a holisitic and complicated definition of the gospel in the most simplistic way I can without compromising the integrity of the argument or the biblical material."[10] He enlists 1 Corinthians 15:1-8 as an item of evidence because Paul "discusses the gospel he preached to the Corinthians and the gospel by which they were saved without mentioning justification by faith. Instead Paul mentions the cross and the resurrection as a summary of his gospel. This observation acknowledges that justification is only one of the many important parts of the gospel."[11] It is puzzling that the writer could say this shows Paul's discussion of the gospel apart from justification by faith when the text is riddled with both the vocabulary of justification and an assumption of its preeminent importance. Paul was defending bodily resurrection by pointing to the resurrection of Christ as essential for the doctrine of justification. "By which you are being saved, if you hold fast to the word I preached to you—unless you believed in vain." "But if there is no resurrection of the dead, then not even Christ has been raised. And if Christ has not been raised, then our preaching is vain and your faith is in vain." "And if Christ has not been raised, your faith is futile and you are still in your sins." (1 Corinthians 15:13, 14, 17 ESV). Paul argues that forgiveness and right standing before God is utterly dependent on the completed work of Christ for sinners, which includes His bodily resurrection, a message to be received by faith. Justification by faith, rather than being absent, is the very core of Paul's argument.

---

10. Ibid., 31.

11. Ibid., 38.

Gospel, he argues again, with some plausibility, "should not be defined exclusively in terms of justification by faith." In discussion of Galatians 1:6-2:14, the writer claims that Paul "uses the gospel vocabulary without mentioning justification" and he claims that Peter's problem in Galatians 2:11-14 was a failure to see the "horizontal component of the gospel."[12] In fact, Paul actually makes the point that Peter had implied a legalism in the vertical relationship for both Jew and Gentile. This kind of isolationism in exegesis makes the reader miss the extended context that Paul subsumes all of these into a discussion of justification by faith in Galatians 2:15-21. Paul then extends the implications of that throughout chapters 3-5 including a discussion of life in the Spirit, who is given because of Christ's justifying work, as a manifestation of freedom from the damning burden of the law. All of it flows from justification by faith.

After an extended discussion of the many ways in which "euangelion" is used in Scripture, the writer concludes, "This observation acknowledges that justification is only one of the many important parts of the gospel."[13] In listing 9 elements of the redemptive work of Christ (overall an impressive synthesis of the benefits the believer has in Christ) he includes "the ability and freedom to live in pursuit of love in the power of the Spirit to thereby fulfill the entire law (Galatians 4:21-5:26)."[14] Though many excellent items for theological reflection are included in this discussion it promotes confusion between the doctrines of justification and sanctification. This view puts the work of the Spirit in transformation as a partner with the work of Christ in giving sinners a right standing before the Law of God. While it is right to look at the work of the Spirit as inextricably united with the work of the Son and the work of the Father in salvation, as Reformed theologians have done for centuries, we must not confuse the

---

12. Ibid., 37.

13. Ibid., 38.

14. Ibid., 38, 39.

standing before God granted in justification with the ongoing transformation effected by walking in the Spirit.

It seems to me, had this writer not been driven by a special interest in a social justice agendum he would not have been prone to this compromising blending of doctrines. This also would explain why he does not think that early evangelicals and early Southern Baptists really understood the gospel. He desires for a denomination that, in his view, "was founded because of white supremacy" (the final evil antithesis) to work harder to remove that flaw. Part of the labor must be to run biblical exegesis through the purifying filter of the "Great Commission task of gospel centered racial reconciliation."[15]

Shared Power and Entitlement:

Social justice takes advantage of our innate tendency to claim entitlement. In Mark 10, James and John asked Jesus for a place of prominence in His kingdom. If an element of the final synthesis is political equilibrium, and perfectly shared authority, then a plausible consequence of social justice theory is shared authority, equal recognition of giftedness, places on the platform. One writer has spoken of the need for those who have "white privileged status" in the SBC to work toward "shared leadership within the SBC." While its "key leaders are white" these leaders have much they could learn from the "many gifted and under-represented minority groups in Southern Baptist life." "We want," the writer says, "our white brothers and sisters to share their leadership and influence with qualified black and brown people." "When Christians deny that skin color currently plays a role in determining who assumes leadership and privilege within the SBC, they make the stain of racism more difficult to remove."[16]

---

15. Ibid., 51.

16. Ibid., 46- 49.

Another writer says, "People of color who are called to serve within SBC life often evaluate reconciliation based on the majority culture's desire to release leadership and influence. When SBC leaders refuse to relinquish leadership and influence, they invariably enforce the perception of placation in the corridors of marginalized hearts. Perhaps the greatest act of faith within our convention will be when SBC entities hire non-whites to give primary leadership to our convention."[17] Is this not exactly the kind of posturing for an exalted position that Jesus warned against when He said, "You know that those who are considered rulers over the Gentiles lord it over them, and their great ones exercise authority over them. Yet it shall not be so among you; but whoever desires to become great among you shall be your servant" (Mark 10:42, 43). No person of any ethnicity should ever seek a position of power as a legitimate expression of gospel justice.

Sensitivity to Personal Offense:

Social justice theory encourages us to examine ways in which we might have been on the receiving of injustice. We complain that we have not been treated fairly, or that other people have criticized us, used references or made substantial suggestions about conduct that have offended us, and should, therefore, be reprimanded in some way. We are therefore tempted to forget our infinite offence against God and the gracious status of justification that has been granted us by God, whose contention against us is truly and absolutely just, and whose reception of us is on the basis of the perfect combination of justice and mercy.

The constant recitation of ways in which injustice, both apparent and real, has been done in our culture, particularly to our tribe, comes to occupy our minds with relentless pressure. It seems noble for it has been provoked by a synthetic ideal of social justice but quickly takes advantage of our self-protective tendency to be easily offended. We lose the benefit

---

17. Curtis Woods in *Removing the Stain*, 119.

of an admonition like, "My brethren, count it all joy when you fall into various trials, knowing that the testing of your faith produces patience." We learn to eschew a quality like patience and want a public recognition of wrongs done in an ongoing way to all succeeding generations. We push aside as irrelevant to the level of offense we have received such a passage as Ephesians 4:31, 32. "Let all bitterness and wrath and anger and clamor and slander be put away from you, along with all malice. Be kind to one another, tenderhearted, forgiving one another, as God in Christ forgave you" (ESV).

Vengeance:

Social justice theory encourages a spirit of vengeance. It looks for ways for persons who are not immediate victims of injustice to exact retribution from classes that have not participated in the remote acts of injustice. Social Justice theory defends the legitimacy of seeking the leveling of "tribes" through payments of influence, position, material resources, It does not encourage contentment with a conscious commitment to the reality of divine justice, that the cries of the oppressed have come up into the ears of the Lord of Hosts. Recently a prolific poster of blogs wrote, "It is one thing to call our congregations to the mandate of scripture to love all people, but another to characterize that as restricting Christians from giving an accurate critique of the status quo. If leaders within the SBC are bullying you into silencing prophetic Black Christians then you are being used as a tool of white supremacy. Do not become 'slaves obey your masters' type of preachers."[18] Perhaps he should add, "Do not become a 'Children obey your parents" type preacher" or a "Wives, submit to your own husbands' type preachers," or "Do not become a 'Husbands, love your wives, just as Christ also loved the church' type preachers." If a biblical

---

18. Black Apologetics, "A Black Church Ecclesiology for Those Continuing to Affiliate with the Southern Baptist Convention." 4mykinsmen, July 4, 2017, https://4mykinsmen. wordpress.com/2017/07/04/a-black-church-ecclesiology-for-those-continuing-to-affiliate-with-the-southern-baptist-convention/.

admonition contradicts the social justice synthesis, so much the worse for the biblical admonition.

Judgmentalism:

Social justice encourages a spirit of judgmentalism, establishing moral absolutes out of issues that are not an element of the moral law. James 4:11 instructs the believer, "Do not speak evil of one another, brethren. He who speaks evil of a brother and judges his brother, speaks evil of the law and judges the Law. But if you judge the law, you are not a doer of the law but a judge." Also, The *Second London Confession,* article 21, in relation to many non-biblical requirements posed by Roman Catholicism stated, "God alone is Lord of the conscience and hath left it free from the doctrines and commandments of men which are in anything contrary to his word, or not contained in it. So that to believe such doctrines, or obey such commands out of conscience, is to betray true liberty of conscience and the requiring of an implicit faith and absolute and blind obedience, is to destroy liberty of conscience and reason also." When persons are seen as righteous who make apologies to those whom they have never offended, to repent of bias and prejudice that has not infected their own minds and hearts, and to see their ethnicity, whether, white, brown, black, tan as imposing upon them sins they did not commit, this is to sit in judgment of the law. The law should have required, so we would assume, certain actions and social postures of people that it, in fact, did not require. We bristle that the Bible did not give a pure and specific condemnation of slavery, does not hold masters as *ipso facto* in a sinful state, and does not endorse our synthesis of the final evil. We look for ways, therefore, to sit as master over the text and thus judge it as inadequate for our context.

Historical Analysis:

Social justice simplifies the manner in which historiography identifies governing factors in historical movements. By "simplify" I mean it engages in a severe reductionism in finding the single issue which either acquits or condemns a person concerning the standard of social justice promulgated. Once that violation is discovered, the broader context and the more substantial traits and accomplishments of the persons so investigated are ignored for the sake of the simple condemnation based on the principle of social justice that has governed the investigation. This can lead one to say that "the evangelical movement in this country was also born within an environment of racial injustice toward black people."[19] Those whose larger context and theological contributions gave gospel and biblical stability to future generations can be simply dismissed as slave-owning racists. So Christopher Columbus, George Whitefield, Jonathan Edwards, Thomas Jefferson, George Washington, Robert Dabney, James P. Boyce, John A. Broadus, James Earl Ray, Sirhan Sirhan, Byron De la Beckwith, and Dylan Roof all are seen as moral equals, under the same censure. This reductionistic principle of historical investigation leads a person to say, "I have more confidence in the Christianity of Martin Luther King than I do that of Jonathan Edwards and George Whitefield." It makes a person embrace the ideas of Malcolm X while despising the theological insights and spiritual theology of John L. Dagg.

Minimize the Eternal, Maximize the Present:

Social Justice moves toward defining Christian ministry in terms of temporal safety and equity to the minimization of eternal concerns. Thabiti Anyabwile lamented this tendency and explained its dynamic in his book *The Decline of African American Theology.* "Second, the emergence of high estimations of man's moral ability leads many to overemphasize political and social freedom. If man no longer needs rescuing from the effects of sin and the wrath of God to come, and if he is capable of ushering in a temporal utopia of sorts, then the logical focus of his energies be-

---

19. Williams, *Stain*, 19

comes societal inequities and social structures. Salvation becomes a matter of reconstructing an inefficient but salvageable society."[20]

Likewise, arguing for the inherent superiority of gospel privileges in Christ, the hope of our complete transformation at His return in glory, and the perfect world of love in heaven to the advantages of some standard of political equity is dismissed as escapism and irresponsible neglect of the more pressing issues of present social equity. Anyabwile, again, noted that in much modern theology that focused on the preeminence of social/racial issues, "reliance on God evaporated into man-centered political programs." In assessing the early African American theology as focused on heaven and eternal life with God, he warned against a Marxian type evaluation of heaven-conscious theology in writing, "We must avoid the mistaken conclusion that earlier generations opted for 'pie-in-the-sky' or 'opiate' forms of religion because they applied their theology in politically less strident or radical ways than we would prefer." He resisted the relentless focus on immanence and horizontal freedom as a more desirable outcome to theological reflection and urged, "We are better off humbly accepting and returning to the wisdom they articulated."[21]

THE GOSPEL, THE GREAT LEVELLER

We should work for and live in hope, that among Christians we can accept the view of reality and the admonition from James contained in the words, "Let the lowly brother glory in his exaltation, but the rich in his humiliation, because as a flower of the field he will pass away. For no sooner has the sun risen with a burning heat than it withers the grass; its flower falls, and its beautiful appearance perishes. So the rich man also will fade away in the midst of his pursuits. Blessed is the man who endures

---

20. Thabiti M. Anyabwile, *The Decline of African American Theology* (Downers Grove: IVP Academic, 2007), 134.

21. Anyabwile, *The Decline of African American Theology*, 98, 99.

under trial; for once he has been approved, he will receive the crown of life which the Lord promised to those who love him" (James 1:9-12 NKJV).

SIX

God's Created Order: Living Justly as Man and Woman

By Jared Longshore

A national commission recently toured the United States considering the viability of drafting American women into the military. This commission plans to deliver its final report to Congress in March 2020. As I watched one of the meetings of this commission, I was left asking, "How do you get to the point where you are honestly considering drafting women, wives, mothers, sisters, daughters, and granddaughters into the military?" How do you have what the apostle Peter calls the weaker vessel, what Paul calls the glory of man, what we all know is the fairer sex, compulsorily strapped with grenades and knives to go fight other men, our enemies? How do you get to the point where men would advocate women being civilly forced in front of them to the front lines? These are women who Solomon called noble daughters with rounded thighs like jewels and bellies like heaps of wheat encircled with lilies, women with breasts that produce milk to nurture babies—with wombs that give life (Song of Solomon 7:1-2). What kind of God-forsaken, woman-hating, oppressive, cowardly, and abusive ideology has resulted in this situation?

It is not a stretch to say our culture has lost its mind on the issue of manhood and womanhood. Amid this sexual insanity, the church must decide where to stand. If we emphasize God's design of male and female, we are going to come into conflict with the world. If we deemphasize the divine order, perhaps we can keep some measure of peace and at least *appear* to be kind. I'm convinced that the church must winsomely and boldly exalt God's design of man and woman. We must do this because God is truth, He is Creator. We must exalt His design because our culture's position on manhood and womanhood is the outworking of a corrupt philosophy—a philosophy which, if adopted, can only lead to despair.

A PAGAN IDEOLOGY

That word ideology is important. I have highlighted a political issue. But politics is downstream from culture and worldview. So what ideology is giving rise to our sexual confusion?

It is an ideology that plainly rejects Genesis 1:1, "In the beginning God created the heavens and the earth." The text is plain. There is a God and we are not Him. He, therefore, *determines what is*. The heavens are the heavens, and the earth is the earth. The heavens could not become the earth even if they tried. God, not his creation, determines *the nature of reality*. God has not only determined what is, but He also has established *the purpose* of what is. The heavens are to be the keeper of the sun, moon, stars, and clouds. The earth is to yield food and give man and beast a place to roam. The earth can complain that it would like the purpose of star-keeping, but it cannot change the purpose for which it has been made.

Furthermore, God not only determines what is, and the purpose of what is, but He has determined the beauty of what is. He created with wisdom, simplicity and complexity, symmetry and asymmetry. He made one creation distinct from Himself. But He immediately went to creating distinctions within that creation, distinctions that sing glorious harmony. The heavens and earth might complain together that things would be more lovely, had God created two heavens and no earth or two earths and no heavens. But they would be wrong.

The worldview that increases around us rejects these things and inverts these things. It is rightly identified as a pagan ideology—*one which claims man is God.* As Paul says in Romans 1, "they turned to worship the creature rather than the Creator." According to this false religion, man, being god, can determine what is. He can determine the purpose of what is. He can determine what is beautiful.

Consider some of our most well-known phrases. Cinderella has been telling us for years, "No matter how your heart is grieving if you keep on believing the dream that you wish will come *true.*" You will determine the truth. When it comes to purpose, we have been saying to children for a couple of generations now, "You can be whatever you want to be when you grow up." You define your purpose. On the beauty front, we say, "Beauty is in the eye of the beholder." In other words, "It's beautiful because I say it is."

It is mind-boggling to see how closely Disney's logic aligns with Playboy's. Hugh Hefner said his Playboy Mansion is,

> a place where one could work and have fun without the trouble and the conflicts of the outside world. Inside, a single man had absolute control over his environment. I could change night into day, screening a film at midnight and ordering a dinner at noon, having appointments in the middle of the night and romantic encounters in the afternoon... Being brought up in a very repressive and conformist manner, I created a universe of my own where I was free to live and love in a way that most people can only dream about.[1]

---

1. Christopher Caldwell, *The Age of Entitlement* (New York, NY: Simon & Schuster, 2020), 48.

This unbiblical worldview, subjective worldview, pagan worldview is expressing itself in our relationships as male and female. We want to redefine the nature of manhood and womanhood according to our own taste. We want a personally crafted purpose unlimited by our sex. We want to blend the sexes, claiming the ambiguity of androgyny as a superior beauty to the complementarity of male and female. Such a worldview, where man sits in God's chair and determines truth, goodness, and beauty, can only lead to nihilism.

Many Christians don't see what the big deal is when it comes to manhood and womanhood. They take a narrow approach to the subject, saying women simply should not be elders in the church, and the husband is the head of his wife in the home. But such a narrow approach is insufficient. Our culture is presently trying to twist the very fabric of reality. The nature of man and woman is a key place where they are making their painful attempt.

The Created Order

God's glorious design appears in Genesis 1. The first thing that jumps out is that both man and woman are created in the image of God. If you only have one man left on the planet, you have the image of God. If you only have one woman left on the planet, you have the image of God. Man and woman are then equal in dignity. But along with this sameness, we see an ordained difference. As the heavens and earth, sun and moon, sea and land, so there is male and female. If man and woman do not acknowledge their complementary nature, then they will not be able to be fruitful and multiply, fill the earth, subdue it, or exercise dominion.

What we see in Genesis 1 is spelled out in more detail throughout Scripture.[2] An emphasis on man's strength and woman's beauty appears in

---

2. The 1 Peter 3, 1 Thessalonians 2, and Genesis 2 observations that follow track points from Kevin DeYoung's message *The Beauty of Biblically Broad Complementarianism.* For a good analysis of the topic see his full message: Kevin DeYoung, "The Beauty of Biblically Broad Complementarianism." CBMW.org, April 4, 2019, https://cbmw.org/2019/04/04/the-beauty-of-biblically-broad-complementarianism-tgc19/.

1 Peter 3. Woman is called the "weaker vessel," implying man's strength. Women are to adorn themselves "with the imperishable beauty of a gentle and quiet spirit." This is not to say that women are not strong, and men cannot be handsome. It is rather to say that God has emphasized strength in men and beauty in women.

In 1 Thessalonians 2, Paul speaks of exhorting fathers and nursing mothers. Paul's words do not strike us as odd because we have lived in the world. We generally see these dispositions in man and woman. They are not watertight categories. Paul himself said he was with the Thessalonians "as a nursing mother." But the fact remains that you expect to see mom putting a band-aid on little Johnny and dad telling him to go and try jumping off the top of the playground one more time—he almost stuck the landing. God designed things this way.

In Genesis 2, we see the pattern of man as leader and woman as helper. Adam is created first, then Eve. Adam is made out of the ground and Eve from the body of Adam. She is a helper fit for him. God gives Adam work to do, and Eve is to aid him in it. Adam names the animals and woman. No, this does not mean that you teach your daughters to submit to men in general. That is an excellent way to get them abused by wicked men. A wife is to submit *to her own husband*. Neither does this mean that women should not lead anything at all, and men should not help. It does, however, mean that God's created order implies man ordinarily taking a posture of leadership and woman a posture of helper.

This brief survey is not an exhaustive analysis of God's created order, but it gives us enough of a foundation to see *where the battle lines are drawn*.

The Church Must Decide

The church must decide to teach what God's Word says about these things or remain silent. We are at a crossroads. We will either be ever so slowly conformed to the world's understanding of male and female or be transformed by Scripture to testify to God's design. There has been much talk about empowering women to the highest levels of leadership in the church. Several Christians advocate women preaching in churches on the Lord's Day.

David Wells is helpful here. He has warned about what happens when pastors become professionalized and borrow the world's principles. He writes, "Rough truth gives way to smooth practice, the jerks and moments of discovery when God's world illumines our own give way to moments in which our world brings His into tame submission."[3] When it comes to God's created order of male and female, the question is, "Will God's world illumine ours, or will our world bring his into tame submission?"

The battle lines are drawn at truth, goodness, and beauty. Let's consider each one.

GOD'S CREATED ORDER IS TRUE

First is the battle line of truth. Christians contend that God's *created order is true*. I am a full believer in the sovereignty of God. God's truth is going to go right on triumphing through this world. Nothing can or will stop it. God made them male and female, and there is no getting around it. You don't break God's order. You break yourself against God's order. These things are true.

And this is also true. If *our generation* would know God's truth, then Christians must live by it. We are truth representatives. We are to shine like stars in a twisted and crooked generation. Indeed Titus 2:5 says that women are to conduct themselves in certain ways so "that the word of God may not be reviled." We live a certain way and, in so doing, "*adorn the doctrine of God*" (Titus 2:10). There is the beauty theme shining through again—women, who display God's created order, show the beauty of God's truth to a watching world. Men have the same responsibility of

---

3. David Wells, *No Place for Truth* (Grand Rapids, MI: William B. Eerdmans, 1994), 248.

representing the truth. Paul says in 1 Corinthians 11 that man is the image and glory of God. He is to radiate the truth about God to the world. 1 Timothy tells us that the church is a pillar and buttress of the truth (1 Timothy 3:15). Supporting and proclaiming the truth; this is our duty.

Our culture's position is that *God's created order is not true*. The feminist movement sought a cultural revolution in which hierarchy was torn down and order done away with. This feminist movement claimed a mission of tearing down the patriarchy, but it truly wanted to tear down the chief Patriarch, the chief Father, God. Radical feminism desires a world that is entirely flat with no truth coming down to us from above.

As a result of this movement, we now have a terrible time with the issue of equality. The question of the day is, "By what standard?" Having torn down God's standard, we are left floundering about trying to find one. It is sad and even a bit humorous, that those who have sought to "tear down men" have now set up men as their standard. The feminist says, "I want you to treat me as an equal." And what is often meant is, "I want you to treat me like a man." They would object to this. But remember, there is no objective standard left in this worldview. All that is left is, "I want everything you have; I want the same treatment."

But a man is not the standard for just treatment of a woman. And a woman is not the standard for just treatment of a man. A human standard though, is the only standard left for a secular worldview. They have "human truth" rather than "God's truth," and the result is women being treated exactly like men, which leads to abuse. The result is women being drafted into the military, men competing in women's sports and taking all of their medals, violent men being sent to women's prisons, and men winning women's beauty pageants. When you neglect God's truth, the consequences are disastrous.

Dr. Mark Coppenger, recent professor of philosophy and ethics at the Southern Baptist Theological Seminary, demonstrated just how badly our society rejects the truth when he spoke in Washington D. C. He was asked to address the United States commission which investigated the viability of drafting women into the military. He pointed out that drafting women into the military goes against nature. He showed this is not merely a Protestant concern, but all sorts of "peoples and nations" have observed something *in nature* that we are missing. He testified,

> Please don't suppose that this is a narrowly Baptist or Protestant concern. Historically, women have not been drafted in majority Catholic countries like Italy and Ireland; in majority Orthodox countries like Greece and Romania; in majority Muslim countries like Saudi Arabia, Turkey, and Indonesia; in majority Buddhist countries like Cambodia and Thailand; in majority Hindu countries like India and Nepal; and yes, in aggressively secular France, whose 18th-century revolutionaries introduced a calendar with 1792 as "Year One," to avoid honoring Christ with *Anno Domini*, AD—the France marinated in the atheistic perspectives of Voltaire, Rousseau, Sartre, de Beauvoir, Derrida, Foucault, Malraux, and Truffaut.[4]

This inversion of nature is not only a problem out there, but it is a way of thinking that threatens the church. Paul warned about just this kind of hollow philosophy in Colossians 2. The threat is subtle. The temptation is for Christians to think, "Whatever is going on with the issues of male and female, we need not fear because we are solid on justification by faith alone." But there are some bedrock truths upon which justification stands. Doug Wilson has helpfully questioned, "Let me try to imagine a place which had heaven and earth muddled, sea and dry land reversed, sun and moon backward, and the female in combat and the male in drag, but where everybody was sound on justification by faith alone. Can't picture that? Neither can I."[5]

It is against the backdrop of this cultural landscape that Christians declare *the truth* of God's created order. The standard for just treatment of a man is God's Word. The standard for just treatment of a woman is God's

---

4. Mark Coppenger, *Please Let's Not Expand Draft Registration to Include Women.* Testimony before the National Commission on Military, National, and Public Service (Washington, D. C), April 25, 2019, https://www.inspire2serve.gov/_api/files/227.

5. Doug Wilson, *Pomosexuality* (Moscow, ID: Canon Press, 2015), 48.

Word. In certain ways, the Word requires us to treat men and women the same, but in many other ways, the Word requires us to treat men and women differently if we would treat them justly.

GOD'S CREATED ORDER IS GOOD

The second battle line is goodness. God's created order is good. It is good because what He has made suits His purpose. Goodness involves suitability to and end. A hammer is good for driving nails, and a screwdriver is good for twisting in screws. But a hammer is not good for twisting in screws. Neither is a screwdriver good for driving in nails.

God created the world for the purpose of glorifying Himself. He created male and female to complement each other to that end. This complementarity includes a whole host of things, not the least of which is coming together in sexual union in marriage to be fruitful and multiply. If posterity would glorify God, then we need nurturing mothers and exhorting fathers. We need the leadership that men, according to nature, bring and the marvelous help that women, according to nature, provide.

There is a lot of talk about purpose today. But the controversial point is that our purpose is *from God*. It is at that very point that the objection comes in. We are fine with a job assignment, but we are not fine with *someone else giving us a job assignment*. Especially God, because as long as we're living, we can't tell Him, "I quit." When it comes to sexuality, God did not ask our permission. He simply thrust manhood on men and womanhood on women.

Moreover, not only is our purpose from God, but our purpose is defined. He did not give you manhood and say, "Do what you will with it." He said, "Here is manhood, and this is how you do it, this is what it's for." John Piper's definitions are instructive. He says, "At the heart of mature masculinity is a sense of benevolent responsibility to lead, provide for and protect women in ways appropriate to a man's differing relationships."[6] So a man cannot claim that *his* manhood runs away when a woman's in danger. Piper continues, "At the heart of true femininity is a freeing disposition to affirm, receive and nurture strength and leadership from worthy men in ways appropriate to a woman's differing relationships."[7] Therefore, if a woman nurture's some scoundrel of a man to do wicked things, then that's not genuine womanhood at work.

Many people are tempted with the false notion that you can be whatever you want to be. This terrible lie leaves many depressed and hopeless. Many get caught up in this lie because you can put a "Christian" veneer on it. When you hear pastors saying, "You have purpose, you have meaning" that's great. But more needs to be said. Even if you say, "God has given you purpose, God has given you meaning," we haven't gone quite far enough. Several people hear that through the lens of this faulty ideology and think, "Great! God has given me a purpose, my very own journey, my venture into the great unknown with no limits or boundaries, *God wants me to be whatever I want to be when I grow up.*"

The solution is to see that God made the sea to hold the fish, the sun to shine, and the rain to water the earth. Man and woman, too, have God defined purposes to fulfill. We go against these purposes at a terrible cost. When you are going about things as God has designed, there is blessing. But the way of the transgressor is hard, Proverbs says. When you go against the grain, things are tough. And you go against the grain when you're striving toward a different purpose than the one for which God made you.

This common notion of an individual's limitless pursuit of nebulous purpose can be seen in a biological man winning "woman of the year." That happened in 2015. The purpose of "woman of the year" is, of course,

---

6. John Piper, *A Vision of Biblical Complementarity*. March 24, 2020, http://cdn.desiring-god.org/pdf/books_bwtd/bbmw_chapter_1.pdf, 29.

7. Ibid.

to esteem the greatest woman. By definition, a biological man cannot fulfill that purpose. But we have so given into the idea that you can determine your own destiny that we are willing to pretend a man can be woman of the year. I don't point these things out to be crude, or mean-spirited. I point them out because this is the world we are living in. There is a reason things are the way they are. Many ideas among us are simply no good.

Christians then stand for Christ as they say, "God has made me what I am. He has told me what to do. Yes, I have failed in many ways. But Christ has died for me. By God's grace in Christ, may the Lord help me to fulfill the purpose for which He has made me." God blesses that attitude. And the world is left with the vivid truth that God's created order is good.

GOD'S CREATED ORDER IS BEAUTIFUL

The third battle line is beauty. God's created order is beautiful. God, being God, not only makes beautiful things, but He determines what is and is not beautiful. When He made man male and female, He saw what He made and said, "It is very good."

The apostle Paul tells us in Philippians 4:8 to think upon that which is lovely. The psalmist tells us to worship the Lord in the beauty of holiness. An exploration into God's created order is just that. It is a meditation on God's beautiful design resulting in worshiping the Lord in the beauty of holiness.

We don't have words to express what arises in us when we consider the wonder of God's design. God made Adam out of the dust, then took his rib to form the lovely creature, woman. Adam says, "This is bone of my bone and flesh of my flesh." That is, there is a *sameness*: bone and bone, flesh and flesh. Yet there are two sets of bones. There is not one flesh but two: distinction. Added to the beauty we see Eve is bone of Adam's bone, an extension of him, not the other way around. And yet God adds to this symphony saying that in marriage, the two shall come back together and become one flesh.

We can only cover our mouths in wonder when Paul says, "Man was not made from woman, but woman from man. Neither was man created for woman, but woman for man... Nevertheless, in the Lord woman is not independent of man nor man of woman; for as woman was made from man, so man is now born of woman. And all things are from God" (1 Corinthians 11:8-12). How are you going to listen to that masterpiece and be distracted by whether you will get the short end of the stick? That's like listening to Bach and claiming, "As a woman, I wish he'd put in more high notes. As a man, I wish he would have emphasized the bass line a bit more." No, Bach knows more about music than you do. Just listen and wonder!

It all is too glorious. We cannot do otherwise than to simply look at man and say with the apostle, "This is the glory of God!" We must look in amazement to the woman and agree, "This is the glory of man" (1 Corinthians 11:7)! For those who are uncomfortable with Paul's terminology here, remember nothing is demeaning about being the glory of the glory of God. Woman is the crown of the crown, the radiance of radiance of God.

But our present world wants none of this harmony and color contrast. The ideology among us rejects the balance, subtlety, and craftsmanship of God. It has lost all appreciation for standards of excellence. It would drain men of valor and fortitude. It would remove from women sensitivity and compassion. In general, there appears to be a hardening of women and a softening of men.

The worldview prevalent among us claims subjective standards for beauty. Strangely enough, with everyone wanting to create their own distinct standards for beauty, the result is an increasing amount of androgyny.

I was reminded of the poor state of modern notions of beauty one night as my wife and I were out on a date downtown. In one of the stores we entered, there was a staircase with a sign that said art was upstairs. So I went up to discover a particular piece of art that was simply several toys scattered on the ground. Orange road cones and caution tape surrounded the scene. I kid you not, this was displayed as art. There was no order, form, no symmetry or asymmetry, no design, just chaos. I thought my children had made their way through the art gallery. Such a pitiful display is a sign of the times when it comes to our society's ill-conceived notions of beauty as it relates to manhood and womanhood.

It is right at this point that Christians have a great opportunity. Things have gotten so ugly out there that people are yearning for true beauty. The world is hungry for male influence and initiative that is not domineering or self-serving. The world is thirsty for female loveliness that is not glamourous or gaudy. This is a time for us to live according to God's created order displaying just how beautiful it is.

God's Created Order And His Gospel

Our culture is has gone off the rails when it comes to manhood and womanhood. They have done so because of a godless ideology that will lead people straight to hell. So let our message be, *there is a God and we are not Him*. He created this world. He created mankind in His own image, male and female. He determines what is true, good, and beautiful.

His gospel says we, created beings, have fallen short of His truth, goodness, and beauty many times. Even so, because of the great love with which He loved us, He sent His Son, who is the truth Himself, goodness Himself, beauty Himself, Jesus Christ, to live, die, and rise from the dead. Trust Him, and you'll be saved from all of your sinful perversions and manipulations of God's design. Trust Him, and He will show you how to live a true, good, and beautiful life according to His design.

SEVEN

ETHNIC GNOSTICISM

By Voddie Baucham

In this chapter, I will address ethnic Gnosticism. I want to share what I intend by that word and why it helps shed light on some of the things evangelicals are dealing with presently.

Gnosticism comes from the Greek word for knowledge. This old heresy occurred around the first century. It involved a specialized, immediate knowledge. By immediate knowledge, I don't mean "right now." I mean knowledge that is not mediated through a source, through the Word of God. This immediate knowledge is intuitive knowledge that separates insiders from outsiders. That is the idea of Gnosticism. I use the phrase ethnic Gnosticism to explain the phenomenon of people believing that somehow, because of one's ethnicity, a person can know when something is racist.

There was a popular saying some time ago, "It's a black thing; you wouldn't understand." The idea is if I go to a restaurant, sit down, and someone looks at me a certain way, *I* know when it is racist. And you can't tell me it is not. I could do the same with the clerk at the store or the police officer who has pulled me over. If someone replies, "Well, no, that's not what I meant." that's just your privilege speaking. According to white privilege, *you don't know what you don't know.* How about *that?* You don't know what you don't know... *but I do.* That's ethnic Gnosticism.

Because of my ethnicity and my position as a minority, I know what oppression is and feels like. I don't necessarily need evidence for it. Additionally, other people, who are not minorities and not being oppressed, actually oppress people without thinking about it and without knowing it. They have privilege that they are not even aware of. So you have to be taught how racist you are. But nobody has to teach me when you're racist. That's ethnic Gnosticism. It's a problematic idea.

The concept is rooted in Cultural Marxism, which reduces everything to race, class, and sex. Cultural Marxism divides people up slightly differently than Classical Marxism. Classical Marxism divides people up into the bourgeoisie and proletariat, the haves and have nots—between those who control the means of production and those who do not. In Cultural Marxism, you divide the world between those who establish and benefit from the cultural hegemony and everyone else. Those who do not benefit from the cultural hegemony are oppressed by it. For one reason or another, they are not a part of the dominant group. Ethnic Gnosticism is rooted in this Cultural Marxist paradigm.

In one sense, I am not merely addressing a black/white thing. Ethnic Gnosticism goes beyond that. The transperson can say the same thing. Such a person just knows when he or she is being judged or oppressed. In this system, the same goes for a homosexual person. A woman simply knows when she is being oppressed or judged for the fact that she is a woman. Being in these particular groups, going through life, and experiencing these things over and over again puts one in a situation where a person just knows. On the other hand, being in a dominant group where you don't have to worry about such things, you literally don't know what you don't know. You are a racist, bigot, homophobic, transphobic, and everything else phobic person, whether you are aware of it or not.

Whether you belong to Christ or not does not matter. Apparently, Christ can transform us and deal with all other kinds of sins, but this one somehow evades the cross. Specific categories of people, whether they're Christian or not, are still suffering from this one.

Ethnic Gnosticism is then rooted in Cultural Marxism. It claims the group to which you belong determines your identity. That is the primary essence of one's identity—your group. It could be your ethnicity, sex, or your so-called sexual orientation. But that is the essence of who I am according to this ideology.

Furthermore, according to ethnic Gnosticism, my identity is understood in the context of *our* struggle—our shared cultural experience and identity. Media portrayals have a great deal to do with this. Interestingly, it is kind of a self-fulfilling prophecy. I am a part of a particular group. For me, I am a black person, born into my ethnicity and environment, and my family shapes my understanding of who I am. But also, when I see images of myself in the media, that can positively or negatively begin to form who I think I am. And we know that portrayals in the media are always accurate!

As an aside, stereotypes are another big part of this issue. Stereotypes are a normal part of life. The other day I was walking with our seven youngest children. Someone was talking about how big they were getting and asked, "Are they playing sports?" "No," I replied, "actually, they are all musicians; they are concentrating on music right now." "Ah, it looks like you ought to have a basketball team." Now you know what many people think: "*That's racist!*" I was speaking with a black family member.

Now, why is it that a black family member can say that to me and it is not racist, but if a white person said it to me, it would be? What's the determining factor? According to ethnic Gnosticism, the determining factor is me, because *I know*. Not only do I know, but you don't know. You can say until you are blue in the face that you didn't mean it that way. But if I receive it that way, then I get the right to determine what it is. Do you see what this does to us?

On the one hand, ethnic Gnosticism is about trusting your heart. Jeremiah 17:9 says, "The heart is deceitful above all things and desperately sick; who can understand it?" I can't understand my own heart, and I'm going to tell you what is in yours? But this is precisely what we are prone to do.

ETHNIC AND NATIONAL IDENTITY

Now, as I say this, let me hurry to acknowledge a couple of things. Ethnicity, culture, and nationality are not bad things. They are good and natural connections. I must say this because some of my dearest friends and brothers, in fact, some who were probably signers of the Social Justice statement, would want to argue for being color blind. But that dog won't hunt. Nobody is color blind, and it would be an affront to God to try to be so.

God didn't give me all this rich, beautiful melanin so you could act like I don't have it. And it is wrong for me to judge you for not having as much. God did this. It is a good and natural thing that God has done. For us to say that we want to be colorblind is for us to say, "I don't care about the variety of color of roses there are. As far as I'm concerned, God just made a rose. Who cares that He made all of those different colors?" If He did, praise Him for it.

I know what we are trying to say when we say we are color blind. But as those should be careful who use the terminology of social justice, so should those who use language like being color blind.

It is funny that when people say they don't see color, they start giving you evidence. The evidence is that they have friends who are *this* color, and they have friends who are *that* color. Oh really? How do you know that if you don't see color? What we're trying to say regarding colorblindness is something different, right, and essential. But let's say what we mean.

What is so good about ethnic and national identity? They are conduits for cultural tradition. When we leave on vacation, we come back with pictures. Usually, we don't take photos of that which is like our culture and tradition at home. Often, we want to show people the beauty of the culture and tradition that is not like our own. That is a good thing. The color blind idea runs us away from that.

Ethnic and national identity teach us dependence and humility. No single group possesses all the good. I belong to a group that has strengths and weaknesses. I look at other groups of people who are strong where I may be weak and who may be weak where I am strong. So I learn dependency and humility.

No single group possesses all knowledge. Here is one of the great things about America. The rich diversity of America is one of the things that has come crashing down on me living in Zambia. I live in a very homogeneous culture. Most of the world is that way. In most countries in the world, people are of the same ethnicity, background, and culture. They look alike. In the Olympics, people from this country look a certain way, and people from that country look a different way—that's most of the world. Then there is America. We have people that look like people from every other country. One of the great things about America is how the highest and best from cultures all around the world come together to make America higher and better. That's good. I don't want to live in a world where we ignore that.

Ethnic and national identity teach providence. Every culture, nationality, and ethnicity has a history that they can trace. My ethnicity teaches me about providence. Knowing who we come from, how we got here, and how by God's grace we survived, teaches us about the providence of God. I have been living and serving in Africa for the last three and a half years. I have been reminded of this almost every day. It is incredible that my ancestors were torn away from that continent and experienced the horrors of slavery, resulting in me being born in the center of the universe. The healthiest, wealthiest, most educated, most prosperous black people on earth are in America. Where else on this planet do black people want to go and live that is better than this? What is that? That's providence. Would anyone have chosen that path? Absolutely not. But you look back on it and see providence. If you ignore culture and ethnicity, you don't see providence.

Ethnic and national identity teaches us about the consequences of sin. We learn a valuable lesson about the multi-generational consequences of sin. One of the reasons we are going through what we are going through right now is because, to quote Malcolm X (and yes, I'm about to quote Malcolm X), "America's chickens have come home to roost." There is great sin in our history. Atrocities that have been committed against people in this country. You don't get to do that and not have consequences later on down the line. Let us not miss that when we talk about our present situation. We need to point to sin's consequences when we speak to our children about these issues. They need to be able to identify more than just a social justice warrior at work. What we are dealing with today is the fruit of horrible sins and atrocities. And you don't have to be a social justice warrior to acknowledge that.

So ethnic and national identity are important. But they are not everything. How do we balance this? I think we have an example in Romans chapter 9:1. There Paul says,

> I am speaking the truth in Christ—I am not lying; my conscience bears me witness in the Holy Spirit—that I have great sorrow and unceasing anguish in my heart. For I could wish that I myself were accursed and cut off from Christ for the sake of my brothers, my kinsmen according to the flesh (Romans 9:1-3).

I love my people. That is what Paul is saying here. "My kinsmen according to the flesh"—Paul is not saying, "I'm colorblind, ethnicity means nothing to me. I'm a citizen of the kingdom of Christ, and I don't even think about those people anymore." He speaks in the most passionate terms imaginable about the group to which he, by God's grace and providence, belonged.

The great irony is some people don't understand this when they see it in certain minority groups. But those same people can tell you what boat their ancestors came over on, and all of these wonderful things about their heritage. Hold on to that. But don't hold on to that and then tell me to forget my ethnicity.

Ethnic Gnosticism is broken and sinful. I'm writing against it. But I don't want you to get confused and think that somehow I'm arguing that one's ethnicity is unimportant. Paul makes this painfully clear—"I could wish that I myself were cursed and cut off from Christ for the sake of my brothers, my kinsmen according to the flesh." You don't get more passionate than that. Then he says,

> They are Israelites, and to them belong the adoption, the glory, the covenants, the giving of the law, the worship, and the promises. To them belong the patriarchs, and from their race, according to the flesh, is the Christ, who is God over all, blessed forever. Amen (Romans 9:4-5).

He is not saying merely our skin color or geographic location is important. He is specific. He looks at providence.

LIMITS TO ETHNIC AND NATIONAL CONNECTIONS

But then there are limits to ethnic and national connections. I love the fact that it is not an either-or. Paul goes on, "But it is not as though the Word of God has failed" (Romans 9:6). You might think that. "I love these people, my kinsmen, and all I want is them, and God, what have you done?" No. It is not as though the Word of God has failed,

> For not all who are descended from Israel belong to Israel, and not all are children of Abraham because they are his offspring, but "Through Isaac shall your offspring be named." This means that it is not the children of the flesh who are the children of God, but the children of the promise are counted as offspring (Romans 9:6-8).

Our connection to Christ is more important.

There is a ditch on both sides of the road. There is a ditch on the side that tries to act like ethnicity does not matter, and it is unimportant. There is also a ditch on the other side of the road that says it is everything. So what is the danger? What does this do?

First, it compromises genuine relationships. Our recent controversies have exposed a false unity. People were brothers from another mother. But now this comes up, and if you say the wrong thing, all of a sudden, you are anathema. That is not a genuine relationship.

Even down on that micro-level you see the problem. If I assume I can read your heart and you "don't know what you don't know," we've created an imbalanced relationship. Such a set up hinders our intimacy. Who wants to have a relationship with someone according to that setup?

I see this all over the place. I get emails several times a week from people telling me of pastors, church members, and leaders of ministries who have been faithful for decades. But they were found to hold the wrong position in some case in the media, or they did not think highly enough about some particular approach to a social justice issue. Now, all of a sudden, they are cast outside the city. We will remove you like a monument at a southern university. We are not even sure if Jonathan Edwards was a Christian anymore. This graceless way of relating hinders genuine relationships when we can't be honest with each other, where we are not free to err.

Second, ethnic Gnosticism fuels the idea of inheriting guilt and innocence from your parents. Thus, white people are inescapably racist, and black people cannot be racist. Remember, the modern definition of racism centers on power. What is the power? The power is the cultural hegemony. If you are not a part of the cultural hegemony, then technically, you cannot be a racist. How about that? So a predominately white church that does not have black members is in sin, but a predominately black church that does not have white members is, well, it just is. One of those groups needs to repent in sackcloth and ashes, and the other—there's nothing wrong.

This unbalanced approach arises from the religion of racialism. It comes along with the idea of tokenism and suspicion. Black preachers in reformed evangelical circles right now are commodities. Sadly the question now is not, "Oh, this guy is at this conference, is he worth hearing?" No, the question is, "This guy is at this conference. Oh, why'd they get that guy?"

Matt Chandler at MLK50 spoke openly in one of his presentations about his church's desire in their church planting to have black leaders of their church plants. He said that if he had to choose between a white guy who is an eight and a black guy who is a seven, "I'm going to take the black guy." That's tokenism. And Matt was speaking out of a passionate desire to see reconciliation.

Let me use that one example because one person's social justice is another person's atrocity. I went to school at the University of Oxford in England. Some people think I went to Oxford because I'm pretentious. Why Oxford? One of the main reasons that I did that is because if I left the United States and went to a school in the UK, no one could accuse the institution of granting me my degree because of tokenism or affirmative action. I was sick and tired of the assumptions that people make because of this attitude that says, "Your skin color makes you the weaker brother, and we have to lower the standard for you." Again, Matt would never say or intend that. But to many, that's exactly what he said.

Here is an interesting thing. If you say something like that amid your penance over your white privilege, you get a pass. Why? Because of the religion of racialism. John McWhorter explains,

> This brand of self-flagellation has become the new form of enlightenment on race issues. It qualifies as a kind of worship. The parallels with Christianity are almost uncannily rich. White privilege is the secular white person's original sin. Present at birth and ultimately ineradicable. One does one's penance by endlessly attesting to this privilege in hope of some kind of forgiveness.

This new cult of atonement is less about black people than white people. 50 years ago a white person learning about the race problem came away asking, "How can I help?" Today this same person too often comes away asking, "How can I show that I'm a moral person?" Another problem is that I'm not sure today's educated whites quite understand how unattainable the absolution they are seeking is.

We have gone from most whites being unaware that racism was a problem for black people at all to whites being chilled to their bones at the possibility of harboring racism in their souls terrified at the possibility of being singled out as a heretic, and forgetting that the indulgences they purchase and the praying they do for their souls has more to do with them than with anyone black and their problems.[1]

The irony of ironies, we are being driven farther apart by this. People who have for decades been serving their communities, loving their brothers and sisters, marching at abortion clinics because of the slaughter of black babies, can now have people say to them, "I don't care about that. I want to know how sorry you are about the latest issue." It is never enough. That will never lead to authentic relationships. In a genuine relationship I have to be free to be wrong. If I am wrong, you have to love me, correct me, and not just dismiss my whole person.

According to the religion of racialization, racism is the new unpardonable sin. This confusion was on display at the Gospel Coalition's MLK50 conference. Martin Luther King was a serial adulterer who denied essential tenants of the Christian faith. People are now arguing that he was OK. But schools are removing Jonathan Edwards' name from their institutions because he owned slaves. And that is an unpardonable sin.

I have quoted Jonathan Edwards. I have quoted Martin Luther King, Jr. I am not willing to go to the place where before I can quote a right and true statement by someone I have to retrace their life to make sure that I

---

1. John McWhorter, "Atonement as Activism." The American Interest, May 24, 2018, https://www.the-american-interest.com/2018/05/24/atonement-as-activism/.

am confident they went to heaven when they died. But, not today. Today where we stand, there is a new unpardonable sin. Those who are presumed guilty of that unpardonable sin must be dismissed, castigated, torn down, and done away with.

RECTIFYING PROBLEMS WITH THE WORD IN LOVE

Now there are great ills, sins, problems, and wrongs that need to be rectified. All of that is true. God has given us a way to deal with those things. He has given us His all-sufficient Word to deal with those problems. Let us trust the Word of God, not our feelings, inclinations, or assumptions.

Let us do what the Book says,

> If I speak in the tongues of men and of angels, but have not love, I am a noisy gong or a clanging cymbal. And if I have prophetic powers, and understand all mysteries and all knowledge, and if I have all faith, so as to remove mountains, but have not love, I am nothing. If I give away all I have, and if I deliver up my body to be burned, but have not love, I gain nothing.

> Love is patient and kind; love does not envy or boast; it is not arrogant or rude. It does not insist on its own way; it is not irritable or resentful; it does not rejoice at wrongdoing, but rejoices with the truth. Love bears all things, believes all things, hopes all things, endures all things (1 Corinthians 13:1-7).

EIGHT

MATURE MANHOOD

By Mark Coppenger

A sked to deliver the prayer for the graduates at my son's M.Div. commencement at Southern, I included this sentence: "I ask that in this terribly confused and willful world that the men gathered here today would be manly, and the women womanly." For some, it was a "Say what?" moment. But I wanted to underscore an important distinction for their ministries, one that other denominations have erased.

It's a distinction that biblicists and secularists alike have addressed. From Christian presses, we have, for example, Darrin Patrick's *The Dude's Guide to Manhood* (Nelson), Bill Delvaux's *Heroic* (B&H), and Tony Evans's *Kingdom Man* (Tyndale). And, then, from Yale University Press, we have Harvard Professor Harvey Mansfield's, provocative book, *Manliness*, whose essence I've heard summarized as "a willingness to put yourself at risk to defend a woman"—Barney Fife saying to Goliath, "If you think you're going to lay a hand on her, you'll have to come over me." And how about Camille Paglia's, December, 2013, essay in *Time* magazine, "It's a Man's World, and It Always Will Be." It drove fellow feminists crazy. In it, she expressed her dismay at the "anything-you-can-do-I-can-do-better" and "who-needs-men" conceit:

> After the next inevitable apocalypse, men will be desperately needed again! Oh, sure, there will be the odd gun-toting Amazonian surviv-alist gal, who can rustle game out of the bush and feed her flock, but most women and children will be expecting men to scrounge for food and water and to defend the home turf. Indeed, men are absolutely indispensable right now, invisible as it is to most feminists, who seem blind to the infrastructure that makes their own work lives possible. It is overwhelmingly men who do the dirty, dangerous work of build-ing roads, pouring concrete, laying bricks, tarring roofs, hanging elec-tric wires, excavating natural gas and sewage lines, cutting and clearing trees, and bulldozing the landscape for housing developments. It is men who heft and weld the giant steel beams that frame our office buildings, and it is men who do the hair-raising work of insetting and sealing the finely tempered plate-glass windows of skyscrapers 50 stories tall.
>
> Every day along the Delaware River in Philadelphia, one can watch the passage of vast oil tankers and towering cargo ships arriving from all over the world. These stately colossi are loaded, steered and off-loaded by *men*. The modern economy, with its vast production and distribution network, is a male epic, in which women have found a productive role — but women were not its author. Surely, modern women are strong enough now to give credit where credit is due![1]

And, of course, it's not just physical. God didn't just pick the strongest man and strongest woman and let them wrestle to see who would enjoy (or suffer) headship, with a coin flip to settle a draw. He'd engineered other characteristics into the genders.

---

1. Camille Paglia, "It's a Man's World, and It Always Will Be." Time, December 16, 2013, https://ideas.time.com/2013/12/16/its-a-mans-world-and-it-always-will-be/.

It's a distinction that Southern Baptists noted in a 2016 resolution against registering women for the draft. I spoke recently to the National Commission on Military, National, and Public service, tasked to bring recommendations to Congress in the spring of 2020. Our panel included a Catholic, a Quaker, a libertarian (atheist?), and a woman, who was a Marine veteran of Iraq, one opposed to drafting women. And in the audience was a remarkable man waiting for open-mic time at the end, retired Navy captain, Robert Miller, whose group, Hope for America, pleads for the maintenance of gender distinctions. (He's a wealth of information, and I've learned much from him, including the fact that the bombing of the USS Cole in Yemen killed a woman sailor who had a child she had left behind in the U.S.)

In my brief opening comments, I said that:

- In opposing draft registration for women, Southern Baptists had cited the male/female distinction in Genesis 1 and noted the difference between men and women on the battlefield in terms of lethality and survivability.

- This wasn't a narrowly Southern Baptist concern, for majority Catholic, Orthodox, Muslim, Hindu, Buddhist, and secular countries did not draft women. (Yes, there's Israel, Norway, North Korea, and a handful of others, but these are extreme outliners for one reason or another.)

- Though my wife Sharon didn't serve in the military, she served the military, as noted by my eldest son, who recently retired from the Marines at Camp Lejeune.

- My four D.C. granddaughters should enjoy the same privilege their mother had, to step away from a White House job offer and a full-ride in the Ph.D. program at Georgetown to be a homemaker and mother.

And I tore a newspaper in two directions to show it had a grain, analogous to the grain in creation.

Of course, it's getting harder and harder to maintain that there is such a creation order. We lionize (or lionessize) women who take "historic" first steps into the realm of traditional masculine activity—Janet Guthrie, Sally Ride—while virtually ignoring those who excel in family heroics, e.g., Susannah Wesley, who raised John and Charles. Yes, Evangelicals can get excited over certain "historic" firsts of their own—first seminary board chairman, first agency head—and ignore a Texas homemaker and deputy county clerk in little Morton, TX (pop. 2,000), 56 miles west of Lubbock. I'm talking about Dorothy Barker, who stood with a handful of male seminary trustees in 1989 to vote against tenure for Southern's heterodox Molly Marshall-Green. Why not recognize Dorothy, who had the wits and gumption to be the "historic" first woman trustee to oppose the first woman theology professor at Southern Seminary?

Of course, we expect the non-biblicist world to be thumbing its nose at biblical distinctions, but Evangelicals are showing themselves susceptible to a similar enthusiasm for cheering on every "advance" in female notoriety, power, and outside-the-home achievement. The "You go girl!" movement is in full swing, and you'd better be on board lest you be branded a "misogynist."

How might this be so? Let me suggest some reasons: In my youth, Southern Baptists and other conservative evangelicals were terrified that they might be considered intellectually second rate, hence, the bargain which was proffered to liberals, "We'll call you Christian if you call us scholars." (Thank God for C. S. Lewis, who gave us some cover). But now the transaction turns upon worship of a new god, *Perceived Sensitivity*, adored by secularists and sacredists alike. If only Barnabas rather than Paul had been tapped to write the epistles, life would be so much easier.

There's that, but let me note a few other forces at play, three maxims which are misappropriated to batter the distinction. Like fire, they can do much good, but, in the wrong hands they can do much harm.

1. "No man on his death bed will say, 'I wish I'd spent more time at work and less time with my family.'" This implies that work is simply a

means to getting ahead in wealth, status, and power, and that the real deal for the man is nurture of and fellowship with the children, whose real deal is to nurture and fellowship with their own children and so on and on. It encourages a feckless circularity, the point of the family being the family. Daddy is at his best in building bird houses with the kids so that they will be tuned up to build bird houses with their kids. Kind of an Amish take on things. So I would push back to say that some men should, in their deathbed reflections, lament, "Mercy, I wish I'd spent more time at my work and less with my family."

2. "God First; Family Second; Ministry/Career Third." As I argued in an ETS paper, this has a number of problems, fifteen by my count, but I'll only mention one. It's epistemological, for unless a decision involves clear violation of a scriptural injunction, it's a lot easier to know what your spouse/family wants than what God wants. So this puts a trump card in the hands of the family, whose interests and motives may be less than anointed. Suppose that "I *feel* God wants me to go on this volunteer mission trip." How could that stand up to your spouse's declaration, "I *know* the kids and I don't want you to go"? And so he doesn't go. (As one minister put it, "Get your people overseas on a mission trip and they'll discover that they're eagles rather than turkeys, and when they get back, it'll be hard to keep them out of the air." But thanks to mom and the kids, dad remains a turkey, when they need an eagle landing in the house.)

Since my college days, I've been part of a University of Michigan survey of family economics. (I'm linked in because my mom was a U of M grad). This year's survey asked how many hours a week on average I joined in housekeeping activities, and there are many who argue that the higher that number, the better the hubby. So, for instance, a 50/50 split on dishwashing is laudable. Thus, the praiseworthy husband does well to scurry home to take up his role as assistant homemaker.

Of course, it's important that the father be a strong, helpful presence in the home. (Indeed, the social wreckage of fatherless homes is everywhere to be seen.) But what of the larger point that men are supposed to be world-changers (or world-protectors) out in the world?

NYU psychology prof, Paul Vitz, put it this way:

> What is the father's major function? ... [T]he father is a kind of Mr. Outside, while the mother is Mr. Inside. She forms the basic character, the emotional life, the interpersonal responsiveness of the child, much more than the father. But the father introduces the child much more often to the outside world. The father symbolized the structure of that world, of law and order, of the activities, of the things that you get involved in when you leave the home.

Antonin Scalia thought so. In a *60 Minutes* interview with Lesley Stahl in 2008 (recounted in an obituary), he said that

> he worked a lot while the children were young and never went to any of their soccer games or piano recitals. Having his father attend his own events as a child was something Scalia wasn't used to himself. "You know, my parents never did it for me ... and I didn't take it personally. 'Oh Daddy, come to my softball game.' No, I mean, it's my softball game. He has his work. I got my softball game.'"

> Scalia's Ivy League-educated wife told Stahl that she juggled most of the events, making sure to show up for a little bit at a time for each of them.

> Scalia is survived by Maureen, his wife of over 50 years, and his middle-aged children — Ann, Eugene, John, Catherine, Mary, Paul, Christopher, Matthew and Margaret. They went on to make their parents proud and gave them more than 30 grandchildren ...

> Paul became a parish priest in Virginia, and Matthew made a successful career in the Army ... Eugene and John became lawyers based in Washington, D.C., while Christopher made a name for himself as a writer. Catherine, Ann, Margaret and Mary each gave birth to a handful of children.

> Scalia married Maureen in 1960— "the product of the best decision I ever made ... The mother of the nine children you see, the woman responsible for raising them with very little assistance from me ... And there's not a dullard in the bunch!"

Nine children! Poor Maureen, or so the cultural narrative goes, a narrative which has crept into Evangelical thinking. Never mind Genesis 1:28, the mandate to be fruitful and multiply. (After all, haven't we filled the earth already, what with over seven billion people crawling all over the planet? Well, not really. The whole lot of us could fit within the city limits of Houston if we stood shoulder to shoulder.) In this connection, I asked two back-to-back, Christ-and-Culture classes at Wheaton whether they thought they had a responsibility to have at least some kids should they marry. Out of the eighty, I think that fewer than ten hands were raised. It seems that, for them, procreation was an elective on the order of eating tofu or visiting New Zealand; take it or leave it. For one thing, it might adversely impact *careers* (another idol we worship).

3. "If you lose your family, you lose everything." Yes, it's very tricky to fault this, but stick with me as I suggest a way this can be weaponized to undermine gender roles. For analogy, consider the maxims, "If you have your health, you have everything" and "If you don't have your health, you don't have anything." Two problems: There are a lot of people with poor health who do great things, including Joni Eareckson Tada and Helen Keller, as well as hymnwriters Fanny Crosby and William Cowper; second, it can drive one to hypochondria, ever anxious at the slightest sign of ill health, causing one to shut down normal living.

The marital version of this is a sort of relational hypochondria, where the husband is terrified at the slightest disgruntlement, ever anxious to curtail his work to keep momma and the kids happy.

All this being said, I submit that the paradigm for a Christian wife is more nearly that of a military or police wife, whose husband maybe deployed at a moment's notice, for dangerous, inconvenient, and prolonged duty. Yes, a lot of unfortunate television drama is built around the complaints of police wives who don't get enough attention and have a hissy when the phone goes off in the middle of a special dinner and such; scripted back-stories of multiple divorces are commonplace. But if you visit the web sites of military and police wives, you'll find inspiring words by and for women handling, with appreciation, the considerable challenges of their status.

For instance, in one, we read,

I am an Air Force Wife.
Guardian of Favorite Blankets and Bedtime Stories.
My Airman's Right Hand.
His Lover and Supporter.
I Defend My Family with My Life.

And then, in the poem, "A Police Officer's Wife," we read,

How many good byes are whispered, joined with a fond embrace?
As duty steals her man, for the danger he must face . . .
She's a mother, lover, chauffeur and nurse,
a living symbol of: 'for better or for worse' . . .
Rich is the man, reaping his rewards in life,
Who chose to be the other half of A Police Officer's Wife.

Which brings us to Proverbs 31. You might read it as a description of a wife whose husband is working undercover for six months or one whose husband is serving in Afghanistan. She isn't a fainting flower, but a woman in full.

Look, I'm not suggesting that all or most men are out there fighting the Taliban, tracking down killers, or bringing sanity to a Supreme Court gone mad. Many of us live in the workaday world of insurance underwriting, bus driving, and manufacturing, and it's perfectly reasonable to expect us home most every night. But the point is three-fold: first, each job can involve being salt and light in a risky way; second, all men are on call to extend their crusades as prompted by God (and not by lust for status and affluence); third, their wives need to be so spiritually constructed as to cheer them on in their strategic, vocational absences.

I served 28 years in the Guard and Reserves and was never called upon to enter combat. But I was ready to go, and my wife would have supported me in it and done the full Proverbs 31 thing in my absence.

We're putting a lot on the wife, and bewailing the plight of the husband who can't rely upon a good one. But, of course, the other tragedy is the difficulty in finding a man who will put it on the line for truth, goodness, and beauty in the world outside the home. Too often, godly women are asked to settle for the less than thrilling. ("Aim low, girls, they're riding Shetlands.") They may not express it, but deep down, many long for a hero.

I think of my surprise when I announced to my wife with caution that I was sensing a call to the pastorate. After all, what could be cooler than being a philosophy professor's wife at Billy Graham's alma mater in Chicagoland? Turns out, she was thrilled. Turns out it was something she'd desired all along, having had such a great experience as a preacher's kid herself. Who knew? So you might be surprised if you showed more boldness in your efforts to glorify God and enjoy Him forever.

Look, I'm not saying that we should shun a Margaret Thatcher when we don't have a Winston Churchill around or that you mustn't hold down the fort in the days when she's landed a job and you haven't. Rather, I'm talking about the default position in God's created order.

One of my favorite movie scenes comes at the end of *Three Amigos*, the story of Hollywood cowboys recruited to deal with bad guys in Mexico. The actors thought they were being asked to make a movie; the villagers thought these guys were the real thing ready to do a real job. Somehow, it all worked out, and some tender relationships developed along the way. Then, as the three were about to "ride off into the sunset," the Steve Martin character, Lucky Day, turned to Carmen and said, "I'll come back some day." To which she replied, "Why?"

I like to image a Christian movie in which the man of the house says to his wife, "I'll be home every night this week?" And then she asks, "Why? Don't you have some important things to do out there some evenings?"

The U.S. Life Saving Service was the precursor to the Coast Guard, and in its day, it was staffed by men who lived with their families in little houses along the coasts—Atlantic, Pacific, Gulf, and Great Lakes. When sailing ships ran aground or were otherwise in distress in their area, these coast watchers were tasked to fire string-and-rope-rigged mortar rounds in hopes of snagging the wreck, allowing them to deploy a breeches buoy to rescue passengers. Failing that, each U.S.L.S.S. man had a life boat to shove into the surf and row to those in danger. The motto was, "You have to go out; you don't have to come back." (I've seen it on the wall of the maritime museum in Astoria, Oregon). The point was this: As bleak as the prospects may seem, don't bother doing the math. Get in the boat and go. If you make it back, great. We may give you a medal. If you don't, you did your duty. And, yes, we may give you a medal for that too. But you have to go.

So we might imagine, Nate Saint, Jim Elliot, Roger Youderian, and Ed McCully (of *Through Gates of Splendor*), dithering over whether to make that next missionary flight to reach the Aucas for Christ. And then Elisabeth Elliot steps forward saying, "Jim, I love you, but you have to go out; you don't have to come back."

Male and female created He them.

NINE

RACIAL RECONCILIATION

By Voddie Baucham

We all love Ephesians chapter 2. We can recite it from memory up to verse 10. But there is more in Ephesians chapter 2. I want to address what follows verse 10 as it relates to racial reconciliation. In the midst of all of these discussions about social justice, race, sex, etc., the central question is: *What does God say about us?*

When we start talking about who we are in Christ, our unity in Christ, our brotherhood in Christ, do we believe that the Bible is sufficient? One of the scariest things about some of the present talk is that we are beginning to see a new hermeneutic. Sin is now institutional as opposed to being in the heart of man. We are reading things differently. Not only that, but we are starting to develop a new canon. If you do not see these issues rightly, people are not saying you need to go to a particular text of Scripture. They are saying, "You need to read *Divided By Faith*." If you are not getting these issues right then, a list of books is provided that you need to read in order to understand the Scriptures rightly as it relates to our unity in Christ. That is a problem.

I believe that the Bible is sufficient, not just inerrant. It is absolutely sufficient for all matters of faith and practice. How we deal with one another across ethnicities is a matter of faith and practice. The Bible is adequate to the task.

I am not arguing that we should not read other things. I quote other books regularly. But the Bible is sufficient. Let me put an even finer point on it. I worry when people suggest that they have had the Bible all this time, and relationships with brethren of different ethnicities, but it was not until they read a particular book that they finally understood God's heart on this issue of justice. People are not saying when they finally read a book that was an exposition of Scripture. No. When they read a particular *sociology book* is when everything changed for them. So now we have sociology overriding and governing our theology. That is not OK. That is very problematic.

I like sociology. One of my degrees is in sociology. I teach an introduction to sociology. It is a wonderful tool as it shows us how worldviews are shaped. Strikingly, few things have been more potent in driving our culture in specific directions (antithetical to biblical truth) than sociology. What is missing in all of this? The text of Scripture. Is the Bible sufficient for racial reconciliation? Can you and I sit down with our Bibles and achieve racial reconciliation? Or are there other texts and ideas that have to inform our reading of the text to achieve justice and righteousness in this field?

I do believe in racial reconciliation. I have to because I believe the Bible. My family and I have been in Zambia for the last three and a half years. In the last three and a half years, we have been in a church where most of the people look like us (granted we are foreigners and outsiders). But before Zambia, it had been over two decades since my family was in a church where most of the people looked like us. That was by design.

In the early '90s, Promise Keepers was a vast movement. I preached at several events. Racial reconciliation was on everybody's agenda. During that time, I was a member of a black fraternity. I married a woman who was a graduate of a historical black college and university. I was the founder of the black student fellowship at Houston Baptist University. I was a member of and preaching at a predominately black church. It was black, black, black, black, black. That was my world. I came to a crossroads in the midst of the Promise Keepers and the racial reconciliation movement. I was hearing from and meeting a lot of my white brethren who were passionate about racial reconciliation. They were asking, "How do we do this? How do we not have our church continue to look like it looks?" I mean no indictment of all black churches. I can only speak to my experience. I looked in my circle and realized that I did not hear that from my side.

I did not know black pastors who were staying awake at night because their churches were too black, on their knees weeping before preaching because most of the faces they were to preach to looked like them. But this is what I was hearing from white pastors. Again, I am not saying that it did not exist. I am saying that in my experience, I did not see it. I was convicted and decided the mid-'90s that my family and I would not continue to go to churches where everybody looked like us. If I was serious about racial reconciliation, then this is something I would do. It was hard.

I took a position at a predominately white church. We faced a lot of things. We rarely faced overt racism. More often than that, it was just insensitivities, ignorance, and the like. But that is what we signed up for. It was hard for my children because they were too young to understand what we were doing and why. It was hard to be the only black kids around.

It was hard having conversations on more than one occasion where people to my face accused me of selling out. I often thought, "Wait a minute. You go to Promise Keepers, and you will do pulpit swaps, but now that I've decided to take this to another level and make a personal commitment with my life and family, I'm selling out? Then what are we trying to do?"

People accused me of robbing the black church of its best and brightest. That one was always difficult, Now, on the one hand, thanks for the compliment! But on the other hand, what do I do with that? On the one side, what a horrible way to think about the church. You are black; therefore, you belong to this group. Your gifts, graces, and talents belong to this group, and it is robbery to take them. But on the other hand, I distinctly remember when I graduated from Southwestern Seminary, receiving a questionnaire from a black Ph.D. student that said less than 15% of all black ministers in this country had a seminary education. His research project was trying to figure out what it was that helped people like me in this direction. Can you see how I would be torn?

I remember having conversations with my wife and children when certain things would happen. I was regularly having to wrestle and struggle with whether opportunities that came to me were tokenism or real. Regardless, I struggled with whether the road I had chosen was the right and necessary commitment or not. I pondered, "If I do have a problem with people's conception of me, can I fault them for not understanding me while not making myself available so they can learn to understand me?" How dare you white people who don't have relationships with black people not understand us! Do you see the dilemma?

It is a double-edged sword. Ironically, that part of my history is often now leveraged against me in this entire discussion—"You don't get a voice in this discussion because you abandoned your people." Seeing it was so hard, why would I do that? And, what did I hold on to during those challenges?

One of the reasons I did it and one of the glorious truths I held to was that our racial reconciliation does not need to be achieved, but *it has been obtained*. It is not something we have to accomplish. It has already been accomplished. The apostle Paul says,

> Therefore remember that at one time you Gentiles in the flesh, called
> 'the uncircumcision' by what is called the circumcision, which is made

in the flesh by hands—remember that you were at that time separated from Christ, alienated from the commonwealth of Israel and strangers to the covenants of promise, having no hope and without God in the world" (Ephesians 2:11-12).

That is bad news. There is a parallel here to the first part of the chapter. In the first part of chapter 2, we start with bad news—"Dead in trespasses and sins." Then we have, "But God." Here we start with bad news, then follows, "But now."

First, consider the bad news. To understand the magnitude of the reconciliation, you have to understand the magnitude of the division. "You *Gentiles* in the flesh called the uncircumcision by what is called the circumcision." The division that God overcomes here is more significant than any we face. Race is arbitrary. Racial classifications are not real classifications. There is but one race. There is virtually no genetic difference between a black and a white man. If we were not of the same race, we could not reproduce with one another. We have the same original parents. We are of multiple ethnicities but one race. The racial distinctions between us are arbitrary distinctions based on certain features we have, but not on real differences.

Consider when the Hutu and the Tutsi experienced genocide in Rwanda. People look at that and think, "I don't get that. These people look the same to me." Do you realize that the genetic difference between the Hutu and the Tutsi is small, but the genetic difference between white and black people is almost as small?

Yet, God Himself established the difference between Jew and Gentile. It was not arbitrary, but real. If God can reconcile those who have real and God-ordained distinctions between them, he can certainly reconcile people who have arbitrary and artificial distinctions between them.

It is not just that the Gentiles were outsiders, related to another ethnic group, or separated from the "cultural hegemony." It is not just that systems were oppressing them, or they lacked access to wealth. They were *alienated from God and Christ.* That is real. That is significant. My point is not to make light of anyone's experience of alienation or separation. But nothing compares to that Jew/Gentile divide. "Having *no hope* and *without God* in the world." What compares to that? Sitting in the back of the bus? No. Lynching? No. Having no hope and being without God is worse than slavery. Slavery is bad news. This is more significant.

Paul goes on in verse 13, "But now in Christ Jesus you who once were far off have been brought near by the blood of Christ." Paul uses temple language. Within the temple, there was the holy of holies. Only one day a year the high priest could go in. Then there was the place for the priest to do his routine work. Beyond that was the court of the Jews and women, then further back, you could have Gentile proselytes who could come but only get so close. But now through the blood of Christ, you, who, were way back there have been brought near. You have been reconciled. How?

Through reading the right sociology books? Through feeling sorry enough about what your ancestors did to someone else's? By having enough of your grievances addressed? No. You are brought near by the blood of Christ. Christ died to reconcile us to Himself and one another. Don't you dare add anything to the blood of Christ. The blood of Christ is sufficient to reconcile us. It is enough. And it is *the only thing* that can reconcile us. Since the blood of Christ reconciles, looking for reconciliation through other means is futile. It cannot be achieved. Not only is it futile, but it is also blasphemous because it becomes the blood of Christ plus something else.

In verse 14 Paul continues, "For he himself is our peace, who has made us both one and has broken down in his flesh the dividing wall of hostility by abolishing the law of commandments expressed in ordinances, that he might create in himself one new man in place of the two, so making peace, and might reconcile us both to God in one body through the cross, thereby killing the hostility."

Four times we see the word *peace*. Christ is our peace. He not only gives us peace and brings us peace. He is our peace. The peace that Christ brings is not just a peace where two sides decide to put down their arms. That is wonderful. We were recently in New Orleans, where we took our children to the national WWII museum. There you go through this process where you start from the beginning, seeing the Nazi build-up. Then you see Pearl Harbor and the construction of the American War machine. Then you experience the road to Tokyo and Berlin. Finally, you behold the victory won and peace treaties. But that is not the reconciliation that Christ brings.

The text says that Christ broke down the hostility *that He might create in Himself one new man* in place of the two. We do not just put down our arms. We become one new man. He makes the two into one. This reconciliation makes us brothers and sisters in Christ. It is so real that there are people in the kingdom of God who are far closer to you than your blood relatives in some cases. Blood might be thicker than water, but it is not stronger than the cross.

What an amazing reality. You can go anywhere in this world and find a church. You do not even have to understand the language. But in the worship of God and the presence of the saints, you are at home with your brothers and sisters. You do not have to read sociology texts to achieve that.

Is it important for us to understand each other? Of course, it is. Houston is a socially diverse city. Our church in Houston experienced a growth spurt in the last six months before we left for Zambia. God sent us people from eleven different nations in six months. Not people whose ancestors were from eleven different nations. But people who were born in eleven different nations—Russia, France, Germany, China, India, Argentina, Nigeria, etc. God did this in a very brief window. Sometimes there were hurdles to overcome. But the Bible was sufficient. I did not have to go get a sociology textbook on each one of those nations to have a brotherly relationship or pastoral commitment to those people.

The power was in the uniting blood of Christ and the grace of God. Our unity was in the power of His Spirit, binding us in the faith, giving us what we needed to come to know, understand, and appreciate each other. There were certain ways that we could grow in our understanding and unity. It was great to go over to the home of the Russian family and have a Russian feast. It was absolutely beneficial, but not necessary. The blood of Christ is the necessary element. The rest of it is gravy.

There is an application here for apologetics. Sometimes we think because a person is a Muslim, Buddhist, or an adherent of some other religion, we need to go study up on that religion to have a conversation with them. Actually, you don't. They are people. They are not a collection of facts. They are not a stereotype. So do not tell me that you have read books about the black experience and therefore now you understand *me*. I'm unique. Black people are unique. We are not all the same.

Ephesians 2:17 says, "He came to preach peace to you who were far off and peace to those who were near." We cannot miss this. It does not matter who you are or where you are; you need Christ preached to you. The Judaizing controversy was about saying, "We have the stuff. You have to get to where we are to come to God. You have to become a Jew before you become a Christian." The Gentiles needed the cross of Christ to be reconciled to God, and so did the Jews. God is no respecter of persons.

Sometimes we think if you really love God, then you must find those neighborhoods where the poor and oppressed are and preach Christ to them. But do we think that rich people automatically know God? Do they not need churches planted among them? Rich people need Christ. They need the gospel. All people need the gospel.

The apostle says in verse 19, "You are fellow citizens with the saints and members of the household of God." In Christ, all people have it better. You could be part of the commonwealth of Israel and be lost. You could have the covenants and promises, and they do nothing but condemn you. But now, in Christ, you have access in one Spirit to the Father. You are members of the household of God. The Redeemer did not merely fix what was broken. He did not just come to repair your dilapidated house. He gave you a new house. He started off talking about what the Gentiles did not have. He ends up talking about what Jews and Gentiles have because of the cross.

Then he finishes, "built on the foundation of the apostles and prophets, Christ Jesus himself being the cornerstone in whom the whole structure, being joined together, grows into a holy temple in the Lord. In whom you also are being built together into a dwelling place for God by the Spirit." That is racial reconciliation. It is not something you and I have to achieve. It is something that you and I have to believe. Because Christ has already achieved it. It is done. It is real. We are one in Christ. The rest of it is just walking in that reality.

It is kind of like a married couple. If they have difficulty, becoming estranged from one another, they do not need to get married. They are still married. You do not just stop being in a one-flesh union because things get hard. It is the same with reconciliation. We are reconciled in Christ. So we need to walk in that reconciliation that Christ has achieved on the cross.

It can sometimes feel like splitting hairs in this current debate. Nobody is going to argue that it is a bad thing to learn about each other and understand our history. But the problem comes when we say if you are relying on the Scriptures, *but these particular sources or perspectives are not informing you*, then you cannot achieve reconciliation in this area. Because you have not done your homework.

To that, I say, the Bible is sufficient. We use the Bible to critique all other books and not other books to critique the Bible. For, "all Scripture is breathed out by God and profitable for teaching, for reproof, for correction, and for training in righteousness, that the man of God may be complete, equipped for every good work" (1 Timothy 3:16-17).

TEN

The Ultimate Injustice: Gospel Privilege and Global Missions

By Chad Vegas

> Romans 1:14-15 "I am under obligation both to Greeks and to barbarians, both to the wise and to the foolish. So I am eager to preach the gospel to you also who are in Rome."

I vividly remember one luncheon at T4G in 2018. I was there with Radius International, a missionary training organization which I helped found and for which I have the privilege of serving as board chairman. My friend (and Radius's president) Brooks Buser was with me. A young pastor, wielding his Masters of Divinity from a respected seminary and an internship at a solid Baptist church, sat across the table from Brooks.

Brooks had just returned from giving a significant portion of his life to a people group called the Yembi Yembi. He spent over 13 years suffering loss for the unsurpassable honor of planting a church among this unreached tribe. He is American-born, of European descent, but grew up in the Iteri tribe in the highlands of Papua New Guinea where his parents planted a church among that formerly cannibalistic unreached people group.

Upon hearing that Brooks had gone to an unreached people group, planted a church, and translated the New Testament, the young pastor clamored for a chance to ask Brooks the most important questions a gospel minister could ask in that moment: "What is your view of white privilege? What do you think about the social justice movement, and how do you think these things inform the Great Commission?" Brooks kindly told him that this is not an issue he dealt with on the mission field. He encouraged the young pastor to consider something which I've somewhat provocatively termed "gospel privilege"—the fact that we have the good news and the word of God in our language, while over 3,100 people groups do not have any access to the gospel. Brooks pointed out that this disparity should be our greatest concern. With complete sincerity, the young pastor responded, "You are not woke."

THE ULTIMATE INJUSTICE

I was stunned by this reply. And more importantly, I was taken aback by its utter lack of Biblical and eternal perspective. You see, my *primary* concern as a gospel minister is not the particular social injustices of our nation, but the gaping chasm between sinners and a holy God.

Yes, injustice exists all about us and anyone who loves God and neighbor must despise it. Racism, sexism, abuse by governing authorities, and the greatest tragedy currently in our nation, abortion, are just a few examples—frankly, we could name innumerable injustices. I am not dismissing, excusing, or denying any of those things. I am also not setting up a contrast between global missions and acting with love and justice toward your neighbor. These behaviors are the fruit of the Holy Spirit in the lives of believers and do not contradict one another. Indeed, where one is, so should the other be also.

But I do want to highlight the difference between the need of the lost to hear the gospel, and the need of the lost to have a more just government. Just governments are good! However, a more just government does not answer the eternal condition of the soul. Our priority is not to transform the government or justice system; "Making America Great Again" should not be our primary concern as followers of Jesus. I'm not saying this as some naive and politically disinterested party. I care deeply about a more just America and have spent many years of my life working toward that end, from running campaigns and holding political office to starting various organizations in order to promote justice. However, what my neighbor—and the world—needs most is not the American Constitution but the word of God. The world needs a holy Christian church preaching a clear biblical gospel far more than it needs equitable government. I mean to plead with you for some biblical and eternal perspective.

Please consider this: there are *thousands* of people groups, representing hundreds of millions of people, with no access to the gospel. I don't mean that they have some anemic, weak churches in their communities that aren't really preaching Christ. No, I'm talking about the thousands of entire people groups who have never heard the name of Jesus, who don't know that there is a book called the Bible. Not only do they not currently have an effective gospel witness, they have never in history had any gospel witness whatsoever. They are dying and facing God's righteous judgement as I write. Stop and ponder this reality: people across the world, our fellow image-bearers, will stand before the ultimate bar of God's justice with no gospel hope. Let that truth hit your soul with the weightiness of grief that it deserves.

Injustice should grieve the children of a just God; it is absolutely right for God's people to stand against it. But we must see justice the way God does. Surely, over 3,100 entire people groups with no access to the saving gospel of Christ is the ultimate gospel and justice issue.

A MISSIONARY LETTER

Christians love Paul's theology, particularly as seen in the book of Romans. If you are like me, you may be the kind of person who pursues the knowledge of God precisely because Christ's Spirit confronted you with the doctrines of grace in this glorious letter. Those of us who love doctrine desire nothing more than to be "masters of divinity" in the manner Spurgeon spoke of: we want to know and teach true theology, and we want to understand the proper use of law and gospel. All of this is clearly found in Romans. Perhaps, like me, when you read Paul's eleven-chapter argument laying out the gospel, your soul is raptured with joy as he concludes:

> Oh, the depth of the riches and wisdom and knowledge of God! How unsearchable are his judgments and how inscrutable his ways!
>
> "For who has known the mind of the Lord, or who has been his counselor?"
>
> "Or who has given a gift to him that he might be repaid?"
>
> For from him and through him and to him are all things. To him be glory forever. Amen (Romans 11:33-36).

But here's a question: how often have you spent time reflecting on this letter to the Romans as a missionary support letter?

We see this focus at the beginning and end of Paul's letter. It brackets the whole book, forming what we call an "inclusio"—a literary device which indicates that everything between those two points has something to do with their theme. In the first few verses of Romans Paul writes, "through whom we have received grace and apostleship *to bring about the obedience of faith for the sake of his name among all the nations...*" (Romans 1:5). Paul wants people from every nation to obey the gospel call to believe in the Lord Jesus Christ and repent of their sins and be saved. And in the very last verses of the book we see the same emphasis:

> Now to him who is able to strengthen you according to my gospel and the preaching of Jesus Christ, according to the revelation of the mystery that was kept secret for long ages but has now been disclosed and through the prophetic writings has been made known *to all nations,* according to the command of the eternal God, *to bring about the obedience of faith*— to the only wise God be glory forevermore through Jesus Christ! Amen (Romans 16:25-27).

Paul also makes his intention for missions clear in Romans 15:24, where we see that he plans to come to Rome to encourage the Roman church in the gospel, to be encouraged, and to seek their help on his way to Spain to make the gospel known where it has not been made known before.

We find it nearly impossible to sound the depths of Paul's theology in Romans, laboring in the worthy effort of hearing what the Spirit is saying to the church regarding matters like sin, propitiation, justification, sanctification, glorification, and election. But in the midst of this rich theological banquet, let us not lose sight of the fact that Paul is a missionary to the nations, and the gospel is why. It is precisely because Paul knew the unmerited love of God in Christ that he was compelled to be an ambassador for Christ.

We should want our churches to know these glorious doctrines of grace, and we should desire to delight in them ever more fully ourselves. However, we should not want to know these doctrines divorced from the missionary imperative. We should not want our churches to fall into the sin that Sinclair Ferguson has warned about when he said he fears that too many reformed folks, "know 'the doctrines of grace,' but do not know the grace of those doctrines." We want our churches and our own hearts to know the grace of God and thus be *compelled* to proclaim that gospel grace to the world. Our understanding of these doctrines must not be locked up in the building where a church meets, or in a classroom, or in some argument on social media. We want these doctrines, which are ultimately about the saving Person and Work of our Lord Jesus Christ, to be proclaimed to all nations.

My neighbor doesn't know Jesus, and he needs to know Him. There are over 3,100 people groups who don't know Jesus, and they need to know Him. Paul knew Jesus, Paul loved Jesus, and Paul believed others needed to know Jesus! It is no mistake that Paul places nearly eleven chapters of the most exalted explication of the doctrine of salvation in a letter that also functions as a missionary support letter—how could it be otherwise? When our hearts are gripped by the gospel they *must* be compelled toward missions.

GOSPEL PRIVILEGE AND GLOBAL RESPONSIBILITY

We have seen that Paul knew his gospel privilege, and so should we—we have the gospel and others do not. Paul also knew that he had a corresponding global responsibility to make the gospel known to the lost. Likewise, if we know our gospel privilege, then we also must know our global responsibility. There are two major implications for us to consider: *we are indebted to global missions* and *we have the honor of global missions.*

INDEBTED TO GLOBAL MISSIONS

Paul writes, "I am under obligation both to Greeks and to barbarians, both to the wise and to the foolish" (Romans 1:14). Greeks, in this context, are highly cultured and educated. "Barbarians," on the other hand, are considered uncultured and unlearned. "Barbarian" is simply an onomatopoeia; when the Greeks heard the speech of a barbarian it sounded like babble to them: "bar bar bar." But here we have Paul saying that he is "under obligation" to both groups of people. In fact, the King James Version translates "under obligation" as "debtor." Paul is a debtor to both barbarians and Greeks—this should be a bit of a shock to us. Why is Paul a debtor to the Greek and the barbarian, both the wise and the foolish? Remember, this is a Jewish man claiming to be *under obligation* to some of the very people oppressing his nation—a phenomenally learned man claiming to be a debtor to the foolish!

Minimally, he is under obligation to them because God has commanded and commissioned him. His introduction in Romans 1:1 makes it clear that he is "a servant (slave) of Christ Jesus, called to be an apostle, set apart for the gospel of God." Notice that in this sense, the whole church is a "debtor"—she has been commissioned by Christ in that most well-known of missionary passages:

> And Jesus came and said to them, "All authority in heaven and on earth has been given to me. Go therefore and make disciples of all nations, baptizing them in the name of the Father and of the Son and of the Holy Spirit, teaching them to observe all that I have commanded you. And behold, I am with you always, to the end of the age (Matthew 28:18-20).

This was spoken to the apostles, but since they are the foundation of the church this commission is now passed to us. It is the whole church's responsibility to make disciples of all nations.

But I think Paul's point goes even further than this. He is a debtor because he knows the grace of God that fellow image-bearers do not know. Notice that Paul has much in common with the Greeks and barbarians: they share a common humanity, a common sin, and a common condemnation. But there is one way in which they are drastically different: Paul knows the gospel. He is the chief of sinners and Christ has saved him! And now the love of Christ compels him, *indebts* him, to share this love with those who do not know it. What is most essential about human beings is not our ethnicity, our skin pigmentation, or our language. Our division in these regards is an effect of the fall into sin. These divisions belong to the old fallen Adamic creation. But Christ has abolished this dividing wall of hostility and created one new man in Himself.

This is why Paul is "not ashamed of the gospel." He uses under-emphasis here in order to make a more powerful point. Imagine my wife asking me how she looks before we go out. If I nod and say a slow, "not bad!," what I mean is "you look great!" Similarly, Paul is *proud* of the gospel! Why? For the gospel is "the power of God for salvation to everyone who believes, to the Jew first and also to the Greek" (Romans 1:16-17). And we all need this news—this righteousness—because Romans 1:18 describes us *all*. We are *all* ungodly and unrighteous. Apart from God's work in us we *all* suppress the the truth; with foolish, darkened hearts we have exchanged the glory of the immortal God for idols. No one is righteous, no, not one. No one is good. No one seeks for God. All stand condemned. Every person will stand before God and their mouth will be shut before the bar of God's justice. Truly, our only hope is the gospel of salvation in Jesus Christ.

Paul was indebted to all people to make this gospel known to those who had never heard. We who call on the name of Jesus share that great privilege; therefore we share his profound indebtedness to make the gospel known where it is not.

We are in an era when many evangelical leaders are shouting from the rooftops about "white privilege." They are consumed with the notion that the church is obligated to work for a definition of justice whereby all people have equal outcomes. In the midst of this debate, I want to throw a concern out there. I'm concerned that while pastors are busy attempting to be sociologists, cultural anthropologists and social justice advocates in an effort to bring about equal outcomes, we are ignoring the weightiest lack of equality there ever could be—we are ignoring the lack of "equal opportunity" to the salvation found in Christ alone!

Once again, there are over 3,100 ethno-linguistically distinct people groups who have zero gospel witness. It bears repeating. Please feel the weight of this: they have no access to the gospel at all! If we have decided that equality is the great virtue, why aren't pastors shouting this inequality from the rooftops? If we are so anxious to shout about what Christ shouts about and to whisper about what he whispers about, then we should be shouting about this. We should be shouting about our *gospel* privilege, and thus our gospel indebtedness to the lost.

We are burning energy on societal injustices, all of which utterly misdiagnose the fundamental problem with man. However much we may have suffered, our greatest problem is not being a victim of injustice. Our greatest problem is that we are wicked, law-breaking offenders against our Holy God. The primary injustice in the world is committed by *us* breaking God's Law. Our greatest need is not for the church to get distracted trying to reorganize society to help people overcome the injustice committed against them. Our greatest need is for the church to remain vigilantly committed to proclaiming the good news of salvation in Jesus Christ alone. Our neighbors need to know that Jesus satisfied the justice of God for them. He satisfied the precept and the penalty of God's law for them. And He graciously offers them salvation and life in His name. They need to hear *that* message and they need the Spirit to regenerate them, to give them life, so that they believe and are saved! This is our greatest need! That's what your neighbor needs to hear; that's what unreached people groups need to hear.

In C. H. Spurgeon's day, education was the social issue which distracted Christians from preaching "Christ and him crucified." Spurgeon, who himself founded a pastor's college, an orphanage and a Christian literature society and educated the pastors of over 200 newly planted churches, had some strong words for the church on this topic:

> It seems to be the opinion of a large party in the present day that the object of Christian effort should be to educate men. I grant you that education is in itself an exceedingly valuable thing… But if the Church of God thinks that it is sent into the world merely to train the mental faculties, it has made a very serious mistake, for the object of Christianity is not to educate men for their secular callings, or even to train them in the politer arts, or the more elegant professions, or to enable them to enjoy the beauties of nature or the charms of poetry. Jesus Christ came not into the world for any of these things, but He came to seek and to save that which was lost; and on the same errand has He sent His Church, and she is a traitor to the Master who sent her if she is beguiled

by the beauties of taste and art to forget that to preach Christ and Him crucified is the only object for which she exists among the sons of men.[1]

Even so, you might be thinking, "Isn't that just something that a privileged white guy in a wealthy country says?" I keep hearing the objection that an appeal to preaching the simple gospel is something that only those in privileged positions have the luxury of saying. Listen to what was recently posted on social media by a "Young, Restless and Reformed" pastor: "Those who say, 'Let's just preach the simple gospel,' usually live where good working social systems are already in place."

This is an interesting point when one considers what life was like for a Jewish Christian in the 1st century under the Roman Empire. Was a 1st century Jewish Christian in a good working social system? Were they members of a privileged majority? On the contrary, they suffered great injustice under an oppressive government. They cared for those in the church in need, they looked after widows and orphans and even rescued abandoned babies. They were too busy loving God and neighbor to put up their collective fist against the Roman Empire.

Let's take the example of Paul: was he a member of a privileged majority? Was he treated fairly by his government? On the contrary, he was slandered and mistreated. He was often left hungry, naked and distressed. He was arrested, beaten, and eventually killed. Yet, how did Paul respond to his severe mistreatment, injustice, and oppression?

> For I decided to know nothing among you except Jesus Christ and him crucified (1 Corinthians 2:2).

> For I am not ashamed of the gospel for it is the power of God for salvation for everyone who believes... (Romans 1:16).

---

1. Charles Spurgeon, "Soul Saving Our One Business." The Spurgeon Center, March 27, 2020, https://www.spurgeon.org/resource-library/sermons/soul-saving-our-one-business#-flipbook/.

Paul was singularly focused on preaching "the simple gospel" precisely because he knew what humanity's deepest problem really was.

Do we really believe that, apart from this gospel message being preached and the Spirit applying it, people will remain dead in their sins and eternally damned by the righteous justice of God? And if we do believe that truth, how does it effect how we pray and preach and send missionaries? C. H. Spurgeon, speaking to Sunday school teachers about prayer, asked them to recall how Elijah prayed for the widow's dead son (1 Kings 17:17-24); he cast himself upon the dead child three times and cried out to the Lord to give him life.

> We see here, as in a picture, that if we would bring spiritual life to a child, we must most vividly realise that child's state. It is dead, dead. God will have you feel that the child is as dead in trespasses and sins as you once were. God would have you, dear teacher, come into contact with that death by painful, crushing, humbling sympathy.[2]

Do we pray this way for our children? Do we cast ourselves upon the Lord and plead for Him to give them life? Do we plead with the Lord for our neighbors, our co-workers, our friends? Do we plead with the Lord on behalf of the nations? Do we really see that they are dead in their sins — that they are blind and deaf? "You must have," Spurgeon says, "...a distinct sense of the dreadful wrath of God and of the terrors of the judgment to come, or you will lack energy in your work, and so lack one of the essentials of success."[3]

And do we beseech the Lord to raise up workers for the harvest to make Christ known? Jesus never commanded us to wait, twiddling our thumbs, for some young person from our church to get fired up about missions at a conference and come back asking about being sent. He commands us to pray that God would raise people up, and to send them! He

---

2. Charles Spurgeon, *The Soul Winner* (New York, NY: Cosmio, 2007), 120.

3. Ibid.

commands us to *"Go."* Grammatically, this is not merely an encouraging suggestion but an imperative. Daniel Wallace convincingly makes the case for "Go" being a participle of attendant circumstance. He also points out the importance of considering the historical context of this commission, as given to ethnocentric Jews:

> These apostles of the soon-to-be inaugurated church did not move from Jerusalem until after the martyrdom of Stephen. The reason for this reticence was due, in part at least, to their Jewish background. As Jews, they were ethnocentric in their evangelism (bringing prospective proselytes to Jerusalem); now as Christians, they were to be ektocentric, bringing the gospel to those who were non-Jews. In many ways, the book of Acts is a detailed account of how these apostles accomplished the command of Matt 28:19–20.[4]

Jesus is not asking us to casually make some disciples while we're walking around doing our normal things. He is *commanding* us, with the strength of His own universal authority and indwelling Spirit, to *"Go* and make disciples." *Going* involves being ektocentric rather than ethnocentric. We are to go, taking the gospel to foreign cultures and languages, precisely because we once were also lost and now are saved. The only hope of the nations, and our neighbors, is what brought us hope too—the preaching of the gospel!

The Honor of Global Missions

This leads to our second major implication of gospel privilege: our gospel privilege doesn't *just* indebt us to global missions, it also gives us the honor of global missions. In chapter 15 of Romans, Paul describes how he preached the gospel from Jerusalem to what is approximately southern Albania, and all the way back. He has made a long, circular journey, and

---

4. Daniel Wallace, *Greek Grammar Beyond The Basics* (Grand Rapids, MI: Zondervan, 1996), 645.

now he says that he has fulfilled his ministry. Even more—and this is fascinating—Paul claims that there is no more work for him to do in all those regions!

There were hundreds of thousands of people in these areas, and probably less than one percent of them had come to Christ at that point. Yet Paul says there's no more room for him to work. Imagine if your pastor stood up to preach one day and announced, "there's just no more room for gospel work here for me—I'm moving on." Whatever city you're from, you would think he'd lost his mind! But Paul says this because his work is a specific missionary work, which he makes clear in Romans 15:20-21: "… and thus, I make it my ambition to preach the gospel *not where Christ has already been named,* lest I build on someone else's foundation."

Paul has planted churches from Jerusalem to Illyricum, expecting that those churches will now reach their cities and areas. We see in the whole body of Paul's letters that he exhorts these young churches to grow in their adoration of Jesus, in their love for one another and in their good deeds for the sake of gospel witness. But as for Paul, he wants to reach the unreached peoples of the world—specifically, he wants to go to Spain next. Paul sees his work as going to lay a new foundation where there is none.

Interestingly, this word "ambition" can also be translated as something like "he has the *honor*" of preaching the gospel where it has not been preached. Paul is seeking a holy honor or ambition, not a worldly ambition, and this holy honor consists in seeking to be honored by God, not by man. This is the honor of suffering for the cause of making Christ known where He is not. This is the honor of bearing in our bodies the afflictions that are lacking in Christ, for the sake of His beloved church.

I mentioned Brooks Buser earlier. His father, Brad Buser, moved his wife and young kids into a formerly cannibalistic tribe, called the Iteri, and lived with them for 20 years in order to learn their language, proclaim the gospel and translate the Bible. When he left America, Carter was President; when he returned to America, Clinton was President. In this time, Brad and his wife suffered immensely from loneliness, disease, and loss. He told me once that he literally wrote down 5,000 reasons to leave. He could only come up with one reason to stay: Jesus commanded it. The Buser's location required them to send their kids to boarding school for much of the year each and every year, so they lost most of the worldly joy we all come to expect from being parents. Further, all three of their sons have gone to other people groups. This means that they have lost the privilege of their company as adults, and have missed out on much of the lives of their grandkids.

I asked Brad how he endures all that loss. He replied that he suffers that loss for the honor of standing before the Lord and presenting the Iteri church to Him. Brad said, "I long for the day when I say, 'Here is the Iteri church, here is how my life was spent. Here is the Yembi Yembi church, and the church in Biem, and here is how the life of my boys was spent.'" That is his crown and his joy. What more godly and holy ambition and honor could there be?

Building more temporary political artifices to make the world more just may be a worthy effort, but it pales in comparison to the real need of mankind. I can build generations of temporary socio-political systems that seem to be more equitable, and yet be guilty of doing nothing more than providing better conditions for folks on their way to eternal Hell. I can raise up armies of "social justicians" and "politicians" and neglect the much weightier and more eternal matters. What does it profit mankind if I gain the whole world for my socio-political cause and forfeit the gospel ministry which saves their souls?

Spurgeon puts it this way:

> Now observe, brethren, if I, or you, or any of us, or all of us, shall have spent our lives merely in amusing men, or educating men, or moralizing men, when we shall come to give in our account at the last great day, we shall be in a very sorry condition, and we shall have but a very sorry record to render; for of what avail will it be to a man to be educated when he comes to be damned?[5]

---

5. Spurgeon, *The Soul Winner*, 201.

Christ has come to save people from every tribe, tongue, and nation, and Paul was ambitious to have the honor of carrying that gospel word to the world and to plant churches. May the Lord be pleased to use our local churches to raise up, train, send, and support many missionaries, for we have glorious good news in Jesus that the world needs to hear. We have the answer to every injustice in Christ. In the Word of truth we have the hope of all the nations. This incredible gospel privilege is ours! May the urgency and weight of our corresponding global responsibility ever more fill our hearts. May God be pleased to make us grateful, and faithful.

IDENTITY POLITICS AND THE BONDAGE OF THE WILL

By Timon Cline

INTRODUCTION

[M]an's will is like a beast standing between two riders. If God rides it, it wills and goes where God wills: as the Psalm says: "I am become as a beast (before thee) and I am always with thee." If Satan rides it, it wills and goes where Satan wills; nor can it choose to run to either of the two riders or to seek him out, but the riders themselves contend for the possession and control of it.[1]

So says Martin Luther in his famous work, *The Bondage of the Will*.[2] The German reformer was obviously concentrated on soteriology in his

---

1. Luther, *The Bondage of the Will*, eds. J.I. Packer and O.R. Johnston (Grand Rapids: Fleming H. Revell, 2004), 103-104.

2. The Latin title of Luther's work (1525) was *De Servo Arbitrio*, which can be more accurately translated as "Concerning Bound Choice." The will or the choice is in enslaved (*in servetium*). It was a response to Erasmus' publication from the previous year, *On Free Will*, or *De libero arbitrio*.

exchange with Erasmus of Rotterdam.[3] For Luther, the will was the stage upon which the drama of salvation was enacted. In the things of salvation, it is only to God that "free-will", acting without compulsion, can be appropriately attributed. Luther's aim in *Bondage of the Will* was to buttress his doctrine of justification by grace through faith, predestination, and divine election over and against his opponents' suggestion of libertarian freedom in man to choose God. Luther argued that this was tantamount to ascribing divinity to man, "a delusion fraught with the most perilous consequences." Man had no inherent power to act apart from God because he is a metaphysically and morally dependent creature, one now fallen and bound by sin. "Free will", in this context, was an empty concept. Man's eternal destiny depends on God alone, not his own striving or self-help, contra Gabriel Biel and late-medieval doctrine.[4] By Luther's estimation (in this context), "[w]hat is sought by means of free choice is to make room for merits." And if merits may justify, then Christ's sacrifice was indeed foolish.

In the 16th and 17th centuries, Lutheran and Reformed theologians alike typically bifurcated their discussions on the will's place in the economy of salvation and its activity in the temporal realm.[5] Man's disposition and ability as it pertains to what is above differs from its relationship to what is below. To this end, writers of the period often said that man's will was "formally" free (and this formal freedom does not deny the brokenness

---

3. "Luther congratulated Erasmus for perceiving what others had missed, that the quarrel [between Luther and Rome, and Luther and Erasmus] centered on the view of man and God." Roland H. Bainton, *The Reformation of the Sixteenth Century* (Boston: Beacon Press, 1985), 24.

4. *See* Heiko Oberman, *The Harvest of Medieval Theology: Gabriel Biel and Late Medieval Nominalism* (Grand Rapids: Baker Academic, 1963).

5. *See e.g.* Harry S. Stout's description of the distinction between the evangelical message of Sunday sermons and the focus on social order of weekday lectures and occasional sermons in Puritan New England in *The New England Soul: Preaching and Religious Culture in Colonial New England* (Oxford University Press, 1986), 6, 23-31 (esp. 27).

of the ideal reflex of the mental faculties of lapsarian man).[6] Though all things fall out according to God's providence and immutable will, He does no violence to the will of "the creature", as the Westminster Confession (1646) states (3.1), "nor is the liberty or contingency of second causes taken away, but rather established."[7]

Luther's own view of the operation of the will outside of soteriological considerations was more complicated and out of scope here. But it was his polemic in the *Bondage of the Will* that has often garnered him a label of determinism.

However Luther's soteriology should be characterized, there is no question that he still affirmed man's moral responsibility as a free agent subject to God's moral law. Affirming that point— that man is a free and knowing creature operating with spontaneous volition— is necessary to designate man inexcusable in his sin (Rom. 1:20). William H. Lazareth summarizes Luther's position well, "Persons are relatively free as subjects/citizens to do some moral good in history; they are absolutely bound as sinners to do no saving good for eternity."[8] In Luther's words,

> [W]e may still in good faith teach people to use it to credit man with 'free-will' in respect, not of what is above him, but of what is below him... However, with regard to God, and in all that bears on salvation or damnation, he has no 'free-will', but is captive, prisoner and bond slave, either to the will of God, or to the will of Satan.[9]

---

6. *See* Perry Miller, *The New England Mind: The Seventeenth Century* (Cambridge: Harvard University Press, 1954), 255-256.

7. The Second London Baptist Confession (1689) and the Savoy Declaration of Faith (1658) feature the same language verbatim, but the former helpfully adds, "... in which appears his wisdom in disposing all things, and power and faithfulness in accomplishing his decree." *See also* The Irish Articles of Religion (1615), XI; The Second Helvetic Confession (1536), VI.

8. William Henry Lazareth, *Christians in Society: Luther, the Bible, and Social Ethics* (Minneapolis: Fortress Press, 2001), 133.

9. *Bondage of the Will*, 107.

In fact, far from denying the operation of man's will, Luther held that man acts out of necessity—depending on which cosmic being is in his saddle— not out of compulsion. "That is to say: a man without the Spirit of God does not do evil against his will, under pressure, as though he were taken by the scruff of the neck and dragged to it... but he does it spontaneously and voluntarily."[10]

Luther's theology was wrapped up in the classical hierarchy of being. It was also profoundly Augustinian and more or less repeated through the ensuing centuries by the likes of John Calvin, William Ames, Petrus von Maastricht, Jonathan Edwards, and Charles Spurgeon.[11] Only when the will is regenerated by the Spirit can man willingly turn to Christ and grasp his promises by faith unto salvation. Prior thereto, he was in bondage to sin by corrupt affections. Absent a regenerating work of God, man's status is that of sin, he can do no other.

Though "God hath endued the will of man with that natural liberty, that it is neither forced, nor, by any absolute necessity of nature, determined to good, or evil,"[12] post-fall "Man... hath wholly lost all ability of will to any spiritual good accompanying salvation," declares the Westminster Confession.[13] But,

When God converts a sinner, and translates him into the state of grace, he freeth him from his natural bondage under sin; and, by his grace alone, enables him freely to will and to do that which is spiritually good;

---

10. *Ibid.*, 102.

11. Spurgeon, "Free-Will - A Slave," Sermon No. 52, *New Park Street Pulpit*, vol. 2, (Dec. 2, 1855), *The Spurgeon Center, Midwestern Baptist Theological Seminary*, https://www.spurgeon.org/resource-library/sermons/free-will-a-slave#flipbook/. *See*, for Calvin's discussion, *Institutes of the Christian Religion* (1559), II.2ff. *See also Ibid.*, I.15.8 (showing that Calvin's focus when discussing freedom of the will in this context is soteriological, *e.g.*, "In this upright state, man possessed freedom of will, *by which, if he chose, he was able to obtain eternal life.*"(emphasis added)).

12. WCF 9.1 (citing Matt. 17:12; Deut. 30:19).

13. WCF 9.3 (citing Rom. 5:6; Rom. 8:7).

yet so, as that by reason of his remaining corruption, he doth not perfectly, nor only, will that which is good, but doth also will that which is evil.[14]

Thereafter, "The will of man is made perfectly and immutably free to good alone, in the state of glory only."[15] Throughout, God's grace does not violate but rather regenerates and sanctifies the nature of man.

Faithful Protestants have, for the past 500 years, continued to affirm Luther's basic insight into the operation of the will and the enslaving power of sin, maintaining that the only route to salvation is a work of God's free grace coming not from within but from without.

Yet, the contemporary proponents of identity politics and critical theory have imposed upon us a different sort of determinism; a new bondage of the will, we might say, and one that nears revocation of a uniquely human faculty and its operation in the things below. It is a bondage drawn not from Scripture and orthodox theology, but from an ideology of more recent vintage that has lately captivated public discourse, even in Christian circles.

I. Defining the Relationship

All the Rage

In their commendable new primer, *Engaging Critical Theory and the Social Justice Movement*, Neil Shenvi and Pat Sawyer note the pervasive-

---

14. WCF 9.4 (citing Col. 1:13; Jn. 8:34-36; Phil. 2:13; Rom. 6:18, 22; Gal. 5:17; Rom. 7:15-23).

15. WCF 9.5 (citing Eph. 4:13; Heb. 12:23; Jude 24).

ness of the language of identity politics in American culture.[16] Everyone from Rosie O'Donnell to Cher to candidates for the 2020 Democratic primary has wittingly or otherwise employed it. On multiple occasions, Beto O'Rourke has claimed without qualification that America is founded upon white supremacy and that he himself is a beneficiary of this.[17] This year, *The New York Times* began publishing, to much fanfare, a collection of essays known as "The 1619 Project."[18] The lead essay in the initiative— named for the year in which chattel slavery was allegedly introduced to the American continent via the Jamestown colony— supports O'Rourke's assessment, arguing that the ideals of the Founding Fathers were bold-faced lies, that the main impetus for American's independence was to pro-

---

16. Shenvi and Sawyer, *Engaging Critical Theory and the Social Justice Movement* (Ratio Christi, 2019), *available at* https://ratiochristi.org/wp-content/uploads/2019/11/E-Book-Engaging-Critical-Theory-and-the-Social-Justice-Movement.pdf. For other helpful overviews from Shenvi and Sawyer, *see* "Gender, Intersectionality, and Critical Theory," *The Council on Biblical Manhood and Womanhood* (Nov. 20, 2019), https://cbmw.org/topics/eikon/gender-intersectionality-and-critical-theory/; "The Incompatibility of Critical Theory and Christianity," *The Gospel Coalition* (May 15, 2019), https://www.thegospelcoalition.org/article/incompatibility-critical-theory-christianity/; "Critical Theory & Christianity," *Free Thinking Ministries* (Aug. 17, 2018), https://freethinkingministries.com/critical-theory-christianity/. *See also* Eboo Patel, "On Wokeness and Power," *Inside Higher Ed* (Nov. 25, 2019), https://www.insidehighered.com/blogs/conversations-diversity/wokeness-and-power (making the case that, in fact, "[T]alking about identity in terms of power, privilege and oppression is no longer the woke insurgency, but rather the cultural establishment. If you talk in this way, you are not showing your subaltern stripes -- you are flashing the badge of insider dominance. The badge of power.").

17. Julio Rosas, " Beto O'Rourke: 'This country was founded on white supremacy'," *The Washington Examiner* (July 10, 2019), https://www.washingtonexaminer.com/news/beto-orourke-this-country-was-founded-on-white-supremacy.

18. "The 1619 Project," *The New York Times Magazine*, https://www.nytimes.com/interactive/2019/08/14/magazine/1619-america-slavery.html. The project has been developed into primary school curriculum. *See* "The 1619 Project Curriculum," *The Pulitzer Center*, https://pulitzercenter.org/lesson-plan-grouping/1619-project-curriculum. Recently, Buffalo joined Newark, Washington D.C., and Chicago in implementing the curriculum in is middle and high schools. Kyle S. Mackie, "'Your story is in the textbooks. Ours isn't.' Buffalo schools adopt The 1619 Project," *WBFO* (Jan. 17, 2020), https://news.wbfo.org/post/your-story-textbooks-ours-isn-t-buffalo-schools-adopt-1619-project. *C.f.* Max Eden, "A Divisive, Historically Dubious Curriculum," *City Journal* (Dec. 3, 2019), https://www.city-journal.org/1619-project.

tect the decidedly sinful institution of slavery, and that America's essence from the word go has been a struggle between white oppressors and oppressed minorities.[19]

One is tempted to summarily dismiss these examples as the nuisance of so-called "political correctness," the mad ravings of social justice warriors, or an inordinate spillover of "wokeness" from academia. It might be equally tempting to breeze over recent stories like the one about teens in Argentina protesting "gendered" Spanish and presume them irrelevant, insular, and extreme instances of juvenile rage.[20]

But these quite natural reactions would be premature and miss the underlying, coherent ideology behind the socio-political, and even moral, vocabulary of the day— a vocabulary that is increasingly enveloping all

19.   Nikole Hannah-Jones, "Our democracy's founding ideals were false when they were written. Black Americans have fought to make them true," *New York Times Magazine* (Aug. 14, 2019), https://www.nytimes.com/interactive/2019/08/14/magazine/black-history-american-democracy.html. Lucas Morel has penned an insightful and measured rebuttal to the alternative history of the 1619 Project. *See* "America Wasn't Founded on White Supremacy," *The American Mind* (Oct. 17, 2019), https://americanmind.org/essays/america-wasnt-founded-on-white-supremacy/. Popular historians James McPherson, who specializes in Civil War history, and Gordon Wood, known for many famous works on the American Revolution, have both denounced the historical interpretation of the contributors to the 1619 Project. *See* Rod Dreher, "Leftists Attack The '1619 Project'," *The American Conservative* (Nov. 29, 2019), https://www.theamericanconservative.com/dreher/attack-on-1619-project-socialists/. The comments by McPherson and Wood have given rise to an online sparring match between the NYT editors and other historians and commentators, some of which have (perhaps, unintentionally and indirectly) evinced the influence of CT in historical analysis. *See generally* Adam Serwer, "The Fight Over the 1619 Project Is Not About the Facts," *The Atlantic* (Dec. 23, 2019), https://www.theatlantic.com/ideas/archive/2019/12/historians-clash-1619-project/604093/; Elliot Kauffman, "The '1619 Project' Gets Schooled," *The Wall Street Journal* (Dec. 16, 2019), https://www.wsj.com/articles/the-1619-project-gets-schooled-11576540494; Peter A. Coclanis, "The 1619 Project is the 2019 Project — and the 2020 Project," *The Spectator* (Dec. 24, 2019), https://spectator.us/1619-project-2019-project-2020-project/; Michael Harriot, "#NotAllHistorians: Some White People Are Upset That the New York Times' 1619 Project Isn't Centered in Whiteness," *The Root* (Dec. 23, 2019), https://www.theroot.com/notallhistorians-some-white-people-are-upset-that-the-1840616511.

20.   Samantha Schmidt, "A Language for All," *The Washington Post* (Dec. 5, 2019), https://www.washingtonpost.com/dc-md-va/2019/12/05/teens-argentina-are-leading-charge-gender-neutral-language/?arc404=true.

areas of social life. Instead, Shenvi and Sawyer say, language of white supremacy, patriarchy, hegemonic power, and the like flows "out of a knowledge area known as critical theory, which seeks to understand human relationships through the fundamental lens of power."

Critical Theory and its Roots

Shenvi and Sawyer coin the term "contemporary critical theory"— some have called it "applied postmodernism"[21]— to explain the most recent manifestations of a remarkably variegated tradition of thought which stretches back to the early 20th century ideas of Max Horkheimer, Theodore Adorno, and Herbert Marcuse of the Frankfurt School, the neo-Marxism of Antonino Gramsci, and the postmodern social theory of Michel Foucault and deconstructionism of Jacques Derrida.[22] Though myriad intellectual strands have come together to form contemporary critical theory—indeed, one of the chief characteristics of critical theory generally is that it is allergic to rigid definition— most agree that the Frankfurt School and the development of western or cultural (or some prefer "humanist") Marxism—Marxist framework applied critique of western culture— played a foundational role in this origin story.

Disillusioned with classical Marxism's inordinate (in their minds) fixation on economics—not to mention Marx's notorious and numerous faulty predictions— and discouraged by the increasingly apparent crimes of Communism in eastern Europe, the members of the Institute for Social Research at Goethe University—what came to be known as the Frankfurt School—shifted their attention from the means of economic production to the means of *cultural* production, specifically in the west. Their contention was that Marxist-Leninism was too rigid and that the preexistent so-

---

21. James Lindsay, "Postmodern Religion and the Faith of Social Justice," *Aero Magazine* (Dec. 18, 2018), https://areomagazine.com/2018/12/18/postmodern-religion-and-the-faith-of-social-justice/.

22. Thomas McCarthy, "The Critique of Impure Reason: Foucault and the Frankfurt School," *Political Theory* 18(3) (Aug. 1990), 437-469. *See also Globalizing Critical Theory*, ed. Max Pensky (Lanham: Rowman & Littlefield, 2005).

cial theory dominant in political science could not account for the radical politics and upheaval of the 20th century.[23]

But they did not discard the basic Marxist framework—the oppressor-oppressed dichotomy and the language of alienation, exploitation, fetishism, and reification. The Frankfurt Schoolers merely altered the content and refocused the application of said framework.[24] To their credit, Horkheimer, Marcuse, Adorno, and others were rightly critical of Nazi Germany, and fascism wherever it cropped up. But by their lights, the Third Reich was part and parcel of a larger problem.

Gramsci too denounced Mussolini's fascist regime in Italy. His famous, posthumously published *Prison Notebooks*, which espoused his revision of Marxism—*viz.*, that civil institutions which imbedded capitalist ideology in western culture were to blame for the failure of Marx's predictions—were a product of his incarceration for his communist leanings. Gramsci rejected as too simplistic Marx's economic determinism—the contention that men are formed by their material environment rather than their consciousness; Gramsci held just the opposite.[25] Capitalism had tak-

---

23. What is often caricatured as the "slight of hand narrative" has been dismissed by many contemporary apologists for the Frankfurt School, though never, as far as I can tell, by critical theorists themselves. In fact, nearly every account of the history of the Frankfurt School and the development of the critical theory tradition reflects the narrative that outlets like the *Hedgehog Review* denounce. *See e.g.* Andrew Lynn, "Cultural Marxism," *The Hedgehog Review* (Fall 2018), https://hedgehogreview.com/issues/the-evening-of-life/articles/cultural-marxism. *C.f. Marxism and the Interpretation of Culture*, eds. Cary Nelson and Lawrence Grossberg (Urbana: University of Illinois Press, 1988) (*see esp.* the introduction by Grossberg).

24. For an article that captures well the background against which the Frankfurt School members were theorizing, *see* Stuart Walton, "Theory from the ruins," *aeon* (May 31, 2017), https://aeon.co/essays/how-the-frankfurt-school-diagnosed-the-ills-of-western-civilisation.

25. *C.f.* Karl Marx and Friedrich Engels, *The Communist Manifesto* (1848). Does it require deep intuition to comprehend that man's ideas, views, and conception, in one word, man's consciousness, changes with every change in the conditions of his material existence, in his social relations and in his social life? What else does the history of ideas prove, than that intellectual production changes its character in proportion as material production is changed?

en root not only in men's material world, but in their mental world too through "fetishistic illusions," which, in turn, allowed capitalist material structures to dig in their heels. In the chicken and egg question faced at the outset by Marxists, Gramsci essentially ordered the superstructure before the substructure (material forces of production).[26] And so, it was Gramsci who cast the gaze of future Marxists toward the cultural institutions that construct the capitalist consciousness.[27] To that end, Gramsci directed his compatriots to infiltrate and transform (if not demolish) western schools, churches, and media, not to mention political and legal structures—a war on all moral and cultural hierarchies and their gatekeepers.

In a recent article at *Themelios*, Robert Smith expertly traces the intellectual development from classical Marxism to Gramsci to the Frankfurt School, and eventually, to critical theory. Smith also includes helpful assessments of key thinkers (i.e. György Lukács and Erich Fromm) not covered here.[28] Accordingly, that detailed history will not now be fully

---

26. This is not to imply that Marx and Engels ignored the influence of the superstructure upon the substructure, but rather to emphasize the difference in priority between Gramsci and his predecessors. *See e.g.* "Engels to J. Bloch
In Königsberg, London, September 21, 1890," in Karl Marx, Friedrich Engels, and Vladimir Lenin, *On Historical Materialism: A Collection* (Moscow: Progress, 1972), 294 – 296.
The economic situation is the basis, but the various elements of the superstructure — political forms of the class struggle and its results, to wit: constitutions established by the victorious class after a successful battle, etc., juridical forms, and even the reflexes of all these actual struggles in the brains of the participants, political, juristic, philosophical theories, religious views and their further development into systems of dogmas — also exercise their influence upon the course of the historical struggles and in many cases preponderate in determining their form.

27. The jury is still out within Marxist circles as to whether it was Gramsci, Adorno, or Lukács who first influenced this shift, and the extent to which there was real interdependence in the ideas of the three.

28. Properly and chronologically speaking, Lukács, a Stalinist and, briefly, the minister of culture for the Hungarian Soviet Republic, was the grandfather of the Frankfurt School. For a short but fair summary of his thought and contribution to the Marxist tradition, *see* Roger Scruton, *Fools, Frauds and Firebrands: Thinkers of the New Left* (London: Bloomsbury, 2015), 117-127.

reiterated.[29] Suffice it to say, out of the work of the Frankfurt School—essentially a cocktail of neo-Marxism, Darwinism, and Freudianism,[30] with some Kant sprinkled in for good measure—an entire field, and sub-fields, of study emerged, namely but not exclusively, critical theory and so-called cultural studies.[31]

Westward Expansion

It must be admitted that the period of history in which the Frankfurt School, founded in the wake of World War I during the Weimar Republic (1918-1933), sprouted up was a good, or at least understandable, time to be pessimistic about western civilization.[32] During the nightmare years,

---

29.   Robert S. Smith, "Cultural Marxism: Imaginary Conspiracy or Revolutionary Reality," *Themelios* 44(3) (2019), https://themelios.thegospelcoalition.org/article/cultural-marxism-imaginary-conspiracy-or-revolutionary-reality/. The influence of the University of Birmingham's Centre for Contemporary Cultural Studies and Raymond Williams, especially upon the direction of the post-war New Left in Britain, should also not be overlooked; but space does not permit due attention here. *See generally*, Dennis Dworkin, *Cultural Marxism in Postwar Britain: History, the New Left, and the Origin of Cultural Studies* (Durham: Duke University Press, 1997).

30.   *See* Joel Whitebook, "The Marriage of Marx and Freud: Critical Theory and psychoanalysis," in *The Cambridge Companion to Critical Theory* (Cambridge University Press, 2004), 74-102 (noting that Adorno, Horkheimer, and Fromm were among the first thinkers to take psychoanalysis seriously and integrate it into their work outside its immediate field); David Held, "Marxism and Critical Theory," *Political Studies* 29(2) (1981), 292-299. *See also* Erich Fromm's highly readable and helpful comparison of Freud and Marx, *Beyond the Chains of Illusion: My Encounter with Marx and Freud* (New York: Simon and Schuster, 1962).

31.   Some critical theorists today, such as Douglas Kellner of UCLA, still explicitly identify themselves with the Frankfurt School. *See* Kellner's helpful article on the ideas of the Frankfurt School and its influence in Britain, "The Frankfurt School and British Cultural Studies: The Missed Articulation," *Illuminations: The Critical Theory Project*, https://pages.gseis.ucla.edu/faculty/kellner/Illumina%20Folder/kell16.htm (retrieved Dec. 8, 2019).

32.   Robert Smith insists that the development of CT must be understood against the backdrop of the horrors of the Great War, the resultant freefall of the European economy, and the rise of anti-Semitism in Nazi Germany coupled with another world war. Smith, "Cultural Marxism: Imaginary Conspiracy or Revolutionary Reality," *Themelios* 44(3) (2019), https://themelios.thegospelcoalition.org/article/cultural-marxism-imaginary-conspiracy-or-revolutionary-reality/. *See also* David Held, *Introduction to Critical Theory: Horkheimer to Habermas* (Berkeley: University of California Press, 1980).

as William Shirer called them, that was the reign of the Third Reich, most of the scholars at the Frankfurt School were forced to flee Germany. Hitler also understood the power of cultural institutions and did not take kindly to communists or Jews—most of the original Frankfurt Schoolers were both—spouting off their subversive ideas in German universities. By 1935, the Frankfurt crew had relocated, after a pitstop in Geneva, to the Institute for Social Research in New York.[33] Marcuse taught in America for the rest of his career and enjoyed considerable influence in the academy, and the sexual revolution and anti-war protests of the 1960s.[34]

Despite the early presence of the Frankfurt School at key universities, critical theory (CT) took root in the American academy most acutely in law schools and the critical legal studies movement (CLS) in the late

---

33. For the history of this period, *see* Thomas Wheatland, *The Frankfurt School in Exile* (Minneapolis: University of Minnesota Press, 2009). In recent days, the Frankfurt School has received renewed press coverage. Alex Ross, "The Frankfurt School Knew Trump was Coming," *The New Yorker* (Dec. 5, 2016), https://www.newyorker.com/culture/cultural-comment/the-frankfurt-school-knew-trump-was-coming; Sean Illing, "If you want to understand the age of Trump, read the Frankfurt School," *Vox* (Jan. 27, 2019), https://www.vox.com/conversations/2016/12/27/14038406/donald-trump-frankfurt-school-brexit-critical-theory; Stuart Jeffries, "Why a forgotten 1930s critique of capitalism is back in fashion," *The Guardian* (Sept. 9, 2016), https://www.theguardian.com/books/2016/sep/09/marxist-critique-capitalism-frankfurt-school-cultural-apocalypse.

34. *See* Kevin Floyd, "Rethinking Reification: Marcuse, Psychoanalysis, and Gay Liberation," *Social Text* 19.1 (2001): 103–28, *available at* https://pdfs.semanticscholar.org/c6fe/0f4bdc4a0947ffd6523d15a1687ef4d9bc3a.pdf.

1970s and early 1980s, which in turn, spawned critical race theory (CRT).[35] CT has made a notable showing of late in education theory (i.e. critical pedagogy[36]) but is prevalent in older disciplines like sociology, history, and the humanities.[37] Additionally, new areas of study have been hatched for the purposes of applying and expanding the insights of CT. We now have

---

35. *See generally* Aja Y. Martinez, "Critical Race Theory: Its Origins, History, and Importance to the Discourses and Rhetorics of Race," *Frame* 27(2) (Nov. 2014), 9-27, *available at* http://www.tijdschriftframe.nl/wp-content/uploads/2016/12/Frame-27_2-Critical-Race-Theory.pdf; Jack M. Balkin, "Critical Legal Theory Today," in ed. Francis J. Mootz, *On Philosophy in American Law* (Cambridge University Press, 2009), *available at* http://digitalcommons.law.yale.edu/cgi/viewcontent.cgi?article=5623&context=fss_papers; Mark Tushnet, Critical Legal Studies: A Political History, 100 *Yale Law Journal* (1991), *available at* https://digitalcommons.law.yale.edu/cgi/viewcontent.cgi?article=7345&context=ylj. For a concise description of CRT, *see* "What is Critical Race Theory?" UCLA School of Public Affairs, https://spacrs.wordpress.com/what-is-critical-race-theory/. For a representative sample of foundational CRT work, *see Critical Race Theory: The Key Writings that Formed the Movement*, eds. Kimberlé Crenshaw, Neil Gotanda, Garry Peller, and Kendall Thomas (New York: The New Press, 1995).

36. Tait Coles, "Critical pedagogy: schools must equip students to challenge the status quo," *The Guardian* (Feb. 25, 2014), https://www.theguardian.com/teacher-network/teacher-blog/2014/feb/25/critical-pedagogy-schools-students-challenge; D'Artagnan Scorza, Nicole Mirra, and Ernest Morrell, "It should just be education: Critical pedagogy normalized as academic excellence," *International Journal of Critical Pedagogy*, 4(2) (2013), *available at* http://libjournal.uncg.edu/index.php/ijcp/article/view/337.

37. *See e.g.* Mohammad Aliakbari and Elham Faraji, "Basic Principles of Critical Pedagogy," *2011 2nd International Conference on Humanities, Historical and Social Sciences IPEDR*, vol.17 (2011); Robin DiAngelo, "White Fragility," *The International Journal of Critical Pedagogy*, 3(3) (2011), 54-70, *available at* http://libjournal.uncg.edu/ijcp/article/view/249/116; Mark Jarzombek, "A Prolegomena to Critical Historiography," *Journal of Architectural Education*, 52(4) (May, 1999), 197-206; David Gillborn, "Critical Race Theory and Education: Racism and antiracism in educational theory and praxis," *Discourse: Studies in the Cultural Politics of Education* 27(1) (2006). *See also* Gerald Horne, "Race from Power: U.S. Foreign Policy and the General Crisis of 'White Supremacy'," *Diplomatic History* 23(3) (Summer 1999), 437-461 (making a fascinating, if mind-bogglingly historically selective, case for white supremacy's influence throughout the history of American foreign policy).

gender studies,[38] post-colonial studies,[39] queer theory,[40] ethnic studies,[41] family theory,[42] and other relative newcomers to academia cropping up in niche journals and course lists at elite universities.[43]

From the start, CT has been interdisciplinary, and in the case of CLS, this was necessarily so since the basic premise of the movement was that

---

38. Mary Zaborskis, "Gender Studies: Foundations and Key Concepts," *Daily JSTOR* (Nov. 29, 2018), https://daily.jstor.org/reading-list-gender-studies/.

39. Harald Fischer-Tiné, "Postcolonial Studies," *European History Online*, http://ieg-ego. eu/en/threads/theories-and-methods/postcolonial-studies ("'Postcolonial studies' denotes a loosely defined inter-disciplinary field of perspectives, theories and methods that deal with the non-material dimensions of colonial rule and, at the same time, postulates the deconstruction of colonial discourses and thought patterns that continue to exert an influence up into the present.")

40. Dinitia Smith, "'Queer Theory' Is Entering The Literary Mainstream," *The New York Times* (Jan. 17, 1998), https://www.nytimes.com/1998/01/17/books/queer-theory-is-entering-the-literary-mainstream.html; "Queer Theory: A Rough Introduction," *Illinois University Library*, https://guides.library.illinois.edu/queertheory/background.

41. Evelyn Hu-DeHart, "The History, Development, and Future of Ethnic Studies," *The Phi Delta Kappan*, 75(1) (Sep., 1993), 50-54, *available at* https://pages.ucsd.edu/~rfrank/class_web/ES-200A/Week%201/Hu-DeHart%20PhiDK%2075-1.pdf. *See also* Dana Goldstein, "Push for Ethnic Studies in Schools Faces a Dilemma: Whose Stories to Tell," *The New York Times* (Aug. 15, 2019), https://www.nytimes.com/2019/08/15/us/california-ethnic-studies.html; Heather MacDonald, "Ethnic Studies 101: Playing the Victim," *City Journal* (Jan. 16, 2020), https://www.city-journal.org/lorgia-garcia-pena-harvard-diversity-debate.

42. Shelley Burtt, "What Children Really Need: Towards a Critical Theory of Family Structure," in *The Moral and Political Status of Children*, eds. David Archard and Colin M. Macleod (Oxford University Press, 2002), 231-253; Mark Poster, *Critical Theory of the Family* (New York: Seabury Press, 1978); Darwin L. Thomas and Jean Edmondson Wilcox, "The Rise of Family Theory," in *Handbook of Marriage and the Family*, eds. M. B. Sussman and S. K. Steinmetz (Boston: Springer, 1987), pp 81-102.

43. On "fat studies," *see generally* Helen Pluckrose, "Big fat lies," *The Critic* (Dec. 2019), https://thecritic.co.uk/issues/december-2019/big-fat-lies/. Even the famous historian of American Puritanism, Perry Miller (cited favorably here often), was a co-founder of the discipline of "American Studies"—sometimes referred to with a "Critical" inserted before "American" for good measure—an interdisciplinary approach to American history and culture that relies on critical theory. Murray G. Murphy, "Perry Miller and American Studies," *American Studies* 42(2) (Summer 2001), 5-18. *See also generally* Richard S. Lowry, " American Studies, Cultural History, and the Critique of Culture," *The Journal of the Gilded Age and Progressive Era*, 8(3) (July 2009), 301-339.

western jurisprudence, far from being based on any transcendent moral law, has been developed for the protection of the structural interests of those in power. To CLS scholars, like the so-called "realists" before them, law does not possess its own integrity or independence.[44] Accordingly, it is economics, sociology, and literary criticism that provides insights into what law *should* be in the pursuit of equity.[45] The unofficial mantra of CLS has always been that law is politics by others means, a play on the famous quote from Carl von Clausewitz's *On War*.[46]

Contemporary Critical Theory: Its concerns and emphases

In general, contemporary CT "divides the world into oppressed groups and their oppressors along lines of race, class, sex, sexual orientation, gender identity, physical ability, age, weight, and a host of other identity markers."[47] The goal of this approach to the world is liberation (primarily political and cultural) of the oppressed groups—a distinctly Marxist *modus operandi*—especially in terms of oppression proliferated through structural or systemic conditions. Liberation is accomplished by

---

44. *C.f.* Jeffrey A. Standen, "Critical Legal Studies as an Anti-Positivist Phenomenon," *Virginia Law Review* 72(5) (Aug. 1986), 983-989 (challenging the conventional narrative and positing instead that CLS was/is a critique of positivism/realism rather than a maturation of the same).

45. *See e.g.* Linz Audain, "Critical Legal Studies, Feminism, Law and Economics, and the Veil of Intellectual Tolerance: A Tentative Case for Cross-Jurisprudential Dialogue," *Hofstra Law Review* 20 (4) (1992), *available at* https://scholarlycommons.law.hofstra.edu/cgi/viewcontent.cgi?article=1752&context=hlr. For an exchange representative of CLS convictions, *see* Richard Delgado and Daniel A. Faber, "Is American Law Inherently Racist?" *Thomas M. Cooley Law Review* 15 (1998), 362-390, *available at* https://scholarship.law.berkeley.edu/cgi/viewcontent.cgi?article=1211&context=facpubs (with Delgado predictably answering in the affirmative to the question posed).

46. The influence of CLS and CRT in America's top law schools has done anything but wane. *See e.g.* Catharine A. MacKinnon & Kimberlé W. Crenshaw, "Reconstituting the Future: An Equality Amendment," 129 *Yale Law Journal Forum* 343-364 (2019-2020), *available at* https://www.yalelawjournal.org/forum/reconstituting-the-future-the-equality-amendment (stating summarily that "White supremacy and male dominance, separately and together, were hardwired into a proslavery and tacitly gender-exclusive Constitution…").

47. Shenvi and Sawyer, *Engaging Critical Theory and the Social Justice Movement*, 2.

undermining the status quo via comprehensive social critique, and highly cynical critique at that. In other words, deconstructing "hegemonic narratives"— especially historical ones— and concomitant social, political, and economic structures that allegedly justify the dominance of oppressor groups in society.[48] It is to Gramsci that the idea of cultural hegemony is attributed.

As Shenvi and Sawyer rightly point out, the CT tradition, begun (more or less) by the Frankfurt School and Gramsci, served as the philosophical basis for the post-war New Left, which includes thinkers as diverse as Louis Althusser, Jacques Lacan, and Jürgen Habermas—all contributors in their own right.[49]

Mentioned already is the fact that the sheer number of notable thinkers connected to CT attests to the impossibility of neat definition. It is the case with any intellectual tradition that its proponents will not be monolithic in their thought. The thinkers of the Frankfurt School and their CT progeny present no exceptions to the rule. Nevertheless, a basic core to the CT tradition can be identified, and an attempt at such is further pursued below.

More to the point, the influence of this multifaceted way of thinking on contemporary culture is undeniable, even in evangelical Christianity.[50]

---

48. Robert Smith makes the important point that, "What must not be missed, however, is that, despite its (hoped-for) positive outcomes, Critical Theory is an essentially negative exercise. It is intentionally destructive and only accidently constructive." Smith, "Cultural Marxism: Imaginary Conspiracy or Revolutionary Reality," *Themelios* 44(3) (2019), https://themelios.thegospelcoalition.org/article/cultural-marxism-imaginary-conspiracy-or-revolutionary-reality/.

49. On the New Left's adoption of Gramscian thought (a.k.a. "cultural Marxism") in particular, *see* Perry Anderson, "The Antinomies of Antonio Gramsci," *New Left Review* 1(100) (1976), pp 5-78, *available at* https://newleftreview.org/issues/I100/articles/perry-anderson-the-antinomies-of-antonio-gramsci. *See also*, Dennis Dworkin, *Cultural Marxism in Postwar Britain: History, the New Left, and the Origin of Cultural Studies* (Durham: Duke University Press, 1997).

50. Neil Shenvi, "Critical Theory Within Evangelicalism," *Shenvi Apologetics*, https://shenviapologetics.com/critical-theory-within-evangelicalism/ (retrieved Jan. 17, 2020).

The contemporary version— the brand being championed at the popular level— maintains the basic framework and outlook of its predecessors; it has not wandered far. The simplest insight to remember going forward is that critical theory divides society along oppressed-oppressor lines.

Hence, per Shenvi and Sawyer, "many critical theorists insist that our identity as individuals is inextricably bound to our group identity." Knowledge of "truth," morality, the very experience of reality itself is strongly shaped by group membership. What matters is one's affiliation with either subordinate or dominant groups— groups defined most often in our immediate context by traits like skin color, ethnicity, gender, age, and physical (or mental) ability. Group membership is by and large, though not exclusively, trait-based—even if the "traits" in question are socially constructed to constitute groups, the organizing principle remains *primarily* trait-based (with a few notable exceptions such as class)—and imposed upon people involuntarily. The "dominant" group is the one that is afforded preference by the (self-serving and nefarious) structures, norms, and narratives of society. In essence, the dominant group has intricately constructed, and continues to control, how a society makes sense of itself and perceives its purpose, customs, and origins in a way that benefits itself and preserves its status.

The dominant group(s) are the oppressors, subordinate (or "subaltern") groups are the oppressed. The act of oppression does not merely invoke the colloquial definition of arbitrary or unjust exercise of power, though it is certainly no less than that. Rather, "oppression" is synonymous with the dominant group's ability to force everyone else to submit to its norms and values ("hegemonic power"), thus necessarily ostracizing the nonconformist "Other", which strips the Other of power. It is a "soft" oppression that is exercised by the oppressors. Their preferences are ingrained in societal experience.

This is why people perceived to associate with the oppressor group(s) are often referred to as colonizers. Not only does this pejorative link them to the ills of historical colonialism, but also subtly invokes the idea of cultural hegemony. The oppressors have colonized the norms of society through everything from its art to social niceties. Even the very thought patterns of the oppressed are not unaffected by the supposed ubiquitous influence of dominant groups. Some CT practitioners even suggest that American schools themselves are products of (epistemic) hegemonic power by way of oppressor control of "learning culture."[51] This is especially the case in history, economics, and the humanities, but STEM disciplines are not unmarred by oppressor culture and ways of thinking.[52] Evangelical Christians might be interested to know that theorists of critical pedagogy have written about the oppression and "harassment" that Christian evangelism imposes upon minority religions (i.e. "Christian hegemony"). This is especially the case, they say, when evangelism is integrated with school curriculums.[53]

For critical theorists, hegemonic power is manifested in heteronormativity, cisgenderism, ableism, racism, and sexism, to name a few.[54] Members of oppressor groups wittingly or unwittingly (it makes no real difference) preserve their dominant status by upholding, or at least not

---

51. Peter DeWitt, "Why Is the Relationship Between 'Learning Culture' and 'Equity Culture' So Lopsided?" *Education Week* (Nov. 24, 2019), http://blogs.edweek.org/edweek/finding_common_ground/2019/11/why_is_the_relationship_between_learning_culture_and_equity_culture_so_lopsided.html.

52. *See e.g.* Chanda Prescod-Weinstein, "Making Black Women Scientists under White Empiricism: The Racialization of Epistemology in Physics," *Journal of Women in Culture and Society* 45(2) (Winter 2020), *available at* https://www.journals.uchicago.edu/doi/abs/10.1086/704991; Elise Takahama, "Is math racist? New course outlines prompt conversations about identity, race in Seattle classrooms," *The Seattle Times* (Oct. 5, 2019), https://www.seattletimes.com/education-lab/new-course-outlines-prompt-conversations-about-identity-race-in-seattle-classrooms-even-in-math/.

53. Maurianne Adams and Khyati Joshi, "Religious Oppression curriculum Design, *Teaching for Diversity and Social Justice*, eds. Maurianne Adams, Lee Anne Bell, and Pat Griffin (New York: Routledge, 2007), 255-284.

54. Helpful definitions for these terms are provided in John Harris and Vicky White, *A Dictionary of Social Work and Social Care* (Oxford University Press, 2018); *see also* Neil Shenvi, "What is Critical Race Theory?" *Shenvi Apologetics*, https://shenviapologetics.com/what-is-critical-race-theory/ (retrieved Dec. 2, 2019).

combating, oppressive structures and norms—the status quo. For this reason, it is membership in the dominant, hegemonically powerful group that determines one's complicity in this system, not one's individual conduct per se (though the latter can certainly compound guilt). Likewise, it is membership in an oppressed group that defines one's measure of innocence and, conversely, one's virtue.

The oppressed also, ironically, have privileged access to superior knowledge. In the CT paradigm, it is the deconstruction of false, oppressive narratives that liberates truth—"truth" being conveniently redefined by Horkheimer as "whatever fosters [emancipatory] social change."[55] It is the oppressed, then, who, by way of their "lived experience" as the Other, have achieved a gnostic-like transcendence of the lies of hegemonic power to higher truth. CRT in particular features the concept of "double consciousness" which affords people of color the power of second sight from the perspective of anti-black prejudice.

It is this aspect of CT that has so confused contemporary debates in the public square. According to contemporary CT, appeals to "reason" and "objectivity" are concealed bids for power by oppressors; a covert means of maintaining dominant thought patterns. Hence, the relatively ineffective efforts of historians to poke factual holes in the openly revisionist historical accounts peddled by the 1619 Project. Arguments containing appeals to objective standards of evidence and the like are couched as dog whistles for racism, misogyny, sexism, and etc.

A public discourse of distrust is the predictable result of this outlook because every statement is interrogated for its embedded, hidden bid for power rather than for its truthfulness.[56] Not only are the responses of ma-

---

55. Martin Jay, *The Dialectical Imagination: A History of the Frankfurt School and the Institute of Social Research 1923-1950* (Berkeley: University of California Press, 1973), 63 (describing Horkheimer's thought).

56. This paragraph is indebted to Neil Shenvi's analysis in "Compromised? A Long Review of Tisby's Color of Compromise," *Shenvi Apologetics*, https://shenviapologetics.com/compromised-a-long-review-of-tisbys-color-of-compromise/ (retrieved Dec. 15, 2019).

jority culture members to claims of racism, oppression, and the rest presumed guilty of what has just been described, but it is further believed by the purveyors of CT that any effort by the marginalized to educate their oppressor counterparts will be ineffective and therefore futile. The subconscious, implicit bias and inbred self-interest (by way of his class membership) of the oppressor will not allow him to fairly consider the claims and explanations of the marginalized, critical theorists suggest. So, why try?[57]

Those of the oppressor class, being ignorant of the subconscious ideologies that protect their systemic power, are therefore cordially invited to "stay in their lane" when it comes to the ever-growing list of topics about which oppressed people have superior competence via lived experience in a hegemonic regime. Social location controls knowledge (or at least perception) of truth.[58] "Lived experience" is a special, indispensable hermeneutical tool possessed by the oppressed. They therefore deserve deference in their judgments. Recently, even evangelical Christians have begun to adopt this sentimentality regarding Biblical interpretation and application.[59]

---

57. Nora Berenstain, "Epistemic Exploitation," *Ergo* 3(22) (2016), https://quod.lib.umich.edu/e/ergo/12405314.0003.022/--epistemic-exploitation?rgn=main;view=fulltext.

58. *See* Shenvi and Sawyer, *Engaging Critical Theory and the Social Justice Movement*, 7.

59. *See e.g.* Esau McCaulley, "Why it matters if your Bible was translated by a racially diverse group," *The Washington Post* (Sept. 23, 2019), https://www.washingtonpost.com/religion/2019/09/23/why-it-matters-if-your-bible-was-translated-by-a-racially-diverse-group/?arc404=true; Jarvis Williams, "Biblical Interpretation for Black and Brown Marginalized Contexts Part 2: The Importance of Reading Black and Brown Authors," *The Witness* (Apr. 27, 2017), https://thewitnessbcc.com/biblical-interpretation-black-brown-marginalized-contexts-part-2-importance-reading-black-brown-authors/. *See also* Denise Kimber Buell and Caroline Johnson Hodge, "The Politics of Interpretation: The Rhetoric of Race and Ethnicity in Paul," *Journal of Biblical Literature* 123(2) (Summer 2004), 235-251 (stating explicitly that 1) "all reading is ideological"; and 2) that the purpose of the rejection by the authors of the Christian egalitarianism and *homogenized* "universalism as non-ethnic" via Gal. 3:28—which allegedly ignores "the racism of our own interpretive frameworks"—and a "naturalized" view of race and ethnicity—which sees race as a "fixed aspect of identity"—is to further "antiracist goals").

Given that there are multiple "lived experiences," even within the oppressed class, the uninitiated observer might be puzzled as to how any single "lived experience" is prioritized over another. Does not some tiering system need to be inserted? So glad you asked.

The Linchpin

How does one determine at the ground level one's group membership? Enter intersectionality. In *Black Feminist Thought*, Patricia Hill Collins defines intersectionality—a term coined by Kimberlé Crenshaw to analyze the unique experiences of black women[60]—as an "analysis claiming that systems of race, social class, gender, sexuality, ethnicity, nationality, and age form mutually constructing features of a social organization," which, in turn, shape the experiences of minorities.[61]

As Barbara Smith explains, these experience-shaping, intersecting (or mutually reinforcing) oppressions cannot be separated; they are "intimately intertwined."[62] Collins concurs: "Race, class, gender, and similar systems of power are interdependent and mutually construct one another."[63] Ashley J. Bohrer recently clarified,

> In its most basic form... intersectionality is the theory that both structurally and experientially, social systems of domination are linked to one

60. Crenshaw, "Demarginalizing the Intersection of Race and Sex: A Black Feminist Critique of Antidiscrimination Doctrine, Feminist Theory and Antiracist Politics," *University of Chicago Legal Forum* 1(8) (1989), *available at* https://chicagounbound.uchicago.edu/cgi/viewcontent.cgi?article=1052&context=uclf.

61. Patricia Hill Collins, *Black Feminist Thought: Knowledge, Consciousness, and the Politics of Empowerment* (New York: Routledge, 2000), 299. Crenshaw has described intersectionality not as merely an analytical tool, though certainly no less than that. Rather it is a "sensibility" or "disposition" which conditions the use of all other analytical tools. Sumi Cho, Kimberlé Williams Crenshaw, and Leslie McCall, "Toward a Field of Intersectionality Studies: Theory, Applications, and Praxis," *Signs* 38(4) (Summer 2013), 785-810.

62. Barbara Smith, *The Truth That Never Hurts: Writings on Race, Gender, and Freedom* (New Brunswick: Rutgers University Press, 1998), 112.

63. Collins, *Intersectionality as Critical Social Theory* (Durham: Duke University Press, 2019), 44.

another and that, in order both to understand and to change these systems, they must be considered together.[64]

It is with the mechanism of intersectionality that relative oppression status is assessed based on intersecting traits of victimhood relating to sex, gender, race, ethnicity, and etc. Intersectionality serves as the measuring stick.[65] For example, a black man is more oppressed than a white man, but an Asian lesbian is more oppressed than either. Her sexual preference and gender give her the edge. An ethnic minority, transgender person would top all three, and so on the analysis goes.

This is the necessary tiering system by which "lived experiences" are measured in terms of their priority. They also determine the authority of a speaker. The person with the most intersectional points, the most perceived victimhood, rules the day. More structurally important, it is via intersectionality that the high-level, binary divide between oppressor and oppressed is informed by lower-level, (socially constructed) trait-based affiliations. Top to bottom the analysis hinges on involuntary group membership.

On this basis, the CT world is organized for the purpose of deconstruction of interlocking oppressive systems of social domination and liberation therefrom.[66] Intersectionality exists for the purpose of expos-

---

64. Bohrer, "Intersectionality and Marxism: A Critical Historiography," *Historical Materialism* 26(2) (July 2018), http://www.historicalmaterialism.org/articles/intersectionality-and-marxism#_ftnref3 (Bohrer's article is especially good at both defining terms relevant to intersectionality and outlining the critiques by intersectionalists of classical Marxists (and vice a versa), *e.g.* "… intersectionality theorists allege that Marxists reduce all social, political, cultural and economic antagonisms to class.").

65. To be fair, Kimberlé Crenshaw and Patricia Hill Collins have both criticized those who endlessly stack up identity markers. The real "work" is the critique and disruption of power structures. *See* Patricia Hill Collins, "Intersectionality's Definitional Dilemmas," *Annual Review of Sociology* 41 (August 2015), 1-20.

66. "Critical theory's pronounced focus on liberation has the effect of minimizing, relativizing, or even negating the existence of other moral duties." Shenvi and Sawyer, *Engaging Critical theory and the Social Justice Movement*, 7.

ing, problematizing, and critiquing hierarchical structures, and especially ideological hegemony. It is this approach to social life that has, in part, produced what is commonly known as identity politics—which can be engaged in by both the left and the right—wherein political capital is acquired in two ways: 1) by the self-flagellation of oppressor class members,[67] and 2) by assertion of victim status (via intersectional analysis) by members of the oppressed class. In both instances, it is a race to the bottom.

It is essential for Christians to grasp that the central purpose of CT is decidedly not merely explanatory. It is, rather, heavily indebted to its predecessors (namely, Sartre and Lukács) for its "totalizing" outlook (see *interlocking* oppressions). As David French suggested last year in a presentation at Southern Baptist Theological Seminary, if all intersectionality endeavored to do was to describe the distinctiveness of the individual and the discrete peculiarities of human experience then no quarrel would be found.[68] In that hypothetical case, intersectionality would just be a fancy way of confirming the priority and dignity of the individual, an idea preached by the western tradition for centuries. To assert that women have concerns and challenges distinct from men, or that black people face unique challenges in America, or that immigrants often undergo social ostracization, or that a majority culture (in any society) can become insular is not particularly revolutionary.

But intersectionality is by its own admission *not* interested in simply asserting individual human dignity and describing observable social phenomenon. The decidedly comprehensive character and activist purpose of intersectionality, as attested to by Bohrer above, must not be missed. This activist instinct connects it again to its Marxist lineage. For it was Marx

---

67. *See e.g.* Cheryl Strayed and Steve Almond, "How Can I Cure My White Guilt?" *The New York Times* (Aug. 14, 2018), https://www.nytimes.com/2018/08/14/style/white-guilt-privilege.html?smid=nytcore-ios-share.

68. Southern Baptist Theological Seminary, "Intersectionality and Identity Politics - Lecture 1: "Introduction to the Concepts" by David French," *YouTube*, Feb. 13, 2019, https://www.youtube.com/watch?v=eDwpzPne7QU.

who criticized philosophers for monotonously interpreting the world rather than seeking to change it.[69] To their credit, the intersectionists are not armchair intellectuals. They are self-consciously activist.

It is difficult, therefore, to be fair to CT (along with its concomitant mechanisms) as a discipline and its self-described objective, and simultaneously refer to its methodology as a set of neutral analytical tools that can be cherry picked at will simply for observatory (which is to say arbitrarily limited) ends.[70] The mechanism of intersectionality, for example, explicitly rejects piecemeal application; the whole point is to identify and evaluate *intersecting* points of oppression for the sake of frustrating the source(s) of oppression thereafter. Intersectionality is certainly an analytical tool, but it is not *merely* an analytical tool. Rather, it is, by intent of the designers, the vehicle by which the insights and aims—shall we say, worldview—of CT are transported to the ground level. It makes the theory of CT (and especially CRT) practical. Intellectual honesty and fruitful theological evaluation on the part of the Christian demands conceiving of CT on its own terms according to its self-prescribed ends.

None of this is to say, of course, that *all* insights produced by critical theorists or even classical Marxists are erroneous. It can readily be admitted, for instance, that capitalist societies are prone to inordinately commodifying all areas of human life, including the family and children. It must also be acknowledged that racism, misogyny, and the like exist; and that people really are subject to oppression (whether from their own sin or the sinful behavior of others). But these true insights are not unique to CT, and nor do they demand the characterization and response that

---

69.   Karl Marx, "Theses On Feuerbach" (1845), *available at* https://www.marxists.org/archive/marx/works/1845/theses/theses.htm ("The philosophers have only interpreted the world, in various ways; the point is to change it.").

70.   Resolution 9: On Critical Race Theory And Intersectionality, Southern Baptist Convention (2019), http://www.sbc.net/resolutions/2308/resolution-9--on-critical-race-theory-and-intersectionality.

CT propounds.

On Group Identity

In a recent talk put on by the British magazine, *The Spectator*, cultural commentator Douglas Murray and novelist Lionel Shriver discussed the advent of identity politics and intersectionality, and the self-proclaimed omnicompetence of its proponents on both sides of the pond.[71] The event surrounded Murray's latest book, *The Madness of Crowds* (2019), which expertly deals with the subject matter at hand. The cultural prognosis given by Murray and Shriver is not a hopeful one. Indeed, the latter suggested that the corrosion of the public square at the hands of identity politics can only be stifled by some catastrophic event that distracts everyone from their previous squabbles. Despite the dejected tone, both contributors presented valuable insight. The whole talk is worth listening to.

Toward the end of the discussion, Murray argued that group identity based on race, gender, or sexual orientation are reductive and inadequate to provide meaningful affiliations that are likely to foster social cohesion. The way that identity politics groups people, said Murray, communicates to people that they only have something in common with others socially, sexually, and ethnically like themselves. Groupings based on a nation or a religion, on the other hand, connect people with those unlike them by uniting them in common cause and mutual obligation. Murray, at this point, invoked the late philosopher Roger Scruton's argument that the nation is the highest possible expression of the first-person plural— an idea introduced in Scruton's *The Soul of the World* (2014)— that a society can achieve. Religion serves a similar function.[72]

This concept— the voluntary affiliation of individuals— creates a

---

71. The Spectator, "Identity Politics: Lionel Shriver & Douglas Murray," *YouTube* (Oct. 30, 2019), https://www.youtube.com/watch?v=ddBKQIomyYI.

72. *See* Scruton, *Our Church: A Personal History of the Church of England* (London: Atlantic Books, 2013).

compound moral person and is indispensable to healthy politics.[73] Emer de Vattel (1714-1767) taught us that this conception of society and nations is what makes the entire post-Westphalian order possible.[74] A state, once constituted by individuals in a state of nature (a hypothetical pre-societal, totally free existence) spontaneously contracting together, stands in for the constituting individuals as a new "person" in relation to other like bodies.[75] The state becomes the individual writ large.[76] Like people themselves, the state is a living organism, so to speak. But this process cannot continue *ad infinitum*. The nation-state is the highest workable expression of such. Any claim to universal jurisdiction frustrates it. The studies of John Figgis and Otto von Gierke proved that international law as a basis for inter-state relations was not possible until the universal jurisdiction of the Papacy was fractured, and the medieval dream of the Holy Roman Empire laid to rest.[77]

---

73. Scruton, "Politics Needs a First-Person Plural," *The Conservative* 5 (Nov. 2017) 7-9. *See also* Scruton, "Populism VII: Representation & the people," *The New Criterion* (Mar. 2017), https://newcriterion.com/issues/2017/3/populism-vii-representation-the-people; Scruton, *The Meaning of Conservatism* (South Bend: St. Augustine's Press, 2002), 43-44.

74. *The Law of Nations, or Principles of the Law of Nature Applied to the Conduct and Affairs of Nations and Sovereigns* (1758), eds. Joseph Chitty and Edward D. Ingraham (Philadelphia: T. & J. W. Johnson & Co., 1883).

75. On the historical development of the artificial "personhood" of the state idea, *see* Quentin Skinner, "A Genealogy of the Modern State," *Proceedings of the British Academy* 162 (2009), 325-370; Skinner, *Visions of Politics: Renaissance Virtues* (Cambridge University Press, 2002), 368-413.

76. Admittedly, fewer and fewer political scientists and historians conceive of the state in this classical fashion (but they did in the 17th century). A recent exception might be Jared Diamond in his latest, *Upheaval: Turning Points for National Crisis*, in which he curiously uses pop psychology and personal anecdotes to frame contemporary national problems. What Diamond offers is a sort of psychoanalysis of ailing states, a decidedly different use (and for different ends) of the compound personhood afforded states by 17th century theorists like Johannes Althusius and Samuel Pufendorf. The analogy was meant to be a theoretical, organizational mechanism, not a predictive, behavioral one.

77. Gierke, *Natural law and the theory of society, 1500 to 1800* (1934); Gierke, *Political Theories of the Middle Ages* (1900); Figgis, *Studies in Political Thought From Gerson to Grotius, 1414-1625* (1907).

Vattel was not innovating. The conviction that in a pre-political, pre-state condition all men are by nature free (excepting the inescapable, concreated compulsion of the natural law) and equal had compelled political writers, especially Calvinist ones, since the late 16th century—most notoriously by the anonymous Monarchomach authors of the *Vindiciae Contra Tyrannos* (1579)— to argue that it is the people who freely constitute societies, form governments, and confer power to rulers. And because governments are formed by free contract (or covenant), the powers of governments must be constitutionally limited and, if abused, revocable (hence Protestant resistance theory). Tyranny is antithetical to this theory of society and government.

Furthermore, it is the contractual basis of society and government that enables subsequent generations to both defend the inherited good and simultaneously adapt to new challenges. In short, it accounts for the freedom of participation. A socio-political outlook based on something other than popular sovereignty and the related doctrines above affords no such freedom—at least not in an intellectually coherent way—to persons not present at the initial founding. Indeed, practically none of the 17th and 18th century theorists had really experienced the hypothetical state of nature, certainly not in a pure sense.[78] Yet, it was a key theoretical mechanism to understand human nature and the nature of societies, locate the foundational source of governmental authority, and limit the distribution of power.

To summarize, a nation or state is the voluntary unification of persons for a common interest. It is a collective, volitional act, and one that must be tacitly affirmed by every generation. Each nation so formed subsequently acts by analogy as an individual as it interacts with other nations. This is the highest level of organization of this kind because any more

---

78. Interestingly, the Vermont constitution of 1777 declared its people to have reverted to a "state of nature." The American Revolution presented a rare opportunity for people in the modern world to be able to say such in earnest.

expansive, global government would necessarily confound the basis of the original, constitutive contract which forms a society and state. In short, people would become members of a society and a government by way of simply existing apart from any exercise of volition.[79]

Human v. Inhuman Categories

As Murray was outlining his objection to group affiliations based on sexual, racial, or ethnic identity, Lionel Shriver interjected. In her estimation, it is more proper to conceive of human affiliations in terms of volitional and non-volitional, whereas identity groups based on race or gender involve no exercise of the will. By contrast, nation-states and a religion not only permit the exercise of the will inside their confines to determine their shape and meaning but are at their very inception products of the will.

I heartily concur with Shriver. But I would add a further qualification. I would opt for organizing affiliations or attachments based on a *human v. inhuman* distinction *depending on* whether they are volitionally based or not. As alluded to above, the dual concepts of, 1) the natural equality of men in a hypothetical state of nature, and 2) the idea of man as a voluntary moral agent, undergird western political systems including our own. They are the basis of popular sovereignty, the rule of law, freedom of expression, and more. It is difficult to conceive of western political norms enduring within a cultural environment that no longer respects the values that support it.

But on a more fundamental, and chilling, level— one that gets at why I favor an associational distinction between human and inhuman designations— the bondage (or negation) of the will advanced by identity politics and CT challenges the very dignity, and unique status, of human

---

79. This theory of politics was pioneered the Conciliarist during the Great Papal Schism of the late-fourteenth-early-fifteenth centuries and was taken up by Protestant jurists like Hugo Grotius and Johannes Althusius, the latter being hands down the greatest Calvinist political theorist to ever live. Their ideas were perpetuated by people like Samuel Rutherford throughout the 17th century. In sum, these ideas were demonstrably Christian in their origin and development.

beings. That prospect should startle Christians into having a care before they adopt the language and concepts of CT presently in vogue.

The best antidote to new challenges is to look backward. History, or rather, an older, forgotten theology can explain my contention, and help us navigate unchartered waters and reassert a Christian anthropology contra the new counter narrative.

II. What is Man?

Samuel Willard, forgotten Puritan

Samuel Willard (1640-1707), a Puritan, congregationalist theologian and preacher of the highest order, is almost totally forgotten today. But in his own day, Willard was, along with Increase Mather, the leading intellectual light in New England, vice-president of Harvard, and a long-time pastor of one of the Old South Church (Third Church) in Boston.[80] His posthumously published *A Compleat Body of Divinity* (1726)— a compilation of 250 expository lectures on the Westminster Shorter Catechism— is the closest thing to a systematic theology that any New Englander of the 17th century produced. Accordingly, as American Puritanism's *summa theologica*, it serves as a window into the Reformed orthodoxy maintained by those noble people who embarked upon an errand into the wilderness.

And yet, as early as the 19th century, Moses Coit Tyler lamented that Willard's *Compleat Body* had been confined to the dust bin of history. Tyler sardonically quipped that the book might still serve to "make men good Christians as well as good theologians— if only there were still left on

---

80. John Langdon Sibley, "Samuel Willard," in *Biographical Sketches of Graduates of Harvard University, in Cambridge Massachusetts*, vol. II: 1659-1677 (Cambridge: Charles William Sever, 1881), 13-36. Willard published many other written works but gained additional notoriety as an opponent of the Salem witch trials. *See e.g.* his anonymously published, *Some Miscellany Observations On our Present Debates Respecting Witchcrafts, In a Dialogue Between S. & B.* (Philadelphia: William Bradford, 1692).

the earth men capable of reading it." [81] At over 900 folio pages, Willard's compendium is not for the faint of heart. It is methodical, but it represents a lifetime of rich, faithful preaching, and can, per Tyler's advice, still offer guidance today. Willard's anthropology, which was totally conventional—indeed, the view of man imbedded in the minds of the authors of the great confessions—during the High Orthodoxy period (1620-1700) of Reformed theology,[82] is of especial interest here.[83]

Man, the Reasonable Creature

Willard portrays man as a microcosm of creation. "There were many beams of [God's] wisdom, power and goodness scattered among other creatures; here [in man] they are all contracted in this little model."[84] Every element or level of the Great Chain of Being is represented in man. He is embodied, which represents the lowest level of existence that even rocks have. He has the power to grow, which corresponds to the "vegetative soul." His ability to move is due to the "locomotive soul." Man's power to perceive, think, and remember belongs to his "sensitive soul" (what we

---

81. Tyler, *A History of American Literature: 1607-1765* (New York: G. Putnam's Sons, 1878), 167-168 ("Samuel Willard, himself, like his book, a body of divinity; a man of inexpressible authority, in those days, throughout all the land.").

82. On the periodization of Reformed orthodoxy, *see* Richard Muller's magisterial *Post-Reformation Reformed Dogmatics: The Rise and Development of Reformed Orthodoxy, ca. 1520 to ca. 1725* (Grand Rapids: Baker Academic, 2nd ed., 2003).

83. Indeed, as Perry Miller observed, the anthropology (and "psychology") outlined below via Willard "was part of the intellectual heritage [from the medieval period] which Puritans accepted without criticism," and was appropriated "as readily as [was] the doctrine of the four causes." *The New England* Mind, 242-243; *and see Ibid.*, at 239-279 (Miller offers a more thorough discussion than can be included here, in which Samuel Willard features heavily throughout). For a much later attestation to the same basic theology, *see* Charles Hodge, *Systematic Theology*, vol. II (Peabody: Hendrickson Publishers, 2016 [1871-1873]), 96-99.

84. Willard, *A Compleat Body of Divinity in two hundred and fifty expository lectures on the Assembly's Shorter catechism wherein the doctrines of the Christian religion are unfolded, their truth confirm'd, their excellence display'd, their usefulness improv'd; contrary errors & vices refuted & expos'd, objections answer'd, controversies settled, cases of conscience resolv'd; and a great light thereby reflected on the present age* (Boston, 1726), 122. [Hereinafter, *Compleat Body*].

might refer to as the instinctive nature) and is shared with other animals. But uniquely, man has a rational soul.[85] He can know, judge, and choose.[86] "There are three lives in man," said John Preston (1587-1628), "there is the life of plants, of beasts or sence [sic], and the life of reason."[87]

Man is a wonderous expression of God's craftsmanship because his being spans the cosmological divide; he is a "Microcosmos." In him is included elements, so to speak, of both the visible and invisible realm, the earthly and celestial. Willard was convinced that no person could totally discard the innate awareness of his special position in creation.[88] As Ernest Benson Lowrie perceives, in Willard's theology, "The distinctive place man holds in the hierarchical order of the universe determines Willard's fundamental anthropological doctrine."[89] It is the whole man that Willard engages. Though a composite creature, his parts cannot be separated and remain man qua man. In Willard's words, "Man consists of two essential constituting parts, *viz.* a body, and a reasonable soul. Neither of these alone is the man, but both in a conjunction... both go together to his

---

85. The assumption here (in classical metaphysical terms) is that, as Thomas Aquinas said, "[T]he soul is the form of the living body...the principle of the acts of life." Aquinas, *Selected Writings*, ed. Ralph McInerny (London: Penguin Books, 1998), 425-426.

86. *See also* Miller, *The New England Mind*, 239-241 (summarizing the same organization of the soul).

87. Miller, *The New England Mind*, 240 (quoting Preston).

88. Willard, *Compleat Body*, 127.

89. Lowrie, *The Shape of the Puritan Mind: The Thought of Samuel Willard* (New Haven: Yale University Press, 1974), 77.

specifications and personality."[90]

That being said, it is man's rational soul that chiefly concerns us because it is this aspect of his being that most acutely distinguishes him from the rest of creation. Most importantly, it is the reasonable soul which fits humankind for his appointed end, that is, "being an active instrument in serving God."[91] It is man's faculties housed in his reasonable soul that are "a mirror of the divine glory," said John Calvin (1509-1564).[92]

The rational soul is fundamentally a "spiritual substance" which can exist apart from the body.[93] It is of a separable essence (and different source) from the body and of a constant nature distinguished from the inconstant nature of the lower "souls" in the hierarchy of being. The body can be perpetuated (or propagated or transmitted) naturally through acts of procreation. By contrast, the soul, as a simple, indivisible, metaphysically infallible substance, is not subject to "seminal generation," division, or multiplication.[94] The key texts in this discussion were, *inter alia*, Ecclesi-

---

90. Willard, *Compleat Body*, 231 (citing Gen. 2:7). *See also* James Boyce, *Abstract of Systematic Theology* (Cape Coral: Founders Press, 2006 [1887]), 195 ("Man alone is possessed of both spirit and body. He is, therefore, the link which binds together the world of spirit and that of matter."); Boyce, *Abstract*, 196,
The union of both body and soul is necessary to constitute man. Of necessity, his conscious individuality is inseparably associated with his spiritual nature, for in him there is no separate animal life in the body from that of the spirit which is united with it. Without that spirit, therefore, the body is but a form of clay. But the spirit alone is but a spirit. It has not all of human nature. It is not a man... If, at any time, therefore, the spirit and body shall be separated, the spirit will not properly be called man until a subsequent reunion.

91. Willard, *Compleat Body.*, 121 (this is done both "actively" and "passively").

92. John Calvin, *Institutes of the Christian Religion* (1559), I.15.4.

93. *See* Francis Turretin, *Institutes of Elenctic Theology*, vol. I, trans. George Musgrave Giger, ed. James T. Dennison, Jr. (Phillipsburg: P&R, 1992), 485 ("For if the soul can act independently of the body, it can also subsist independently of the body, for the mode of operating follows the mode of being.").

94. Willard, *Compleat Body*, 194-195 (denouncing the propagation, multiplication, division, and seminal generation of the soul). *See also* Turretin, *Institutes*, 477-482; Boyce, *Abstract*, 202-207 (refuting "Traducianism"). That spirits are metaphysically incorruptible is not, however, to say that they are infallible, a characteristic of all created substances. *See* Boyce, *Abstract*, 216.

astes 12:7, Genesis 2:7,[95] and Hebrews 12:9.[96] "The [rational] soul is not traduced or derived from the parents, but is immediately created by God himself," says Willard.[97] Hence, the rational soul is immortal.[98] Though man as a whole—the inconstant body and the constant soul— is mortal, the soul in itself is not.[99]

Calvin wrote in his *Institutes* that man's soul is "an immortal though

---

95.   Willard, *Compleat Body*, 123 (Man's soul "is an *Immortal Spirit*. Man by reason of it, is called a *Living Soul*, Gen. 2.7. i.e. Immortal. There was no pre-existing Matter of which it was made, being made immediately out of *Nothing*."). Later on, in the same paragraph, Willard cites to 2 Cor. 4:16, Matt. 32:33, Ex. 3:15, 1 Peter 3:19, and (again) Eccl. 12:7.

96.   On this point, Willard cites the passages above as well as Zech. 12:1, Isaiah 57:16, and Job 10:9-12. *Compleat Body*, 194-195. *See also* Numbers 16:22; 27:16: "And they fell upon their faces, and said, O God, the God of the spirits of all flesh, shall one man sin, and wilt thou be wroth with all the congregation?" "Let the Lord, the God of the spirits of all flesh, set a man over the congregation."

97.   Willard, *Compleat Body.*, 194. *See also* Turretin, *Institutes*, 485 ("If, therefore, the soul is spiritual, it neither is produced from the power of a material, nor depends upon it—not in becoming or in being—because it has a peculiar mode of subsistence and so does not die with the body, but can subsist separated from it."); Boyce, *Abstract*, 190 ("The Scripture doctrine thus revealed is that man was created by God, being formed, as to his body, from earthly material, and as to his soul, by direct creation." (citing, *inter alia*, Ecc. 12:7, "Then shall the dust return to the earth as it was: And the spirit shall return unto God who gave it.")); *Ibid.*, 194-195 (presenting the same basic hierarchy of being and stating that "Man alone is possessed of both spirit and body. He is, therefore, the link which binds together the world of spirit and that of matter.").

98.   Willard's fellow New England divine John Norton affirmed that the soul is "created by God of nothing, immediately infused into the body as the proper form thereof by which man is, liveth, is sensible, moveth, understandeth, willeth, and is affected." Miller, *The New England Mind*, 240 (quoting Norton).

99.   Calvin, *Institutes*, I.15.3 ("For though the whole man is called mortal, the soul is not therefore liable to death, nor when he is called a rational animal is reason or intelligence thereby attributed to the body."). It may shock modern readers to know that so serious was this matter in Willard's day that the first law against heresy (1646) enacted in the Massachusetts Bay Colony listed denial of the immortality of the soul as a punishable (via banishment) offense. H. L. Osgood, *The American Colonies in the Seventeenth Century*, vol. I (Gloucester: Peter Smith, 1957), 215-216. Francis Turretin exposes one of the many grievances of the Reformed against Anabaptists and Socinians when he claims that the latter two groups had followed in the footsteps of the Sadducees and Epicureans in defending "a night of the soul," meaning that the soul, upon the death of man, enters limbo until the resurrection. Turretin, *Institutes*, 482-483.

created essence" and constitutes man's "nobler part."[100] It is properly what designates him the *Imago Dei*.[101] Francis Turretin (1623-1687), who began his treatment of this topic with Christ's dispute with the Sadducees in Matthew 22:32, agreed. The substance of the soul is "immortal intrinsically and as to its faculties," all of which "belong eminently and most perfectly to God."[102] Therefore, even after the entrance of sin, man is still said to be made in the image of God (James 3:9).

In this delineation of the soul, Samuel Willard was doing no more than, along with his Reformed predecessors, elaborately affirming inherited medieval doctrine. His theory of the soul, as Perry Miller recounted, was the heritage of the grand western tradition. Though Thomas Aquinas and Albertus Magnus had loomed large in their articulation of the classical "faculty" psychology, the theory was more accurately an eclectic product, a more or less centuries long collective commentary on Aristotle's *De Anima*.[103]

Excursus: Aristotelianism and Sola Scriptura

The adoption of Aristotelian logical principles (e.g. the principle of contradiction), four-fold causality, and terms and categories—like the distinction between "substance" as the composite of "matter" and "form," and "accidents" as the incidental characteristics of the substance; or the differ-

---

100. Calvin, *Institutes*, I.15.2.

101. Willard, *Compleat Body*, 122 ("Now Man was made a Reasonable Creature, Because he had not been otherwise capable of the Image of God: For that shines forth only in Rational Beings."). *See also* Turretin, *Institutes*, 464-470 (discussing the fourfold image of God); *Ibid.*, 482-488 (on the immortality of the soul); Boyce, *Abstract*, 196 ("Thus is it, that through this union [of body and soul], man, probably along, with the exception of God, introduces and accomplishes direct results of conscious purpose in the material universe.").

102. Turretin, *Institutes*, 466, 478 (on Genesis 2:7). *See also Ibid.*, 483 (distinguishing between "extrinsic" and "intrinsic" immortality) and 485 ("For whatever is spiritual and free from the contagion of matter is immortal. For being in the highest degree simple and indivisible, it is devoid of contrariety...and there is nothing by which it can be corrupted intrinsically or perish. That at length is mortal which is material and compound and consists of contrary qualities contending against each other.").

103. Aquinas produced a commentary on Aristotle's *De Anima* around the late 1260's.

ence of "potency" from "act"—by the early modern Reformed, however, did not represent a wholesale or uncritical adoption of Aristotelianism.[104] Rather, the basic language presented by the Philosopher, and preeminent in the theological discipline, was eclectically and strategically employed by Christian theologians for centuries in various doctrinal areas systematically to organize and communicate scriptural truths.[105] Richard Muller has done much to correct the old assumption that the Reformation represented a total repudiation of Aristotle and that, thereafter, the 17th century scholastics plunged Reformed doctrine back into the arms of classical philosophy. More accurately, as Reformed theologians sought to sharpen their doctrinal assertions over and against their external and internal opponents and for use in higher education, precise definitions and distinctions were needed. The result was the establishment of a (in some ways) distinctly Protestant prolegomena and metaphysics built upon the pre-existent framework of the scholastic method and Aristotelian language.[106]

This work was not done in an historic or intellectual vacuum—many of the theological questions posed to the Reformed were already couched in predetermined forms—but rather in dialogue with friend and foe alike, as well as the authorities of the past and the grand tradi-

---

104. Richard A. Muller, "Reformation, Orthodoxy, 'Christian Aristotelianism,' and the Eclecticism of Early Modern Philosophy," *Nederlands archief voor kerkgeschiedenis / Dutch Review of Church History*, 81(3) (2001), 306-325, 315-316 (listing examples of key Aristotelian terms employed by 17th century theologians). On the reception of Aristotle by Aquinas and medieval theologians on the question of contingency and necessity, *see* Muller, *Divine Will and Human Choice: Freedom, Contingency, and Necessity in Early Modern Reformed Thought* (Grand Rapids: Baker, 2017), 83-138.

105. *See generally* T. Theo J. Pleizier and Maarten Wisse, "'As the Philosopher Says': Aristotle," in ed. William J. Van Asselt, trans. Albert Gootjes, *Introduction to Reformed Scholasticism* (Grand Rapids: Reformation Heritage Books, 2011), 26-44 (contending that, for example, the Reformed use of *natura*, *essentia*, and *attributa* were distinct from Aristotle's); *Ibid.*, 41 (noting that even the sixth century commentary of Boethius on Aristotle's works, written to accommodate his translation, was "more Christian than Aristotelian in bent.").

106. Muller, "Reformation, Orthodoxy, 'Christian Aristotelianism,'" 315.

tion within which Aristotle's thought and categories were ingrained.[107] Muller concludes that, "[T]he Protestant theologians and philosophers of this generation viewed Aristotelian metaphysics as a crucial source for definitions and arguments needed in the construction and defense of their theological systems."[108]

Importantly, Muller has demonstrated that Aristotelianism was significantly modified by the realist tendencies and Augustinian impulses of western theologians to coincide with their Christian worldview.[109] In short, the adoption of terms did not imply the acceptance of content. Much content, such as the idea of plentitude, was outright rejected.[110] The label can therefore only be loosely applied to the Reformed orthodox of the 17th century; their product was eclectic and unique.[111] The scholastic methodology and Aristotelian categories did not serve as an alternative method of inquiry or interpretation, but rather as (at the time, nigh inescapable) organizational mechanisms for the construction of a Reformed systematic theology that could withstand assaults on multiple fronts and

---

107. Pleizier and Wisse, "'As the Philosopher Says'," 30 (providing the example of the consistent appeal to the law of contradiction by the Reformed to combat Socinian and Roman Catholic polemics).

108. Muller, *Post-Reformation Reformed Dogmatics*, vol. III, 107.

109. Muller, "Reformation, Orthodoxy, 'Christian Aristotelianism,'" 309 ("The Reformation can hardly be said to have ended the intellectual hegemony of modified Christian Aristotelianism.").

110. Primarily because the idea leads to belief in an eternal world and determinism, neither of which were orthodox beliefs from the position of the Reformed.

111. Muller advises that if a strict view of Aristotelian is applied then Aristotle was in a class of one, the only Aristotelian to ever live. Alternatively,
If... Aristotelianism is defined as a view of the universe that affirms both a primary and secondary causality, that assumes the working of first and final causality through the means of instrumental, formal, and material causes, and that, using this paradigm, can explain various levels of necessary and contingent existence, then a large number of Aristotelians appear on the horizon.
Muller, "Reformation, Orthodoxy, 'Christian Aristotelianism,'" 313-314.

evidence its catholicity.[112]

The goal, at all times, from Aquinas to Willard, was a *Christian*, which is to say biblical, philosophical model. Per Muller, "The object of the scholastic [whether medieval or early modern] theologian… was, typically, not so much to be 'Aristotelian' as to be the formulator and mediator of a Christian philosophical model that both used and refused various elements of the classical tradition."[113] A mere cursory search of early modern Reformed sources (especially the confessions) will reveal that the principle of *sola scriptura* as the starting point and bedrock of doctrine was not in any way discarded or compromised by this effort of systemization and explication.[114] The theology surrounding the origin and duration of the soul and the order of the human faculties was developed over centuries through painstaking exegesis of the relevant biblical texts and the careful reasoning of hundreds of theologians in conversation with one another.

More in service to the subject at hand, Willard and his Puritan compatriots in the late 17th century "retained without substantial change [medieval] orthodox scholastic ideas of the soul, of its composition and its faculties."[115] The central presupposition underlying these ideas was the *scala naturae* ("ladder of being"), developed fully by scholastic scholars, like

---

112. Indeed, the term "Aristotelian," in this context, requires significant qualifications. *Ibid.*, 313ff.

113. *Ibid.*, 314. Pleizier and Wisse, "'As the Philosopher Says'," 32 ("The question in the scholastic tradition is therefore not whether the use of a distinction is Aristotelian but whether the application of the distinction can solve a theological issue.").

114. As Muller notes, even the "Ramists," who sought to simplify Aristotle's logic and of which Willard would have been one, "did not give up the basic assumptions taken from Aristotelian physics and metaphysics." Even extreme critics of Aristotelian metaphysics in theology were unable or unwilling to shake off the system of causality inherited from the Philosopher. Muller, "Reformation, Orthodoxy, 'Christian Aristotelianism,' and the Eclecticism of Early Modern Philosophy," 310-311.

115. Miller, *The New England Mind*, 244-245. Another classical (hierarchical) assumption was that there was in man's faculties a natural subordination; the inferior faculties received their motion and direction from the superior ones. *See* Miller, *The New England Mind*, 252-253.

Aquinas in his *Contra Gentiles*, and rooted in Aristotle's *Historia Animalium*. The classical hierarchy (or "chain") of being, with God at the top and men sitting only a little lower than the angels (Ps. 5:8), served for centuries as the basis for truth and epistemology until the advent of Cartesianism.[116] Preaching his messages which comprised the *Compleat Body*, Willard was acting as a last bulwark against a rather glacial but radical shift toward a new metaphysics.[117]

Man, a Spontaneous Agent

Though, as stated, the body and the soul are essential to human nature, it is the rational soul that qualifies man as a voluntary (free) moral

---

116. Nicolas Laos, *The Metaphysics of World Order: A Synthesis of Philosophy, Theology, and Politics* (Eugene: Pickwick, 2015), 58-63; *see also generally* Seymour Van Dyken, *Samuel Willard, 1640-1707: Preacher of Orthodoxy in an Era of Change* (Grand Rapids: Eerdmans, 1972). Muller, *Post-Reformation Reformed Dogmatics*, vol. I, 120:
It should also be clear that the shift in philosophical perspective that took place in the latter half of the seventeenth century, as the older Aristotelianism gave way before various forms of rationalism was a shift that was recognized at the time as having a massive impact on Christian theology… with the alteration of philosophical perspective at the close of the seventeenth century, there was also a fundamental alteration of theology and of the exegesis that underlay its formulations.

117. "The Puritan version [of the theory of the soul] was not altered until the last decades of the [17th] century, when it was modified to suit the criticisms of Descartes, and was not really abandoned until the beginning of the eighteenth century, when the *Essay on the Human Understanding* swept it into the discard." Miller, *The New England Mind*, 245. *C.f.* Norman S. Fiering, *Jonathan Edwards' Moral Thought and Its British Context* (Chapel Hill: University of North Carolina Press, 1981) (rejecting as exaggerated Miller's estimation of the influence of Locke's *Essay* upon Edwards specifically and American thought generally).

agent and therefore *like* God.[118] It was common for Puritans to designate man "a cause by counsel," a reference to his active and personal self, capable of making a thoughtful and deliberate choice.[119] Per Willard,

> Man can both propound to himself his own end and make choice of the means or way leading unto it. He can deliberate with himself about these things, and take that which likes himself, and leave that which is not grateful to him. None can either compel or hinder him in his choice, but he can follow the dictates of his own understanding. From whence it follows, that all his *human* actions are voluntary and deliberate.[120]

A voluntary agent, in Willard's formulation, is necessarily distinct from what he calls a "natural agent." In describing the nature of an action, Willard writes,

---

118. *See also* Calvin, *Institutes*, I.15.3 ("For though the divine glory is displayed in man's outward appearance, it cannot be doubted that the proper seat of the image [of God] is in the soul."). In this section, Calvin thoroughly refutes Osiander's contention that it is not in the soul of man that the image of God is found but in the *whole* Adam, body and soul. In I.15.5, Calvin clearly denies that this "likeness" implies any transference of substance or essence from God to man as implied by the Manicheans and Servetus. Therefore, the image of God in man does not afford man divinity. "[W]e are [God's] offspring... not in substance, however, but in quality, inasmuch as he has adorned us with divine endowments." *And see* Boyce, *Abstract*, 196,

The union of body and soul is necessary to constitute man...Without that spirit, therefore, the body is but a form of clay. But the spirit alone is but a spirit. It has not all of human nature. It is not a man...If, at any time, therefore, the spirit and body shall be separated, the spirit will not properly be called man until a subsequent reunion. Until then it would be known and spoken of as the spirit of the man, or the soul of the man, but not as the man himself. Accordingly, the Scriptures speak thus of all men during the period intervening between death and the resurrection of the judgment day.

119. Willard, *Compleat Body*, 214 ("That which makes the action sinful, is, *because the exorbitation is voluntary*. It is certain that sin can be charged upon no creatures, but such as are causes by counsel." (emphasis in original)); *Ibid.*, 124 ("By [the rational soul] Man becomes a Cause by Counsel.").

120. *Ibid.*, 124 (emphasis added). *See also* Willard, *Mercy magnified on a penitent prodigal, or A brief discourse, wherein Christs parable of the lost son found, is opened and applied, as it was delivered in sundry sermons* (Boston, 1684), 149 ("Man is a reasonable Creature, and a cause by counsel of his own actions: The understanding in man is the light in him, by which he regulates all his wayes, and as he seeth so he practiseth.").

> In every agent we consider a power which is in it, and that seated in the faculties, and is in them a principle of operation, which is called the habit, and is that whereby it is fitted to serve to its end. And there is such a power in every faculty... according to the end and use of it... Now whensoever [sic] this power is exerted by any faculty in the creature, that is properly an action, and that is always by applying to an object.[121]

He goes on, "Now these actions are some natural and some rational and spontaneous. Hence the distinction between natural and voluntary agents."[122]

In sum, an agent (of any kind) is that which has the power to act, according to the appointed end, in itself. A natural agent is one that acts by an action that originates instinctually (i.e. without the ability to deliberate and choose). A rational or "spontaneous" agent is one that acts without being compelled by instinct but by free deliberation and choice (both of the means and the end). The free agent is capable of self-determination. Of course, as mentioned above, humans possess the sensitive (or "sensual") soul and therefore act in some things as a *natural* agent. Not every action is, in fact, voluntary. But "all [man's] *human* actions are voluntary and deliberate."[123]

Man, a Cause by Counsel

In classical fashion, Willard divides (though only "notionally") the rational soul into the understanding (or the intellect) and the will (which often encompassed the affections), two inseparable faculties of the same power. Teleologically speaking, the proper object of the understanding is

---

121. Willard, *Compleat Body*, 212.

122. *Ibid.* (Willard adds that voluntary actions can further be divided into *elicit* and *imperate* actions. The former is those that immediately proceed from the will; the latter is "such as are performed by the other powers in man at the command of the will.").

123. *Ibid.*, 149.

truth; that of the will is goodness.[124] Accordingly, logic is concerned with the well-ordering of intellect toward truth, and ethics with the directing of the will toward the good. These two faculties operating in tandem as "an ability of knowing, and electing, or choosing and refusing" make man a moral creature. For what is true is also good and what is good is true.[125] Willard makes clear that the two faculties are distinct but interdependent and complimentary, and that both are free. "As without knowledge there can be no judgment passed, so without liberty, there can no election be made."[126] The former he more frequently calls the understanding, and the latter he calls the will. The understanding discerns things, and judges them either desirable or undesirable. The will is that whereby we "resolve upon our actions."[127]

It is in the act of "passing a judgment" that man exceeds mere empirical cognition or awareness and becomes, as it were, *truly human*, capable of seeking and discerning wisdom. It was stated earlier that the sensitive soul possesses a certain power of cognition or "cogitation." Willard restricts this ability to matters of fact, simple perception of reality. This level of "thinking" is required for instinctual actions to take place. But, as Lowrie

---

124. The presupposition here is that *essentially* sin does not corrupt either faculty. The intellect must pursue truth and the will must desire the good. However, post-fall, the apprehension of the true and the good is corrupted such that the intellect and will waiver in their joint pursuit. But the will cannot pursue evil as evil and the intellect cannot pursue falsehood as falsehood. *See* Turretin, *Institutes*, 663ff.

125. In the words of Aquinas, "[T]ruth and good include one another; for truth is something good, otherwise it would not be desirable; and good is something true, otherwise it would not be intelligible." *Summa Theologiae*, I, Q. 79, art. 2. Contra older assessments of New England Puritanism which espoused a radical break from medieval theology (and method), Aquinas and other notable medieval scholastics (but especially Aquinas) were not only present but prevalent in the study of philosophy at Harvard during the 17th century. *See* Norman S. Fiering, *Moral Philosophy at Seventeenth Century Harvard: A Discipline in Transition* (Chapel Hill: University of North Carolina Press, 1981).

126. Willard, *Compleat Body*, 454.

127. *Ibid.*, 454. *See also* Miller, *The New England Mind*, 240-241 (outlining the process of perception, assessment, and judgment in man's rational soul, including a brief discussion on the concept of "phantasm" and the role of the imagination).

summarizes, "What cogitation can never do is penetrate through to the being of the thing [which is perceives] in itself."[128] It cannot evaluate experience morally; it cannot discern and pursue metaphysical truth.

In the *Compleat Body*, Willard continues unpacking these distinctions in extreme detail. Imbedded in the discussion is the age-old theological debate regarding the priority or precedence of the intellect or understanding over the will, and vice a versa, which would be out of scope here.[129] However, one final point must be added. Willard makes clear what should be implicitly obvious already: knowing and choosing are different things. The former bears some resemblance to operations of the sensitive soul, whereas the latter is the unique province of the rational soul. Due to the aforementioned interdependence of the rational faculties, the choosing faculty (the will) acts in light of the understanding's value judgments. Man is an understanding, reasonable creature,[130] and this means *both* faculties of the rational soul are *both* in play in his choices and actions.

This gets at the meaning of "cause by counsel," (as opposed to cause by "coaction," or coercion). "[E]very choice," says Willard, "ariseth from a rational and convincing discovery of the suitableness of the object chosen."[131] To act according to unbridled passion is to be a mere sensual creature. That being said, Willard also acknowledged that the will could in some way dictate the work of the intellect "by intending a Thing, which it will have that contrive; and so the Will is

---

128. Lowrie, *Shape of the Puritan Mind*, 88.

129. For a sweeping overview of the debate as it stood in Willard's day, *see* Norma S. Fiering, "Will and Intellect in the New England Mind," *William and Mary Quarterly*, 29:4 (Oct., 1972), 515-558 (dubbing the issue the most hotly debated topic of moral philosophy in 17th century New England).

130. WCF 4.2 ("After God had made all other creatures, he created man, male and female, with reasonable and immortal souls, endued with knowledge, righteousness, and true holiness, after his own image.").

131. *Mercy Magnified*, 149.

the First Mover."¹³² John Cotton (1585-1652) described the will (or the heart) as "the doore of the soule." Likewise, many Puritan divines like John Preston and Thomas Hooker (1586-1647) declared the will "the driver of all faculties, the Lady and Queene of humane acts," and the "commandresse of the soule."¹³³ The intellect instructs and conditions the will—it is "as the palate is to the stomacke"—but it does not absolutely command it.¹³⁴ Hence, in terms of man's eternal destiny and status before God, it is the attachment of sinful will (or affections or love) to idolatry, not intellectual misjudgment per se, that leads him to sin. Even though man knows God and the moral law by nature (Rom. 2:14-15), he rejects right reason and suppresses revelatory truth (Rom. 1:19-21) willingly because he is bound by sinful, false love.

To summarize Willard's assertions thus far,

---

132. Miller, *The New England Mind*, 250 (quoting Willard). *See also* Willard, *Compleat Body*, 124 ("[The will] can set all the Powers of the Soul and Body on work; it can determine concerning the Acts of them all at its Pleasure: It hath the highest Object, viz. *Goodness* it self [sic], and the best Rule, viz. *Divinity*.").

133. Miller, *The New England Mind*, 249-250, 253 (quoting Cotton, Preston, and Hooker). The resurgence of what Fiering calls "scholastic voluntarism" (contradistinguished from the traditional intellectualism) in the 17th century amongst both Catholics and Protestants attests to the underappreciated influence of Duns Scotus during the period, especially in Reformed theology. The debate centered on exegesis of Romans 7:14-28 and involved distinctly Augustinian convictions but included, if in the periphery, the thought of Scotus, Anselm, and Bernard. *See* Fiering, "Will and Intellect in the New England Mind," 528-529. On the influence of Scotus on the Reformed theology of the period, *see generally* Richard Muller, *Calvin and the Reformed Tradition: On the Work of Christ and the Order of Salvation* (Grand Rapids: Baker Academic, 2012); *Divine Will and Human Choice: Freedom, Contingency, and Necessity in Early Modern Reformed Thought* (Grand Rapids: Baker Academic, 2017).

134. Miller rightly perceives that "Puritanism would have lost all grounds for individual moral responsibility had it held that the psychological reflex, once inaugurated by the senses, was automatic and irresistible; there had to be a break somewhere, a power that could refuse to play the mechanically consistent part, that could deviate voluntarily from the norm." *The New England Mind*, 250; *see also Ibid.*, 251 ("The will must not choose without a reason, but it is not therefore enslaved to reason.").

[A] voluntary action is the action of a reasonable creature applying him-self to his object, not upon compulsion, nor by the force of instinct, but by the inclination of his own mind; so that as he doth it willingly, he also (and therefore) doth it rationally, or upon some apprehended grounds.[135]

Once the will, informed by the judgments of the intellect as to what is good and desirable (the object), has elected to act, the whole being of man is oriented toward pursuing the object properly. Upon the heart or affec-tions—often used synonymously with the will in Puritan writings—being fixed upon an object, the "whole man" follows headlong. This discussion is not one of soteriology, so I will not now address how this plays out in that respect. The comments here by Willard are general and necessary to grasp before any talk of man's regeneration and salvation can be had. They are even more basic prerequisites for theory of society and politics.

Man, and the Pursuit of Happiness

Man, being a "purposive" creature centers his entire life on whatever his rational faculties have judged to be his chief and good end. That end which will provide him with felicity, rest, and satisfaction. Willard calls this inclination of man toward an infinite good— his lifelong project— the pursuit of happiness. He is "insatiably desirous of happiness." More than an inalienable right, the pursuit of happiness is an immutable fact of man's natural disposition.

It should be evident that "happiness" is conceived of here in the clas-sical, and not a licentious, sense.[136] *Happiness* is man living with his facul-ties harmonized and according to that which is suitable to his nature. It is seeking virtue and living life at one with one's self *Coram Deo*. In Willard's mind, "happiness" is man's subjective end whilst the glory of God is his objective end. But in truth, the two are so inseparably bound that the *true*

---

135. Willard, *Mercy Magnified.*, 176.

136. *See* Aquinas, *Summa Theologiae*, I.2, Q. 1-5.

pursuit of one is the *true* pursuit of the other.[137] This pursuit of happiness would be impossible, indeed, unimaginable, for any creature other than a rational, free, and moral one. As established above, only a creature such as man is fit for God's service and worship.

Man, a Sociable Creature

All this talk about man's moral agency and individual freedom must not only be considered abstractly. For man to express his agency, in a sense, he must do so amongst, and in partnership with, others like him. It was deemed by the Creator that it was not good for man to be alone (Gen. 2:18). This is not lost upon Willard.

Not only is man a metaphysically dependent and contingent creature vis a vis God, he is a dependent creature within his own species. Willard, sounding very much like the great Calvinist juris Johannes Althusius, acknowledges that man is not only a reasonable creature but also a "sociable" one.[138] "The comfort of mankind is maintained by mutual intercourse and communion... one man hath a great deal of dependence upon another, without which the affairs of this life cannot be carried on for the support of our livelihood."[139] Man is not meant to proceed through life alone. His existence is at least more meaningful when shared with others. However, it is not life with others (i.e. society) that makes man a moral agent. God creates the agent. Society is merely the immediate and appropriate context of man's agency. Indeed, it is man's agency that forms society, not the other way around.

The basic presupposition of man's inherent sociability— an idea with its roots in Aristotle's *Politics*— was commonplace in Willard's time, and

---

137. *See* Miller, *The New England Mind*, 254 (quoting Willard on this point).

138. Althusius referred to politics as the "art of associating men for the purpose of establishing, cultivating, and conserving social life among them." He therefore frequently referred to it in his *Politica methodice digesta* (1603/1610/1614) as "symbiotics." *See generally* "Introduction to Althusius's *Politica*," in *An Abridged Translation of Politics Methodically Set Forth and Illustrated with Sacred and Profane Examples*, ed. and trans. Frederick S. Carney (Indianapolis: Liberty Fund, 1995).

139. Willard, *Promise-Keeping a Great Duty* (Boston, 1691), 19.

frequently served as the most basic starting point in political discussions. Man's sociability was often referred to as something bordering on instinct, but the expression of sociability was necessarily volitional. And in Puritan writings specifically, the manifestation of this sociability in human relations mimics the relationship between God and man. It possesses a covenantal structure and character and carries on the mandate to flourish given to Adam in paradise (Gen. 1:28).[140]

The first outgrowth of man's desire to relate with others of his species is the covenant of marriage which naturally produces families. Subsequently, the eventual relations of multiple families give rise to society. For the sake of order and tranquility, societies then form governments by covenantal means as well. Inherent in the covenant idea is the operation of volition amongst all parties involved. Each association in the sequence requires it. Indeed, to Willard and other Reformed theologians of the 17th century, societies could only be formed on such a basis. They were fundamentally voluntary organisms, as mentioned above. In the hypothetical state of nature (pre-society) man was subject to none but God himself. The only way man's natural liberty could be limited by his equals was through *willing* relinquishment of certain freedoms for the sake of covenantal affiliation.

Volition, then, is key to forming any sustainable society, and especially those beyond the family. To invoke Roger Scruton again, "Our world is imbued with will, directed from past to future." And like the internal operations of human faculties, a collective reason informs our organic social life, the operations of the will, to form a "constitution," and self-image— all driven by man's inherent sociability. "Hence," adds Scruton, "there is a

---

140. To Willard and his Puritan brethren who espoused the federal theology, that man is dealt with by God by way of covenant, and that man subsequently mimics the condescension of his Maker between himself (man) and others of his own species is a reflection of, and necessary accommodation to, his reasonable nature. *See* Willard, *Compleat Body*, 213 ("God having made man a reasonable Creature, transacts with him as such... he made a rational creature, able to know and chuse [sic] his own actions, and thereby capable of being treated with in the way of Covenant.)

distinctly political process, which is not the process of revolution, nor the mere pursuit of power," but rather wrapped up in human nature itself.[141]

Man's exercise of volition is also intricate to his living out the Garden mandate, continuing to rule, cultivate, and organize the world around him. Most importantly, it is the exercise of the will in joining with other humans in societal and governmental associations that sets man apart as the *imago Dei*.[142] Aristotle famously said that it was life in the *polis*—a concept that implies more than simply municipal existence[143]— that distinguished man from both gods and beasts; the former has no need for the *polis* whilst the latter cannot aspire to it.[144]

III. Defining the Relationship, Again

CT, the Will, and the Imago Dei

The CT paradigm, by its bondage of the will, cannot supply meaning and purpose in a way that respects man's God-given, faculties of the soul which mark him out in creation as the *imago Dei*, nor can it cultivate the full exercise thereof. CT cannot lead man to his deepest longing. In short,

---

141.   Scruton, *The Meaning of Conservatism*, 43.

142.   Even royalists of the 17th century like Thomas Hobbes, William Barclay, and Jean Bodin agreed that legitimate government must originally have arisen from an act of free contract or covenant. Skinner, *Visions of Politics*, vol. 2, 397-398.

143.   As Jean Bodin said, "[I]t is neither the wals [sic], neither the persons, that maketh the city, but the union of the people under the same soveraigntie [sic] of government." Quoted in Skinner, *Visions of Politics*, vol, 2, 399.

144.   "Man is by nature a social animal; an individual who is unsocial naturally and not accidentally is either beneath our notice or more than human. Society is something that precedes the individual. Anyone who either cannot lead the common life or is so self-sufficient as not to need to, and therefore does not partake of society, is either a beast or a god." Aristotle, *Politics*, 1253a2. The Philosopher asserts this conception of man at multiple points in the *Politics*, for example, "[I]t is evident that the state is a creation of nature, and that man is by nature a political animal. And he who by nature and not by mere accident is without a state, is either above humanity, or below it; he is the 'Tribeless, lawless, heartless one,' whom Homera denounces—the outcast who is a lover of war; he may be compared to a bird which flies alone." By "political", Aristotle is referring to man's instinct to associate with others.

CT, for all its focus on justice and equality and the eradication of human suffering, denies the fullness of the image of God in man, which is to say, his dignity. The organization of the world according to identity politics and CT foists upon man categorical, political associations that are not volitionally based, and are therefore fundamentally *inhuman*.

As *inhuman* categories they cannot lead man to happiness because they necessarily frustrate the very nature of man. These categories make primary— as a lens for all of life— features, traits, and phenomena that are non-volitional and attempt to organize social and political life accordingly. By not positively engaging the unique faculties that separate humans from the rest of creation— indeed, the very faculties that evidence his designation as the *imago Dei*— CT-informed categories improperly relegate man to a lower order in the hierarchy of being where his will and intellect, his ability to deliberate, freely associate with others based on a common purpose are of little to no use. No longer is he allowed to "both propound to himself his own end and make choice of the means or way leading unto it," to use Willard's words.

Affiliations which do not consider, or rather are not created by, man's volition are not only *inhuman* but are not properly "affiliations," a word that necessarily implies the operation of volition or will. "Affiliating" is an act. It is the willful (in the first instance or by passive or active consent in the second) connecting or relating with others. It is at root a political idea, and dependent for its intelligibility on the presupposition of man's inherent sociableness. This is why people become understandably defensive and even outraged when they perceive that they are being wrongly affiliated with others against their will and intent—it is a denial of their most basic faculties and, in a very real sense, their humanity.

In an effort to make sense of the world, it is certainly natural for people intellectually to organize the objects and experience according to non-volitional categories; indeed, Adam did just that with the animals in the garden. What is *not* appropriately *human* is to make non-volitional categories and affiliations politically actionable, which is exactly what the

CT worldview endeavors to do. Furthermore, it is especially egregious to supply non-volitional affiliations with moral weight (another aim of CT).

Argued above is the fact that political life is founded upon the presumption of man's free, spontaneous action and sociable desire to associate freely with others like him. Returning to Scruton once more,

> Social life should be founded in free association and protected by autonomous bodies, under whose auspices people can flourish according to their social nature, acquiring the manners and aspirations that endow their lives with meaning.[145]

In other words, it is through free association that people form social institutions and governmental bodies, which *should*, in turn, be dedicated to encouraging the cultivation of the social instinct in people that formed the institutions in the first place. Human flourishing will not be found in those institutions that have abandoned care for the principle, the intrinsic human faculty, upon which they were founded, becoming instead obsessed with combating the undesirable (e.g. oppressive) by-products (real or perceived) of free human activity.

Watch Your Language!

It cannot be overstated that this aspect is what is so insidious about some of the rhetoric of identity politics, supplied by the ever-expanding, ever-morphing vocabulary of CT. On the most basic level, the identity politics game makes a living, so to speak, by designating non-volition, im-

---

145. Scruton, *Fools, Frauds and Firebrands*, 282-83. This volume by Scruton offers a nuanced but biting critique of the chief thinkers affiliated with the New Left, many of which have been instrumental in developing CT. The chapter on Sartre and Foucault (pp. 69-113) is particularly good. *See also* Scruton, "Jeremy Corbyn's Labour would crush civil society," *Unherd* (Nov. 13, 2019), https://unherd.com/2019/11/thirty-years-on-we-forget-the-lessons-of-communism/ ("All free associations were seen by the communists as places of danger, where hierarchies, distinctions, privileges and deals could challenge the role of the [Hungarian] Vanguard Party in its fight for equality and "social justice". Reflecting on this, I came to see why freedom of association belongs with freedom of speech... Those two freedoms are the foundation of civil society, and the necessary shield against the abuse of political power.").

posed categories as primary—assuring everyone that their race, gender, or sexual orientation is the definitive aspect of their personhood— and then hurling said categories upon people against their wills creating a mass scale guilt by non-volition, unintended affiliation—what has lately been called "adjacency."[146]

There is no room here for exercise of deliberation, reasoned discourse, or free association. The identity markers, handed down from on high at the outset, dictate one's group affiliation and relative social status. Coalitions are built around inherent traits rather than common purpose. Interests pursued are determined not by concern for volitionally based affiliations like religion, nationality, family, or any other free association. Indeed, like their Marxist predecessors, CT theorists conceive of organized religion, the nuclear family, and nationality as constructs promulgated by the dominant class (at least in the form in which they now appear). They must necessarily be critiqued and deconstructed if liberation is to be had. Accordingly, political interests and alliances are defined by the prioritization of concerns most relevant to a person's racial, ethnic, or sexual identity.

Entry into these alliances is controlled by either one's involuntary possession of the favored traits, or one's ability to acquire "ally" status. The requirement of an ally is to promote the interests of the trait-based group by fading into the background, divesting one's self of unearned privilege by becoming lower than the Other.[147] Only in this way, by effectively removing themselves from the situation, does a privileged person attain the chance to stifle the oppression their existence inherently causes the marginalized in society, but we're getting ahead of ourselves. Insofar as the

---

146. Anna Holmes, "Black With (Some) White Privilege," *The New York Times* (Feb. 10, 2018), https://www.nytimes.com/2018/02/10/opinion/sunday/black-with-some-white-privilege.html.

147. Ana Valens, "Here's what a good LGBTQ ally looks like," *Vox* (Jun. 22, 2019), https://www.vox.com/identities/2019/6/22/18700875/lgbtq-good-ally (criticizing Taylor Swift for garnering too much of the spotlight in her activism for LGBTQ+ causes).

will of the individual is in play, its activity is conditioned by predetermined social group categories.

These non-volitional affiliations of identity politics are then plugged into the oppressor-oppressed dichotomy to inform the preliminary analysis for political and social engineering in pursuit of equity. For instance, a white person is deemed, by some, inherently and irreconcilably racist, by way of their membership in the privileged class and the majority culture which affords them privilege.[148] The idea of "white privilege" is fairly simple. As a result of living in a majority white culture, wherein the world is "coded" white (and where whiteness is "centered"), white people are not only the majority but the "default." Conversely, "blackness" is the Other and is allegedly viewed with suspicion. At the most basic level, then, white privilege is "an absence," as the British journalist and activist Renni Eddo-Lodge writes in her bestseller, *Why I'm No Longer Talking to White People About Race*. White people, it is maintained by CT practitioners, live unaffected by the consequences of racism; structural discrimination is absent from their lives; they are unconfronted by the stark realities of oppres-

---

148. *See* Peggy McIntosh, "White Privilege: Unpacking the Invisible Knapsack," *Peace and Freedom* (July/August, 1989), *available at* https://psychology.umbc.edu/files/2016/10/White-Privilege_McIntosh-1989.pdf. Thirty years on, McIntosh's article still exerts considerable influence and is frequently referenced at the popular level. *See e.g.* Gina Crosley-Corcoran, "Explaining White Privilege To A Broke White Person," *HuffPost* (May 8, 2014), https://www.huffpost.com/entry/explaining-white-privilege-to-a-broke-white-person_b_5269255?guccounter=1&-guce_referrer=aHR0cHM6Ly93d3cuZ29vZ2xlLmNvbS8&guce_referrer_sig=AQA-AAEFzreBvg1FEVqUdmEQ4dMDZvk6iR2kHLQywzTE6WmF1CyVqbfmwawx598ee-jMveVVFSIc__0q7iL1NdKCZgzAxj7NzUok0-VlRKEm7C-MbHmDEsPZ-zlNp2mJJ3tUq14X91h7sO4nGgQhwjeVvTBFtoXKTX0OcaC_te83zKxrEYA.

sion.[149] Most importantly, as whites coast through life in a white culture they are decidedly unaware of the privilege their skin color, culture, and etc. afford them within their cultural context. They, namely due to their fragility, never notice the positive impact on their life trajectory that their whiteness brings. White privilege, therefore, is most often referred to as a sort of extreme complacency toward the status quo (which, it is believed, is of singular benefit to them).[150]

In service to the functionality of these accusations, the meaning of "racism" has also been altered.[151] The old definition was something like, "prejudice, discrimination, or antagonism directed against someone of a different race based on the belief of the discriminator that his own race is superior."[152] Today, "racism" stands for everything encompassed by the old definition but coupled with power derived from dominant culture status.[153]

---

149. Throughout the opening passages of the chapter referenced here, Eddo-Lodge essentially (and anecdotally) unpacks McIntosh's proverbial knapsack. *Why I'm No Longer Talking to White People About Race* (London: Bloomsbury, 2017), 86. Reni Eddo-Lodge is a journalist and well-known feminist activist, and therefore not directly involved in academia's CT project. Nevertheless, her book has been immensely popular and represents contemporary CT well; even the writing style—part biographical monologue, part socio-political polemic—follows that of DiAngelo and Kendi. As proof of CT's influence on Eddo-Lodge's thought, *see* her remarkably short bibliography, *Ibid.*, 241-242 (citing, *inter alia*, Theodore Allen, Kimberlé Crenshaw, Audre Lorde, and bell hooks).

150. Eddo-Lodge explains,
White privilege is one of the reasons why I stopped talking to white people about race. Trying to convince stony faces of disbelief has never appealed to me. The idea of white privilege forces white people who aren't actively racist to confront their own complicity in its continuing existence. White privilege is dull, grinding complacency. It is par for the course in a world in which drastic race inequality is responded to which a shoulder shrug, considered just the norm.
Why I'm No Longer Talking to White People About Race, 87.

151. Remember, "white privilege is instrumental to racism." *Ibid.*, 115.

152. John McWhorter, "Racist Is a Tough Little Word," *The Atlantic* (July 24, 2019), https://www.theatlantic.com/ideas/archive/2019/07/racism-concept-change/594526/.

153. The same goes for sexism. *See e.g.* Anita Sarkeesian, @femfreq, "There's no such thing as sexism against men. That's because sexism is prejudice + power. Men are the dominant gender with power in society," *Twitter*, Nov. 4, 2014, https://twitter.com/femfreq/status/5 33445611543363585?lang=en.

But even if the old definition has not been tossed out wholesale, the emphasis has shifted. Now prejudice or bias is assumed of all people.

As Eddo-Lodge tells us,

> There is an unattributed definition of racism that defines it as prejudice plus power. Those disadvantaged by racism can certainly be cruel, vindictive and prejudiced. Everyone has the capacity to be nasty to other people, to judge them before they get to know them. But there simply aren't enough black people in positions of power to enact racism against white people on the kind of grand scale it currently operates at against black people. Are black people over-represented in the places and spaces where prejudice could really take effect? The answer is almost always no.[154]

Eddo-Lodge rightly understands that all people are *capable* of racial hatred and prejudice.[155] But in her book, what makes one a "racist" is their social location; it is all about systemic impact, the social and political implications, not intent. Hence, white people in America are necessarily racist. Never mind probing beneath the surface to determine their actual views vis a vis prejudice or bias based on their behavioral record.[156] This unavoidable racism, of course, works hand-in-glove with inherent "white supremacy" which, we are told, is on the rise if in morphed form.[157]

---

154. Eddo-Lodge, *Why I'm No Longer Talking to White People About Race*, 89.

155. Eddo-Lodge's language is somewhat softer here in comparison to that of Ibram X. Kendi or Robin DiAngelo. The latter two are much more forceful in asserting that *all* people not only have *potential* for prejudice but, in fact, *are* prejudiced.

156. Kelefa Sanneh, "The Fight to Redefine Racism," *The New Yorker* (Aug. 12, 2019), https://www.newyorker.com/magazine/2019/08/19/the-fight-to-redefine-racism.

157. Gary Younge, " The Truth About Race In America: It's Getting Worse, Not Better," *The Nation* (Mar. 21, 2014), https://www.thenation.com/article/truth-about-race-america-its-getting-worse-not-better/; Carol Anderson, " America is hooked on the drug of white supremacy. We're paying for that today," *The Guardian* (Aug. 13, 2017), https://www.theguardian.com/commentisfree/2017/aug/13/america-white-supremacy-hooked-drug-charlottesville-virginia; Christina Pazzanese, " Probing the roots and rise of white supremacy," *The Harvard Gazette* (Mar. 18, 2019), https://news.harvard.edu/gazette/story/2019/03/harvard-fellow-examines-rise-and-roots-of-white-supremacy/.

Shifting Sands

The definitions of "oppression" and "white supremacy," and "whiteness," mind you, have been redefined in recent days (also without the consent of anyone beyond the ivy-covered walls of elite institutions). A cursory search of recent commentary at the nation's predominant new outlets will evidence this definitional shift. Being racist, which is to say, white, has nothing to do with melanin content[158] and everything to do with real or perceived power dynamics[159] and half-baked history that offers a unitary explanation for all events.

"Whiteness," from the CRT perspective, is a euphemism of sorts for privileged individuals and groups within a socially constructed racial caste system. Those socially, economically, and politically privileged persons are not only typically unaware of their status (like the proverb of the fish in water) but are inherently resistant to acknowledging such. They naturally exhibit a certain "fragility," a lowered stamina for "racial stress," regarding any talk of race or class as it pertains to their privilege. This is due to living in a racist world, and a society constructed to reinforce white privilege.[160]

According to Richard Delgado, "[T]he phenomenon of white power and white supremacy, and the array of privileges that come with membership in the white race," are the result of whiteness as socially constructed in the west. Hence, any crimes of white supremacy and the like— an in-

---

158.   Brent Staples, "How Italians Became 'White'," *The New York Times Magazine* (Oct. 12, 2019), https://www.nytimes.com/interactive/2019/10/12/opinion/columbus-day-italian-american-racism.html.

159.   Teresa J. Guess, "The Social Construction of Whiteness: Racism by Intent, Racism by Consequence," *Critical Sociology* 32(4) (2006), 649-673, *available at* https://www.cwu.edu/diversity/sites/cts.cwu.edu.diversity/files/documents/constructingwhiteness.pdf.

160.   "White people in North America live in a social environment that protects and insulates them from race-based stress." DiAngelo, "White Fragility," *The International Journal of Critical Pedagogy*, 3(3) (2011), 55. *See also* NBC News, "Think: Author Robin DiAngelo: Debunking the most common myths white people tell about race," *NBC News*, commentary by Robin DiAngelo, Sept. 25, 2018, https://www.nbcnews.com/think/video/debunking-the-most-common-myths-white-people-tell-about-race-1328672835886.

creasingly expansive list— are imputed to any and all members of groups deemed white by the CRT definition which includes identity-based groups ranging from Catholics and Jews to Polish and Italian immigrants.[161] Whiteness is only tangentially related to white skin. It is more so a political idea rooted in an alleged legacy of power, genocide, and plunder embodied by those who operate within, and profit from, the status quo.

Furthermore, not only is the designation of whiteness involuntary, so is the expression of such. It is a poisonous fume that naturally exudes from whites and their culture. Sandra Kim has described the dynamic of racial (and otherwise) minorities living in a white society as akin to traveling through a "polluted city."[162] Mere proximity to white people in a white society is like climbing the Mountains of Shadow into Mordor every day.

---

161. Richard Delgado and Jean Stefanic, *Critical Race Theory: An Introduction* (New York: New York University Press, 2012), 85. *See also* Richard Dyer, "The Matter of Whiteness," in *White Privilege: Essential Readings on the Other Side of Racism*, ed. Paula S. Rothenberg (New York: Worth Publishers, 2008), 9-14; James E. Barrett and David Roediger, "How White People Became White," in *White Privilege*, 35-40.

162. Kashmira Gander, "Healing from Toxic Whiteness: The Woman Behind a Course Helping White People Tackling Internalized Racism," *The Independent* (Feb. 23, 2017), https://www.independent.co.uk/life-style/toxic-whiteness-healing-white-people-internalised-racism-woman-sandra-kim-new-york-a7595216.html.

It is toxic and oppressive.[163] *The very air you breath is a poisonous fume.*[164]

The intent of white people, involuntarily grouped with others of the alleged privileged class, is irrelevant (more on that later). Moral culpability is assigned simply by one's existence in the dominant group of the majority culture. So too is their knowledge, for it is not informed by the *right* "lived experience." It is therefore devoid of the *right* kind of knowledge and opinions. White oppressors may not even be aware of their own inherent bias against the Other. Nor do they notice how their daily behavior, manners, and thoughts perpetuate the white-cis-heteronormative-patriarchy. Oppressors are, by nature, as it were, *unknowing* creatures, or at least willfully blind so that they can preserve their acquired power. They

---

163. Similar is the language of Eddo-Lodge. Both she and Kim (and others) frequently discuss white privilege and related concepts in terms of environmental, (to an extent) disembodied, mechanicalistic forces:
White privilege is a manipulative, suffocating blanket of power that envelops everything we know, like a snowy day. It's brutal and oppressive, bullying you into not speaking up for fear of losing your loved ones, or job, or flat. It scares you into silencing yourself: you don't get the privilege of speaking honestly about your feelings without extensively assessing the consequences.
And a little later she adds that, "White privilege is deviously, throat-stranglingly [sic] clever" because of its simultaneous ubiquity and secrecy. Eddo-Lodge, *Why I'm No Longer Talking to White People About Race*, 92-93.

164. This invocation of Boromir's quote from Peter Jackson's film trilogy, now immortalized on the internet through memes, does not risk caricature of CT. It is common to encounter in CT-informed commentary references to the *literal* physical and mental detriment experienced by persons of color living in western society because of pervasiveness of structural and cultural whiteness. The most notorious expression of this kind of language lately is Jonathan M. Metzel, "Dying of Whiteness," *Boston Review* (June 27, 2019), https://bostonreview.net/race/jonathan-m-metzl-dying-whiteness. Somewhat ironically, the case has been recently made that whiteness harms the health of whites. Jonathan Goolsby, "Racialized social system of whiteness benefits whites' health in some ways, study finds," *Phys.org* (Oct. 20, 2017), https://phys.org/news/2017-10-racialized-social-whiteness-benefits-whites.html; Jennifer Malat, Sarah Mayorga-Gallo, and David R. Williams, "The effects of whiteness on the health of whites in the USA," *Social Science & Medicine*, 199 (Feb. 2018), 148-156. See also *See also* Rhea W. Boyd, "Despair doesn't kill, defending whiteness does," *The Lancet*, 395(10218) (Jan. 11, 2020), https://www.thelancet.com/journals/lancet/article/PIIS0140-6736(19)33147-2/fulltext?mod=article_inline ("When confronted with self-inflicted or white on white violence, scholars, the media, and the public are evading the logical conclusion—one Metzl both illuminates and eschews—despair isn't killing white America, the armed defence [sic] of whiteness is.").

certainly lack the requisite lived experience to see the hard truth of, well, almost anything relevant to social and political discussions.

The only acceptable response by white people is a continual penance that is the divestiture of whiteness; a relinquishment of their privilege. The exact process of divestment remains ambiguous by design, and as Robin DiAngelo has made clear on multiple occasions, the process is necessarily perpetual.[165] White people simply are innately privileged and racist by nature of their existence in a white, western, colonial context. All people have prejudices, admits DiAngelo, but only whites possess the systemic privilege to fulfill the *power* element in the *prejudice plus power* definition of racism.[166] Accordingly, the manifestations of racism may be indiscernibly subtle and even subconscious because, as we are told, racism changes forms over time.[167] Even being "nice" is racist because it purportedly allows whites to avoid the reality of their own tyranny over the Other.[168] To be fair, DiAngelo's logic is amazingly consistent within her own paradigm. She, a white woman, considers herself no less racist

---

165. Robin DiAngelo, "White Fragility," *International Journal of Critical Pedagogy*, 3(3) (2011), 54-70, *available at* https://libjournal.uncg.edu/ijcp/article/viewFile/249/116.

166. To critical theorists, and contrary to colloquial use, *bias, prejudice, bigotry*, and *racism* are not interchangeable. *See* Judith M. Katz, *White Awareness: Handbook for Anti-racism Training* (Norman: Oklahoma University Press, 1978), 37.

167. Evergreen State College, "Coming Together Speaker Series: Dr. Robin DiAngelo," *YouTube* (Mar. 9, 2016), https://www.youtube.com/watch?v=wVddM1hzmvI; Nosheen Iqbal, "Interview: Academic Robin DiAngelo: 'We have to stop thinking about racism as someone who says the N-word'," *The Guardian* (Feb. 26, 2019), https://www.theguardian.com/world/2019/feb/16/white-fragility-racism-interview-robin-diangelo ("Everyone has racial bias but, as DiAngelo is determined to establish, 'when you back a group's collective bias with lingering authority and institutional control, it is transformed.'").

168. Robin DiAngelo, "White people assume niceness is the answer to racial inequality. It's not," *The Guardian* (Jan. 16, 2019), https://www.theguardian.com/commentisfree/2019/jan/16/racial-inequality-niceness-white-people.

as, say, Donald Trump.[169] For both, like fish in water, have been inescapably conditioned by their environment; they have been unavoidably socialized into whiteness.

What is remarkable about DiAngelo's thought is that she simultaneously condemns whiteness but (nearly) removes moral weight from the idea of racism. This is not to say that critical theorists like DiAngelo make no moral claims. They find oppression to be highly immoral. It is the unforgiveable sin. But the sin of oppression is largely imputed to people via their group affiliations and the sin of racism is attached thereto as a sort of necessary companion. But the sin of racism itself, upon being redefined, has lost any *direct* moral connotation. It is simply a given fact which receives little evaluation by DiAngelo.

The "Good/Bad Binary," as she calls it—wherein people who do not exhibit explicitly racist (in the old sense of the word) activity are morally upstanding, but those who do commit extreme acts of prejudice and violence are bad—is actually an impediment to discussions about race, a function of white fragility.[170] This commonly held binary, "the idea that racism is conscious bias held by mean people," is "[t]he most effective

---

169.   Isaac Chotiner, "Why White Liberals Are So Unwilling to Recognize Their Own Racism," *Slate* (Aug. 2, 2018), https://slate.com/news-and-politics/2018/08/white-liberal-racism-why-progressives-are-unable-to-see-their-own-bigotry.html. DiAngelo is a bit confusing on this point. In the interview, she does distinguish between herself and someone like Steve Bannon or Donald Trump in that they are "avowed" racists whereas she considers herself an "implicit" racist. The distinction lies in the fact that DiAngelo has confronted her racism and working to divest herself of whiteness; she is therefore situated at a different point on the continuum than Bannon and Trump. At the same time, she also suggests that this is essentially a distinction without a difference. In her words (emphasis added),
You asked me, "What would you call the difference perhaps between Trump and me?" But I actually think, yeah, we both are racists. I see that as a continuum that I'm on and will be on for the rest of my life. In any given moment, I have to ask myself, "How am I doing on this continuum? What end am I behaving closer to? How do I know?" He and I may be on different spots on the continuum, but we're both on it. *I don't tend to distinguish between the two of us, which probably shocks some readers*, but if you're asking me to somehow identify that difference, I would say "avowed" versus maybe "implied" or "implicit."

170.   DiAngelo, *White Fragility: Why Its So Hard for White People to Talk About Racism* (Boston: Beacon Press, 2018), 71-72.

adaptation of racism over time," DiAngelo claims. It is, in fact, a racist construct developed by white people (perhaps, unconsciously) to avoid the difficult task of dismantling the racist systems that benefit them.

As a product of living in a society in which "racism is the bedrock," all people are affected by the "forces of racism;" their worldviews are shaped by it. Hence, "The simplistic idea that racism is limited to individual *intentional* acts committed by unkind people is at the root of virtually all white defensiveness on this topic. To move beyond defensiveness, we have to let go of this common belief."[171] It is much more useful, says DiAngelo, to think of one's self on a "continuum," an essentially inescapable one at that. "Racism is so deeply woven into the fabric of our society that I do not see myself escaping from that continuum in my lifetime."[172]

Though it is a difficult shift to trace, it is doubtless connected to the removal, or at least severe limitation, of the volition in the social and moral calculus. Throughout her book and lectures, DiAngelo repeatedly dismisses the connection between racism and intent. Insistence on any such connection, she maintains, only delays productive discussions on race and perpetuates white fragility. Appeals to intent expose, or rather confirm, the racism of the appellant. What is imposed upon people *a priori* is a socially constructed status from which they cannot escape. First and foremost, racism is something you *are* not something you do. This premise being established, discrete actions are then evaluated.

This too is a muddled maneuver. On the one hand, DiAngelo holds that all white people do exhibit racist tendencies because they are socialized by a racialist society. The analogy often employed is that of a fish in (racist) water. But at the same time, even if the racist fish were plopped down in a non-racist society (water), they would still be racist. The depth of the effects of socialized racism, once acquired, is too deep to simply be

---

171. *Ibid.*, 73 (emphasis added).

172. *Ibid.*, 87.

socialized back out. Furthermore, it is really the racial society (the water) that is being evaluated, not the individual (the fish). Therefore, every fish is necessarily racist because the water is racist. And since the fish has only ever experienced racist waters, his gills are attuned, and conditioned by, it, such that if he were transported to unpolluted water he would, it is presumed, still behave (and think and breath) as he did before. Obviously, the analogy has begun to break down at this point, but hopefully the reader gets the picture.

Racism is an inescapable condition predicated on one's membership in the socially constructed dominant group in a racialized society, not an action or attitude or discernable characteristic per se, though DiAngelo assures us that the latter necessarily follows from the former. Any attempt by a dominant, oppressor group member to deny the label (since it is not so much an accusation anymore) of "racist" serves as proof positive that the denier is a racist. As Neil Shenvi, summarizing DiAngelo, astutely puts it, "[One] can either admit that he is racist and fragile. Or he can demonstrate that he is racist and fragile by denying that he is racist and fragile."[173]

What *is* highly immoral in DiAngelo's estimation is for an oppressor group member to *not* confront their racism and actively divest themselves of their power and privilege (to the extent that such a feat is possible) in the pursuit of "antiracism"—another new term introduced into the popu-

---

173. Shenvi, "The Worldview of White Fragility – A Review of Robin DiAngelo's White Fragility," *Shenvi Apologetics*, https://shenviapologetics.com/the-worldview-of-white-fragility/ (retrieved Dec. 9, 2019).

lar vocabulary by CT—and equity (i.e. equality of outcome).[174]

No Highway Option

Make no mistake, there is no middle ground available in a CT-infused world. Ibram X. Kendi's wildly popular *How to Be an Antiracist* makes that abundantly clear.[175] One cannot acceptably be simply non-racist, and especially not color-blind. "[T]here is no neutrality in the racism struggle. The opposite of 'racist' isn't 'not racist.' It is 'anti-racist'... One either allows racial inequities to persevere, as a racist, or confronts racial inequities, as an antiracist. There is no in-between safe space of 'not racist.'" says Kendi.[176] The claim of non-racism or of neutrality is a "mask for racism," as is the claim of colorblindness.[177] Kendi could have written the

---

174. Earlier use of the term "antiracism" can be found in Judy H. Katz's well-known *White Awareness: Handbook for Anti-racism Training* (Norman: Oklahoma University Press, 1978). Antiracist training has begun to crop up especially in the field of education. *See e.g.* Jenn Fields, " Training white people in Colorado to be "anti-racist" (not just "not racist") is one step in the fight to correct historic wrongs," *The Colorado Sun* (Dec. 17, 2019), https://coloradosun.com/2019/12/17/colorado-anti-racism-training-surj-regan-byrd/ (the curriculum covered by the *Sun* includes the works from Kendi and DiAngelo mentioned here). It should also be noted that Kendi's and DiAngelo's books in particular have been increasingly (and publicly) recommended by pastors, theologians, and Christian writers. *See e.g.* Bryan Loritts, "Top 10 Books I Read in 2019," *Dr. Bryan Loritts* (blog) (Nov. 25, 2019), https://bryanloritts.com/blog/top-10-books-i-read-in-2019; Mark Vroegop, "Eight Unique Books on Racial Reconciliation," *Mark Vroegop* (blog), http://markvroegop.com/eight-unique-books-on-racial-reconciliation/ (retrieved Jan. 20, 2020). For use of the antiracism concept as applied directly to churches, *see* Joseph Barndt, *Becoming an Anti-Racist Church: Journeying toward Wholeness* (Minneapolis: Augsburg Fortress Publishers, 2011). For an excellent review of Barndt's take, *see* Neil Shenvi, "Anti-Racism as Rebirth: A Review of Barndt's Becoming an Anti-Racist Church," *Shenvi Apologetics*, https://shenviapologetics.com/anti-racism-as-rebirth-a-review-of-barndts-becoming-an-anti-racist-church/ (retrieved Jan. 20, 2020).

175. Kendi's book is rightly (and revealingly) described by *The Guardian* (with approval) as a "memoir and political guide." Afua Hirsch, "How to Be an Antiracist by Ibram X Kendi review – a brilliantly simple argument," *The Guardian* (Oct. 11, 2019), https://www.theguardian.com/books/2019/oct/11/how-to-be-an-antiracist-by-ibram-x-kendi-review; *C.f.* Coleman Hughes' thoughtful critique of Kendi's book, "How to Be an Anti-Intellectual," *City Journal* (Oct. 27, 2019), https://www.city-journal.org/how-to-be-an-antiracist.

176. Ibram X. Kendi, *How to Be an Antiracist* (New York: One World, 2019), 9.

177. *Ibid.*, 9-10.

words of Luther in *Bondage of the Will*: "The truth of the matter is rather as Christ says, 'He who is not with me is against me.' ... He does not say 'He who is not with me is not against me either, but merely neutral.'"

The issue is not whether one actively discriminates against people based on their skin color of ethnicity. What matters is whether they are pursuing equity on every level of social life. "There is no such thing as a nonracist or race-neutral policy," Kendi writes. "If discrimination is creating equity, then it is antiracist. If discrimination is creating inequity, then it is racist."[178]

As it turns out, to Kendi, people who pursue race-neutral dealings with his fellow man are the most dangerous breed of all. "[T]he most threatening racist movement is not the alt-right's unlikely drive for a White ethno-state, but the regular American's drive for a 'race-neutral' one." Neither is persuasion pursued in good faith on the table. Power dynamics comprise all reality. Accordingly, "An activist produces power and policy change, not mental change." Kendi's politics is not one of deliberation and compromise. In Kendi's world, man is a power animal, not an intellectual, volitional, sociable one. And it is ironically binary. Man is like a beast between two riders. He is either bridled by racism or antiracism; he is either oppressor or oppressed; he is either an ally or a detractor.

Christians should take notice particularly of Kendi's ideas, in conjunction with the description of intersectionality provided earlier. The idea that analytical mechanisms like intersectionality can be limited in application to race issues is a fantasy, and a logically, methodologically inconsistent one at that.[179] As Kendi writes,

---

178. *Ibid.*, 19.

179. More basically, such a suggestion also misunderstands intersectionality, which must invoke *at least* to axes of analysis (e.g. race and gender, or gender and class). [Thanks to Neil Shenvi for pointing this out].

> We cannot be antiracist if we are homophobic or transphobic... To be
> queer antiracist is to understand the privileges of my cisgender, of my
> masculinity, of my heterosexuality, of their intersections.

In case you didn't quite catch that, let's review. First, to be an anti-racist is not simply to oppose racial discrimination. Established above is the fact that "racism" is no longer simply prejudice against others of another race, but prejudice *plus* power, with an emphasis on the latter since the former is assumed (per DiAngelo).[180] To Kendi's credit, and distinct from some others writing on the subject, he ardently rejects the idea that ethnic and racial minorities (and specifically black people) are incapable of racism.[181] Second, we must add that as Kendi sees it, discrimination is neither here nor there. The question is whether equity is being pursued. The means justify the end.

Finally, Kendi provides a great application of intersectionality as it is intended to operate and incorporates that analysis into his definition of antiracism. To be an antiracist—which most people either covet or are made to feel that they should—means actively combating the oppressive socio-political structures and narratives constructed by the dominant, oppressor class at it pertains to race. Antiracism is a euphemism which, like intersectionality, encompasses advocacy (discrimination unto equity) for the entire gambit of oppressed identities discerned by CT. Racism, sexism, homophobia, transphobia, and others mentioned above, per intersection-

---

180. In the interest of further specificity, Kendi, being very focused (at least abstractly) on public "policy" throughout his book, defines a "racist" as "[o]ne who is supporting a racist policy through their actions or inaction or expressing a racist idea." "Racist policy" is defined as "any measure that produces or sustains racial inequity." In turn, a "racist idea" is "any idea that suggests one racial group is inferior or superior to another racial group in any way." *Ibid.*, 13-20.

181. *Ibid.*, 136 (stating that the claim that "Black people can't be racist because Black people don't have power" is "illusory, concealing, disempowering, and racist."). *C.f.* Manisha Krishan, "Dear White People, Please Stop Pretending Reverse Racism Is Real," *Vice* (Oct. 2, 2016), https://www.vice.com/en_us/article/kwzjvz/dear-white-people-please-stop-pretending-reverse-racism-is-real.

ality, are interlocking systems of oppression. Antiracist activism, if it is to maintain its coherence and shape, is necessarily inseparable from feminist activism, LGBTQ+ activism, and the like. It is all or nothing.

Bringing down an entire, multifaceted system of oppression which, being centuries in the making, has an array of identities under its boot, is quite a tall order for the average American layperson. Luckily, whilst many CT proponents are heavy on analysis of the problem and light on solutions, Kendi offers guidance. The way to "fix" America is to establish an administrative body, with nigh unlimited purview over any and all social policy, and tasked with ensuring anti-racist policy.[182] Apparently, even the separation of powers must be sacrificed to Kendi's omnipotent administrative agency so that the *right* kind of discrimination can be applied to society in the pursuit of equity. Andrew Sullivan insightfully retorts, "There is a word for this kind of politics and this kind of theory when it is fully and completely realized, and it is totalitarian."[183] It is the full-fledged expression of one who has imbibed the resentment of Derrida and the cynicism of Foucault, wherein power is the only currency of social and political activity. And yet, paradoxically, Kendi maintains a distinguishing mark of any CT thinker, the optimistic prospect of an equitable utopia.

---

182. Ibram X. Kendi, "Pass an Anti-Racist Constitutional Amendment," *Politico Magazine*, https://www.politico.com/interactives/2019/how-to-fix-politics-in-america/inequality/pass-an-anti-racist-constitutional-amendment/. According to Kendi, his proposed anti-racist constitutional amendment would:
[E]stablish and permanently fund the Department of Anti-racism (DOA) comprised of formally trained experts on racism and no political appointees. The DOA would be responsible for preclearing all local, state and federal public policies to ensure they won't yield racial inequity, monitor those policies, investigate private racist policies when racial inequity surfaces, and monitor public officials for expressions of racist ideas. The DOA would be empowered with disciplinary tools to wield over and against policymakers and public officials who do not voluntarily change their racist policy and ideas.

183. Andrew Sullivan, "A Glimpse at the Intersectional Left's Political Endgame," *New York Magazine* (Nov. 15, 2019), https://nymag.com/intelligencer/2019/11/andrew-sullivan-the-intersectional-lefts-political-endgame.html.

The Great (Hopeless) Game

The sole option left to those poor souls born into an *a priori* affiliation with whiteness is to play the demoralizing and unwinnable game of virtue signaling— feigned righteousness and moral outrage intended to make the signaler appear morally superior by condemning others (or themselves)— which operates as our modern system of indulgences.[184] Johann Tetzel would have made a great contemporary critical theorist and prosecutor general of the new moral revolution. And it is, indeed, a *moral* revolution. To public intellectuals like DiAngelo and Kendi facts are in many ways secondary. Their project is *not* one of science, sociology, or politics of the kind we are used to. It is rather one of moral realignment according to the insights of CT. As Alexandria Ocasio-Cortez has instructed, one can be factually incorrect but morally right.[185]

Those who choose to indulge in the indulgences game will soon find that, try as they might, their virtuous performance, their interminable divestment of power, is insufficient even to exonerate their ancestors, and the original sin imputed therefrom (i.e. "ancestral guilt"). Much less will it be enough to safeguard them from the inevitable transgressions that they commit in their own lifetime— which could be something as innocuous as being "nice", unintentionally mis-gendering someone, or appealing to scientific empiricism[186]—or what Horkheimer called "instrumental rea-

---

184. This type of behavior was addressed by the Bible long before this new label was applied to it: Luke 18:9-14.

185. CBS News, "Alexandria Ocasio-Cortez: The Rookie Congresswoman Challenging the Democratic Establishment," commentary by Anderson Cooper, *60 Minutes* (Jan. 6, 2019), https://www.cbsnews.com/news/alexandria-ocasio-cortez-the-rookie-congress-woman-challenging-the-democratic-establishment-60-minutes-interview-full-transcript-2019-01-06/.

186. Chanda Prescod-Weinstein, "Making Black Women Scientists under White Empiricism: The Racialization of Epistemology in Physics," *Signs: Journal of Women in Culture and Society*, 45(2) (Winter 2020), *available at* https://www.journals.uchicago.edu/doi/full/10.1086/704991.

son."[187] More common still is the crime of "epistemic exploitation," which is "when privileged persons compel marginalized persons to educate them about the nature of their oppression," resulting in "unrecognized, uncompensated, emotionally taxing, coerced epistemic labor," on the part of the marginalized person.[188] This phenomenon is, we are told, "ubiquitous" and "masquerades as a necessary and even epistemically virtuous form of intellectual engagement, and it is often treated as an indispensable method of attaining knowledge," enabled by "[s]tandard conversational norms" like

---

187. Max Horkheimer, *Critique of Instrumental Reason*, trans. Matthew J. O'Connell (London: Verso, 2012). Even former president Barack Obama has come under fire for criticizing cancel culture and questioning the "woke" rhetoric of the day. Michael Arceneaux, "I respect you immensely, Barack Obama, but I don't need lessons about 'being woke' and 'cancel culture'," *The Independent* (Oct. 30, 2019), https://www.independent.co.uk/voices/obama-woke-meaning-michelle-cancel-culture-foundation-chicago-a9178436.html.

188. On the flipside is "epistemic oppression," which "refers to persistent epistemic exclusion that hinders one's contribution to knowledge production." Kristie Dotson, "Epistemic Oppression," *Social Epistemology*, 28(2) (2014), 115-138. It is in between epistemic exploitation and epistemic oppression that so-called antiracist "white affinity groups" fit. The formation of these groups is essential for antiracist work in that they provide a space for whites to develop their own racial identity in relation to antiracist ends whilst not epistemically "taxing" persons of color with requests for education on, or proof of, racism and systemic oppression in a given cultural context. Affinity groups more or less provide a "safe space" for whites to grow into effective and culturally conscious antiracist allies without hindering the antiracist work of black, brown, immigrant and indigenous persons of color. Indispensable activities of an effective white affinity group include *practicing* talking about race outside of "interracial dialogues" so as not to burden persons of color with white ignorance, coming to terms with the "internalized racism" of (white) members, and learning actively to confront systemic racism. *See* Ali Michael and Mary C. Conger, Susan Bickerstaff, Katherine Crawford, Garrett, and Ellie Fitts Fulmer, " Becoming an Anti-Racist White Ally: How a White Affinity Group Can Help," *Perspectives on Urban Education* (Spring 2009), *available at* https://www.racialequitytools.org/resourcefiles/whiteaffinitygroup.pdf.

curiosity and the desire to learn.[189]*Abandon all hope ye who enter here.*

It is a miserable, Sisyphus-like existence upon the lowest slopes of Dante's island mountain for which they must prepare themselves. And the prayers of the non-canceled cannot help them; neither is Beatrice waiting at the top as the prospect for redemption. No matter how much gold in the casket rings, no soul from purgatory springs.

As these "white" souls suffer in this social purgatory of cancel culture,[190] they must also accept the basic— and we must say again, ironic— inequality of the whole affair. There is no Virgil supplied to graciously guide them through this brave new underworld. Earnest questions are typically denounced as textbook "epistemic exploitation" and met with a derision that is only out done by the ridicule served upon those who misstep more materially. The god of the CT religion is not abundant in mercy and long suffering.[191] He is not tolerant in the classical liberal sense of the word. He possesses a Marcuseian tolerance, which is to say, "liberating tolerance": intolerance of *wrong* opinions and inequity. This god is, therefore, highly

---

189. Nora Berenstain, "Epistemic Exploitation," *Ergo*, 3(22) (2016), https://quod.lib. umich.edu/e/ergo/12405314.0003.022/--epistemic-exploitation?rgn=main;view=fulltext. To be rightly comprehended and analyzed, says Berenstain, epistemic exploitation must be situated within "a framework of epistemic oppression." Only then can we "illuminate the structural disparities that allow it to take place and reveal the role it plays in reproducing active ignorance and maintaining systems of oppression." Key to the concept unpacked by Berenstain is the dynamic of "unpaid labor;" highlighting that marginalized persons must educate their non-marginalized counterparts on the oppression proliferated by the majority culture. In Berenstain's opinion, this uncompensated work reveals that epistemic exploitation (in all its masked forms) is really a tool "to keep the oppressed busy doing the oppressor's work [i.e. correcting white, male ignorance]," constituting "a diversion of energies [i.e. opportunity cost, especially for women of color] and a tragic repetition of racist patriarchal thought [quoting Audre Lorde]."

190. Meghan Murphy, "Soon we'll all be cancelled," *UnHerd* (Oct. 7, 2019), https://unherd.com/2019/10/soon-well-all-be-cancelled/.

191. *See* Brian J. Shaw, "Reason, Nostalgia, and Eschatology in the Critical Theory of Max Horkheimer," *Journal of Politics* 47(1) (Feb., 1985), 160-181 (couching the project of Horkheimer in a religious motif, *e.g.* "Horkheimer committed himself to the self-appointed task with the zeal of a prophet charged with the salvation of a world crowded with unrepentant sinners.").

censorious; suppressive of *repressive* opinions.[192] Free discourse, after all, has historically been cover for the domination of white ideas and the ostracization of minority ideas and thought patterns, so the disciple of CT believes and monotonously parrots.

But the god of CT, along with the demi-god of social justice, —the latter acting as the Wormwood to the former's Screwtape—is not arbitrary, though he is a respecter of persons and a promulgator of a double-standard.[193] (Once the presuppositions of CT are adopted their internal logic and external application are admirably consistent). On the one hand, he pronounces swift judgment on impenitent oppressors via his kangaroo Twitter courts. The lukewarm—those not sufficiently anti-racist—particularly nauseate him, as the apostle Kendi proclaimed to us. With glee the CT deity vomits the unsavory "non-racists" into purgatory. We are all Laodiceans now (Rev. 3:14-21).

At the same time, members of the oppressed class may at will unleash untrammeled, vicious vitriol upon a member of the oppressor class with impunity. In fact, the act is celebrated as propelling society at breakneck speed toward utopia, whilst Charon rows the disdainful and discarded detractors elsewhere.

Conclusion: Ideas Have Consequences (and Analytical Tools Do Too)

Under a CRT-informed conception of the world, the crime of white supremacy, or whiteness (the two now being synonymous), no longer in-

---

192. Herbert Marcuse, "Repressive Tolerance," in *A Critique of Pure Tolerance*, eds. Robert Paul Wolff, Barrington Moore Jr., and Herbert Marcuse (Boston: Beacon, 1965), 81–117.

193. *C.f.* Rom. 2:11.

cludes a *mens rea*,[194] a volitional or intent-based element which was once indispensable to western legal theory.[195] Instead, it is a disease for which its carriers may be condemned and subjected to a kind of social eugenics now in vogue. For all its apparent concern for the dignity of oppressed peoples, by casting out both the volitional and intentional elements of the moral calculus, CT is ironically un-dignifying.

Reasonable people still clinging to the old settlement of liberal society with its norms of procedural fairness and civility would be blameless in assuming that if white supremacy and racism of this kind are inherent, never to be *fully* divested, that the carriers of this ailment would be off the hook. But such is not the case. The *mens rea* has been removed but guilt and condemnation remain; so too has any knowledge element.

Christians would agree that people should be held accountable for sin. And the presumption is that all are sinners—both in capacity for evil deeds and default posture before God. On the ground level, however, people can only be taken to task by their fellow man for the sins they evidence. Humans are not omniscient (1 Cor. 2:11). That all people are sinners in terms of moral status does not guarantee that they will commit

---

194. Noteworthy is an insight presented by Boyce's *Abstract*, 198 (citing Charles Hodge's "Outlines," 299-300), *viz.*, that the Greek and Roman philosophers referred to the rational soul as νους or πνευμα or *mens*. By contrast, the animal soul was called ψυχη or *anima*. Hence, linguistically (if on a somewhat superficial level) we see the early connection between the doctrine of *mens rea* and respect for man's rational soul. Boyce concludes that Paul uses these terms, including σωμα or *corpus* to signify the body, to express the full, composite being of man (*e.g.* 1 Thess. 5:23; Heb. 4:12; 1 Cor. 15:44).

195. CRT scholars regularly decry Supreme Court decisions like *Washington v. Davis* (1976) (and *Personnel Administrator of Massachusetts v. Feeney* (1979), applying the standard to sex discrimination) for its insistence on an intent/motive element ("discriminatory purpose") in nonexplicit discrimination analysis. In short, the intent element imbedded in American jurisprudence frustrates CRT scholars' ability to critique unconscious bias and systemic oppression. *See e.g.* Pamela S. Karlan, "Discriminatory Purpose and Mens Rea: The Tortured Argument of Invidious Intent," 93 *Yale Law Journal* 111-134 (1983), *available at* https://digitalcommons.law.yale.edu/ylj/vol93/iss1/3; James Morsch, "The Problem of Motive in Hate Crimes: The Argument against Presumptions of Racial Motivation," 82 *Journal Criminal Law & Criminology* 659 (1991-1992), *available at* https://scholarlycommons.law.northwestern.edu/cgi/viewcontent.cgi?article=6710&context=jclc.

all kinds of sin. When people are confronted about a particular sin, they, for good reason, expect to be confronted with evidence of the sin in question. That all men are in some measure prideful does not mean that pride outwardly and discernably exudes from everyone at all times. Doubtless, all men contain within their hearts the prideful instinct to feign moral superiority based on standards that most suit confirmation of such unto themselves. This fact attested to by Scripture is confirmed by experience. The racists that perpetuated chattel slavery in the American south, as well as the current peddlers of identity politics, suffer from the same spiritual, moral ailment that all of us do.

Nevertheless, sin must explicitly manifest before it can be prosecuted. It is the prerogative of God alone to deal with those hidden sins that go unexposed on earth (Deut. 32:35). Applying a *guilty until proven innocent* standard to sin is both uncharitable and unsustainable. Assuming that every white person is de facto a white supremacist by way of their membership in the majority culture is to presume gross immorality—the cruelty and narcissism of an oppressor. Though every person has the capacity to be truly oppressive (and racist), and though this capacity is often magnified and materialized by group dynamics (as Reinhold Niebuhr taught us), the presumption at the outset is decidedly unChristian, and all the more so when predicated upon an *inhuman* worldview.

Even without deeply contemplating established standards of evidence or due process, we can readily observe that on its face CT's approach to sin, as a basis for social policy and political norms, is not only unjust but unworkable. Societal cohesion can simply never be achieved on this double-standard, *ex post facto* basis. The present political unrest in the west serves to demonstrate this.

This chaotic result should not be surprising. A standard built upon fundamentally *inhuman* categories can never promote societal or political tranquility because they strike at the very nature of man—his volitional character, the prerequisite for the exercise of his sociable disposition and insatiable desire for happiness. Identity politics can never provide the good life, the ultimate happiness, for which *all* people strive. And we cannot expect humans to treat one another humanely when the only acceptable tools given to them to govern and navigate their relations—to assess one another and construct social relations—are fundamentally *inhuman.*

When human beings have their distinguishing faculties bound unrest will ensue. Without the free operation of the will, no political settlement is possible. Indeed, as Douglas Murray points out in *The Spectator* talk, compromise is not the end goal of the identity politics overlords. It is total, unqualified acquiescence they desire. There is no *via media.* The identity politics game of oppressor v. oppressed is a winner-take-all cage match. Christians should at least realize what they are being forced to give up as a condition of entry into this zero-sum game. If they insist upon entering, they should at least know that the very God-given faculty which constitutes their unique status in the Great Chain of Being is being checked at the door.

Postscript: Moving Forward

Admittedly, it is always simpler, and a good deal more cathartic, to critique ideologies than it is to respond with positive solutions. Doubtless, proponents of CT identify *real* problems in the world. But though critique must always be the first step to correction, there is something monotonous and arid about criticizing *ad nauseum* a way of looking at the world, the lifeblood of which is perpetual criticism of the world it is looking at. Christians should certainly identify and reprimand falsehood where they find it, but they must also assert a positive replacement derived from their own epistemology, anthropology, ontology, and a teleology— one that transcends a unitary explanation for the world, e.g. an oppressor v. oppressed dichotomy. It seems to this writer that a good response to hyperactive deconstruction is renewed construction.

It has been argued above that CT is, at its root, diametrically opposed to historic Christian beliefs about the nature of man as the *imago Dei.* The appropriate and effective response is to reassert with vigor and conviction the truths of the Bible, the historic Protestant confessions and ecumenical creeds, and catholic orthodoxy.

Looking to our own past and tradition of thought can provide surprisingly helpful insights and guidance for present challenges. The thought of Samuel Willard summarized above represents just *one* strategy for navigating but *one* facet of the present gathering storm. I would encourage all Christians to adopt the *ad fontes* spirit of the Reformation as they wade through difficult social and political questions rather than assuming at the outset that the criticism of the critics—that our theology as it stands is inept in such instances—is true.[196] This may be a long, tedious road but it is one worth traveling.

---

196. Michael Lynch, "Returning to the Sources: The Scholarship of Richard Muller," *Mere Orthodoxy* (Jan. 7, 2019), https://mereorthodoxy.com/richard-muller/.